*The Evolution of Altruism
and the Ordering of Love*

The Evolution of Altruism and the Ordering of Love

Stephen J. Pope

GEORGETOWN UNIVERSITY PRESS / WASHINGTON, D.C.

Georgetown University Press, Washington, D.C.   20007
© 1994 by Georgetown University Press. All rights reserved.
Printed in the United States of America
10 9 8 7 6 5 4 3 2
THIS VOLUME IS PRINTED ON ACID-FREE OFFSET BOOK PAPER.

Library of Congress Cataloging-in-Publication Data

Pope, Stephen J., 1955-
    The evolution of altruism and the ordering of love / Stephen Pope.
        p.   cm.
    1. Altruism.   2. Helping behavior--Religious aspects--Catholic
Church.   3. Love--Religious aspects--Catholic Church.   4. Evolution-
-Religious aspects--Catholic Church.   5. Catholic Church--Doctrines.
I. Title.
    BJ1474.P65   1994   241'.042--dc20
    ISBN 0-87840-597-6   93-37489

It is to my wife,
Patricia Curtis Pope,
whose generous, steadfast, and tender love has
sustained and inspired me,
that I dedicate this book.

Contents

Editor's Preface

Moral Traditions & Moral Arguments, as a series, presents systematic, scholarly accounts of major themes in Christian ethics in order to critically examine those insights that, perduring through the ages, have shaped and continue to shape Christian lives and communities. These books are intended to provide scholars with a precise understanding of moral traditions as well as an appreciation of their contribution to contemporary life.

Published by the Georgetown University Press, these first two titles inaugurate a series whose complex of careful analyses and broad scope offer books of interest and use to scholars in ethics, theology, religious studies and philosophy. Edward Vacek's *Love, Human and Divine* and Stephen Pope's *The Evolution of Altruism and the Ordering of Love* are an auspicious beginning for an important series of publications which concern the "heart of Christian ethics."

Weston School of Theology   JAMES F. KEENAN, S.J.,ED.

Preface

Catholic philosophers and moral theologians have found it difficult to write about love and impossible not to do so. Since the time of Christ, love has proven to be both the center and the enigma of Christian ethics, fundamental and at the same time elusive, the center of the moral life and also a mystery that escapes human comprehension.

Our times offer no exception from this history. Indeed, they may underscore and heighten it.

Two major currents have streamed into contemporary Catholic ethics and shaped its understanding of the role of love in the moral life.

Personalism has exercised a critical influence. It advanced Catholic moral theology beyond the austere and abstract "benevolence" featured in the neo-scholastic manuals. Affective and relational models of the I-Thou dialogue came to new prominence in the understanding and tone of monographs on Christian thought and practice. Personalism, however, also bespoke its limitations, unable to address serious difficulties in the encounter with multiple and conflicting objects of loyalty, responsibility, and love.

The "Preferential Option for the Poor" has drawn Catholic reflection to a serious examination of moral norms and virtues and to the development of a new hermeneutic that takes its point of departure in the misery that marks the lives of so many human beings. Still, like Personalism, even this advance failed to develop the distinctions and hierarchy of moral priorities that would respond to the concrete experience and ordering of nature intrinsic to human life.

It is curious that in recent years neither Personalists nor advocates of the "Preferential Option for the Poor" have attended to the scientific treatments of human nature recently made available through work in evolutionary theory and behavioral biology—perhaps doubly curious since much in these treatments speak to something from the genius of the

Catholic tradition, the "ordering of love" or the *ordo amoris* in the classic treatment of Thomas Aquinas.

The last fifteen years have witnessed an explosion of scientific works on human social behavior. They have explored the evolution of human sociality, cooperation, and altruism. Evolutionary theorists have produced major volumes on attachment and bonding, cooperation and alliance formation, reciprocity, sympathy, and a variety of related concerns.

One cannot help but notice that no Christian theologian, Catholic or Protestant, has registered these inquiries nor attempted to examine them for their relevance to something so central to Christianity as the love of one's neighbor.

It is perhaps even more puzzling that most Catholic ethicists have ignored the possibly telling contribution that these new scientifically-based studies on human nature and prosocial behavior could make to an understanding of charity. For the Catholic tradition has insisted powerfully that grace does not repudiate nature but brings it to its completion. The repeated acknowledgment in magisterial social teachings that human beings are "social animals" follows from this classic axiom and provides yet another encouragement for scholars to examine current literature on natural sociality. Earlier in this century, Catholic thinkers were properly suspicious of social Darwinism and its description of human nature as relentlessly egoistic, competitive, and opportunistic—an understanding not held by Darwin himself. But the neo-Darwinians of today have advanced beyond this primitive and ideologically-biased perspective. These evolutionary theorists construe human nature in a far more sophisticated, complex, and nuanced manner, and their findings and speculative proposals deserve at least an honest and critical hearing in contemporary ethics and moral theology. If human nature is actually constituted by predispositions to both egoistic and altruistic behavior, then Catholic reflection should encompass these data within its discernment and evaluations.

These scientifically-based studies of human social behavior have generated an important group of closely related questions. If altruism is naturally channelled in certain directions more than others, what significance does this have for the meaning and application of the command to love the neighbor? If human beings are naturally predisposed to develop strong bonds of attachment to specific people with whom they live, to love some people more than others, to develop special bonds with close kin and friends, and to exhibit greater generosity and higher degrees of self-denial for their loved ones, what relevance does this have for efforts to understand the hierarchy of moral responsibilities for various neighbors?

Is it possible to appreciate the necessity and value of establishing priorities among objects of love while retaining a lively and critical sense of the universal scope of neighbor-love? In short, what is the significance of recent theoretical developments regarding the evolution of sociality, cooperation, and altruism for Catholic interpretations of neighbor-love? This book attempts to address these questions and proposes that the natural gradation of altruism can be positively incorporated into a Catholic understanding of the "ordering of love."

Acknowledgments

I would like to express publicly my gratitude to those who have helped me throughout the writing of this book. Special thanks are due to my friends and teachers at the University of Chicago, especially professors James M. Gustafson, Robin W. Lovin, and Don S. Browning. During the writing of my dissertation I enjoyed employment as a lecturer of theology at the Saint Paul Seminary, St. Paul, Minnesota, and I will always be grateful for the kind sponsorship of its rector, Fr. Charles Froehle, and the academic dean, Dr. Victor Klimoski. After having completed my dissertation, I began teaching at Boston College, where I have gained immeasurably from the generosity, kindness, and wisdom of my colleagues there, particularly Jim Rurak, Lisa Sowle Cahill, and David Hollenbach, S.J. Various friends have helped me to think through the contents of this book, and I would like to acknowledge the assistance I received from Charles Hefling, Tom Shannon, Ed Vacek, S.J., Jim Keenan, S.J., Jack Gallagher, and Martin Cook.

Portions of this book have appeared in abbreviated form in articles I have published previously and entitled "The Order of Love and Recent Catholic Ethics: A Constructive Proposal," *Theological Studies* 52 (1991): 255–88, and "Agape and Human Nature: Contributions from New-Darwinism," *Social Science Information* 31 (1992):509–29. Both essays are cited with the permission of the editors of these journals.

I have a profound sense of gratitude for the love lavished on me by my parents, Pat and John Pope, whose unflagging support and care have made this book possible; to my uncle, Michael J. Buckley, S.J., whose friendship has always sustained and inspired me; and to my grandparents, Michael and Eleanor Buckley, who are models of the kind of Christian "ordering of love" examined in this book. Finally and most importantly, I want to register my deep appreciation for the support given to me by my immediate family. Over the years I have been loved, sustained, and entertained by my wonderful children, Michael, Katie, and

Stevie. My deepest debt of gratitude is owed to Patti, my wife, whose steady love, encouragement, and patience have been far in excess of what I deserve. The Bible speaks for my life when it proclaims, "Happy the husband of a good wife. . . . A good wife is a generous gift bestowed upon him who fears the Lord; Be he rich or poor, his heart is content, and smile is ever on his face" (Sirach 26:2,4). Thanks, Patti.

Introduction

Twentieth-century Christian ethics has been marked by extensive research and writing on the topic of love, so much so that one would assume to the subject matter to have been discussed exhaustively. Earlier in the century Anders Nygren's *Agape and Eros* triggered intense debate among Christian ethicists and generated a massive body of books and articles devoted to the meaning of neighbor love, its distinctively Christian character, and its relation to justice.[1] The increased interest in the topic of love in Catholic ethics during the second half of the century reflected a widespread desire to find an alternative to the neo-Thomistic manuals that dominated moral theology up to the Second Vatican Council. Major moral theologians abandoned the legal paradigm of the manuals and placed active and responsive neighbor love at the center of the Christian moral life. Despite the ground broken by this movement, however, questions and controversies over the meaning and moral implications of love persist to this day.

In this book I intend to focus on one significant lacuna within Catholic ethics: the question of the order of love. My own perspective accords with that of James M. Gustafson when he writes that, "the 'natural' ordering of life has theological and moral dignity" and that through the natural "ordering of love," particularly in marriage and family, God is "enabling and requiring us to be stewards, deputies, and custodians of one another and of life itself."[2] It also concurs with Stephen G. Post's judgment that certain currents within contemporary Christian ethics, particularly those most influenced by Kant, fail to recognize the moral significance of naturally-rooted human affections and interdependencies.[3]

Much Catholic writing tends to confine its analysis of love to dyadic, one-to-one interpersonal relationships. Liberation theologians, however, and other Catholic authors committed to social justice, insist that the church embrace a special regard for the poor, the marginalized, and the oppressed. Both perspectives are valuable but incomplete, and therefore misleading. Important and valid in their own right, a one-sided

1

preoccupation with either friendship or social concern can lead to a neglect of other aspects of the moral life. Neither approach provides an account of the role played by primary relations of marriage and family in the Christian moral life. Both tendencies ignore the fact that people in ordinary life are often confronted with multiple objects of love that make different and at times competing claims on them. In general recent Catholic accounts of Christian love have given little attention to the conflict between multiple relationships, to the need to develop priorities among our various loyalties, and to the kinds of issues that used to be entertained in discussions of the "order of love," the *ordo amoris.*[4]

Neglect of the *ordo amoris* is directly related to avoidance or insufficient treatment of what, for want of a better term, has been called "human nature." Human nature is a concept regarded with a great deal of suspicion in contemporary ethics, both philosophical and theological, for complex reasons that can only be mentioned here. Some critics object on social scientific grounds that no such thing as human nature exists, or, that if it exists, it cannot be properly or meaningfully characterized. Others argue on philosophical grounds that human nature is essentially egoistic and therefore cannot be regarded as normative. Finally, some critics charge on moral grounds that human nature is a code word employed by political conservatives or reactionaries to suggest that certain political, social, or economic arrangements are inevitable rather than the product of human choices that are therefore subject to rational intervention.

Suspicion of biologically-based accounts of morality in particular is easily understood given their misuse in the purported justification of, for example, female domesticity, white supremacy, Nazi eugenics, and euthanasia. The social application of Darwinism, illustrated in John D. Rockefeller's Sunday school message that success of capitalist monopolies fulfills the law of nature (i.e., the "survival of the fittest"), has been held suspect by moralists since its inception.[5]

Yet the abuse of a source does not invalidate its proper use. The failure to appropriate relevant insights from evolutionary theory is more understandable in theological traditions that employ primarily biblical sources, than in Catholic circles that rely on various forms of natural law argumentation. Yet Catholic moral theologians have generally kept their distance from Darwinism, despite Pope Pius XII's official acknowledgment in the 1950 encyclical *Humani generis* that evolutionary science is not necessarily at odds with Christian doctrine.[6]

Contemporary acceptance of the "turn to the subject" has been accompanied by a unfortunate tendency to avoid discussing human nature in all its dimensions. Personalists and existentialists have proclaimed the need to move Catholic ethics from "respect for blood relationships" to "respect for the human subject" as such.[7] Earlier in this century, a number of personalists, in Catholic circles most notably Jacques Maritain, criticized older organic notions of society for reducing the individual person to a mere part of an anonymous collectivity.[8] More recently, since the repeated attacks by moral theologians on the "physicalism" implied in magisterial prohibition of artificial birth control, many progressive Catholic ethicists have reacted with repugnance to arguments employing the category of "nature," especially "biological nature." Those who do continue to employ "nature" reduce it to autonomous reason precisely in order to avoid "physicalism."[9] They do so, however, at the cost of eliminating certain important components from their consideration of human nature.

The most well-known contemporary evolutionary approach to human nature is sociobiology, which E. O. Wilson defines as the systematic study of "the biological basis of all social behavior."[10] The neglect or deliberate avoidance of this resource in Catholic ethics is understandable, given its frequent assumption of scientific materialism and its reductionistic tendencies. One can find in sociobiological literature simplistic claims that religion is an enabling mechanism for individual survival and reproductive fitness,[11] that morality is a means by which people manipulate others into acting more altruistically toward oneself and one's kin than vice versa,[12] and that Christianity advocates a morality fit for "suckers."[13] Typically inferred from this view of morality is a reciprocity ethic, something like Freud's Golden Rule, "Love thy neighbor as thy neighbor loves thee."[14] In sociobiological language, this translates into something like the maxim, "cooperate with cooperators, but defect against defectors"[15] —a far cry, needless to say, from Jesus' "new commandment": "love one another as I have loved you" (John 15:12 N.R.S.V.).

These and other kinds of claims do not suggest an immediate kinship between sociobiology and Catholic ethics, though it should also be said that a number of other modern sources that have significantly influenced contemporary Catholic ethics, for example, Nietzsche, Marx, and Freud, have been equally or even more hostile to religion than sociobiology. Simplistic claims can be found in most intellectual innovators, but at times further development can give rise to nuanced and reasonable reflections from the same perspective. Intellectual bias at times undercuts openness to valuable insights that might be forthcoming from unexpected sources.

The cumulative result of these various negative responses to the use of biology in Catholic ethics has been not only a general practice of eschewing the evidence of science from ethics (except in certain special areas, notably biomedical and environmental ethics) but also a fairly consistent neglect of the biological roots of human nature—that, as philosopher Mary Midgley puts it, "We are not just rather like animals; we *are* animals."[16] The effect of this oversight is certainly felt in Catholic accounts of love, and it is at odds with the characteristically Catholic conviction that there is, at bottom, no real contradiction between science and Christianity, properly understood. A persistent failure to incorporate scientific knowledge about natural sociality is difficult to reconcile with the church's theological recognition of the goodness of the natural, material world and its conviction that grace retains and perfects, rather than obliterates, human creatureliness.[17]

In this book, then, I will indicate the significance of current scientifically-based theories of human nature for recent Catholic ethics. A great deal of attention is given to human sociality, altruism, and cooperation in contemporary behavioral biology as I attempt to show the significance of this theory, or more accurately this cluster of theories, for a Catholic understanding of the ordering of love.

Definitions

To avoid misunderstanding, it may be helpful to clarify the meaning of certain key terms as they are used in this book. The term "behavioral biology" is one label by which evolutionary theorists identify the study of human behavior in "neo-Darwinian"perspective. By "neo-Darwinian" I refer to the "modern synthesis," begun in the 1930s, which incorporated into one synthetic theory the Darwinian principle of natural selection and Mendelian genetics.[18] Prominent disciplines within neo-Darwinian behavioral biology include "ethology," "behavioral ecology," and "biosociology," along with sociobiology. These subdisciplines have different connotations, but they all agree that human beings should be understood in the context of a vast global ecosystem, interacting with millions of other evolving species. Behavioral biologists attempt to provide a scientifically-based account of the natural, "evolved," context of human life and of the evolutionary basis of the fundamental capacities, inclinations, and needs that comprise human nature.

The critical object of evolutionary theory employed by this book is "altruism." "Altruism," a term of more recent vintage than "love," was originally coined by August Comte in opposition to "egoism."[19] Altruism is by no means interchangeable with "love." The former term is ordinarily used to refer to any behavior performed to benefit another person without the intention of receiving rewards from external sources.[20] Altruism is typically defined by philosophers as action intended to benefit another person or persons,[21] but it need not entail valuing others' welfare more than one's own or valuing it so much that one is prepared to make heroic sacrifices for others. It is, more modestly, to value the welfare of others for their own sakes and to be willing to undertake some forms of self-denial on this basis.

Altruism is found in a broad array of behavior, from simple acts of kindness to what Durkheim called acts of "altruistic suicide," displayed, for example, when soldiers jump on hand grenades to save their comrades.[22] It always involves a significant degree of other-regarding motives and intentions. By this definition the magnificent displays of generosity in the potlach festivals of Native Americans in the Pacific Northwest should not be regarded as altruistic because they are intended to promote the sponsor's social status; and the same is true of charitable donations motivated by the desire for income tax deductions, and the behavior of Christians who hid Jews from the Nazis primarily for monetary reward.[23]

Simple moral altruism is distinguished from sociobiological interpretations of altruism, which, as we will see in more detail below, involve the sacrifice of one individual's "inclusive fitness" for that of another, non-related, individual.[24] As Trivers puts it, in sociobiology:

> An altruistic act is one that confers a benefit on someone at a cost to the other. Since cost is measured by a decrease in reproductive success, we know that altruistic acts are opposed by natural selection's working on the actor.[25]

Thus, unlike the ordinary moral sense of altruism, sociobiological "altruism" involves neither motives nor intentions but only consequences regarding reproductive success.[26] Consciousness is considered irrelevant to sociobiological notions of altruism, which only make sense given the fact they have been constructed to account for behavior of all social species—including, for example, "altruistic" soldier aphids who sacrifice their own reproductive potential to better promote that of others.[27]

Overview

Earlier forms of Catholic personalism and existentialism encouraged a movement in moral theology from "respect for blood relationships" to "respect for the human subject."[28] I would like to argue for an incorporation of both the need for a universal love of neighbor and a Catholic incorporation of the moral centrality of natural priorities. My argument can be summarized concisely. Formally, I argue (1) that recent Catholic interpretations of love display certain characteristic weaknesses, (2) that the ethics of Thomas Aquinas did not suffer from these weaknesses, in part because Thomas used available scientific sources, and (3) if contemporary Catholic ethicists would employ the scientific sources available today they could avoid these weaknesses. Substantively, I argue (1) that recent Catholic interpretations of love ignore the issues surrounding the "ordering of love," (2) that Thomas's ethics did not suffer from this weakness, in part because he employed contemporary biological accounts of the human within an anthropology which took seriously this dimension of human nature, and (3) that if contemporary Catholic ethicists would consider more seriously the biological dimensions of human nature they would be better able to attend to the issues surrounding the ordering of love.

The book proceeds sequentially. The argument proper begins in the first chapter with an interpretation and assessment of contemporary Catholic interpretations of love. I examine key works of several particularly influential and persuasive authors, for example, Robert Johann and Gustavo Gutiérrez, to illustrate what I take to be typical approaches to love in recent Catholic ethics; alternative theologians and philosophers could have been used to exemplify the same tendencies. These authors draw on material from the Christian theological tradition (especially Augustinian-Thomistic), recent philosophical movements (especially personalist, phenomenological, and existentialist), and human experience broadly conceived, but they ignore scientific theories regarding human nature.[29] This basic disregard of science contributes to a number of unfortunate consequences, most generally to an unnecessary and counterproductive rift between interpretations of love and charity on the one hand, and human nature and natural law on the other. This separation leads to the major problem that this book addresses: an inattentiveness to the periodic conflict between, and need to prioritize, various "objects" of love.

The second chapter examines Thomas Aquinas's employment of the available scientific theories in his interpretation of the natural basis of primary relationships. (i.e., those of family and friendship) in the *ordo amoris*. I draw upon Thomas because he provides the clearest example of a classical position that uses biological material and thereby avoids the deficiencies and general problems that characterize contemporary Catholic interpretations of love. His appropriation of available biological interpretations of human nature set a major precedent within the tradition. I do not criticize recent Catholic authors for departing from Thomas per se, but for failing to draw as he did on the full range of available knowledge relevant to their subject matter.

The third chapter, entitled, "Thomas's Order of Love and Evolutionary Theories of Altruism" attempts to draw attention to certain functional equivalences between Thomas's *ordo amoris* and contemporary behavioral biology. It should be noted, however, that I will not argue that behavioral biologists are making claims identical to those advanced by Thomas. My focus is on "function," a term which refers to "the contribution which a partial activity makes to the total activity of which it is a part."[30] Thus this chapter examines certain similarities or equivalences between the way biology *functioned* in Thomas's moral theology and how it functions in the writings of some of the behavioral biologists today.

Chapter four, "Evolution and Altruism" offers a more extensive discussion of the analysis of altruism provided by neo-Darwinism. It reviews several standard criticisms of sociobiology and presents the aspects of evolutionary analyses of altruism and sociality that I take to be the most plausible and relevant for my purposes. Readers particularly suspicious of my use of this source may want to begin here with my clearly selective (but, I think, fair) use of neo-Darwinism, before proceeding to the first chapter.

Chapter five, "Human Nature and the Ordering of Love" advances the central argument of the book, namely, that accounts of human altruism developed by behavioral biology can be used to correct the deficiencies of recent Catholic interpretations of love, particularly regarding the place of humanity in the natural world, the kind of ordering that characterizes human nature, and the natural gradation of affections, assistance giving, and related notions. Sociobiology in particular provides significant insights into the natural limits of love, the need for an ordering of love, and the biological basis of the human preference for near kin and close friends. Behavioral biology, I argue, provides a natural basis for attending to a broader viewpoint of human relations, a wider and more complex range of moral concerns, and a deeper appreciation for the moral priorities of primary relations, without thereby necessarily compromising the universality of *agape*. I propose that contemporary biological interpretations of interhuman and human-natural interdependencies can be used to develop a more extensive and inclusive range of moral responsibility than is suggested by recent trends in Catholic ethics.

The concluding chapter offers both a summary of the argument of the book and a brief discussion of wider unresolved issues that would need to be addressed in a comprehensive theory of the ordering of love.

The Use of Behavioral Biology

My general starting point for using behavioral biology and sociobiology is well-expressed by philosopher Mary Midgley when she argues that

> we cannot deal with sociobiology on tribal lines. It is neither a heresy to be hunted down, nor a revealed doctrine necessary to academic salvation. It is the usual kind of mixed picnic hamper which needs to be unpacked, filled with the usual mixture of the nutritious and the uneatable, insights and mistakes, old and new material.[31]

Sociobiologists attend to ways in which widespread behavioral tendencies lead human behavior to maximize "inclusive reproductive fitness," that is, the reproductive success of the agent's descendent and nondescendent genetic relatives. Rather than argue simplistically that human behavior contributes in a direct way to inclusive reproductive success, sociobiologists inquire how selection pressures and previous environments may have interacted to produce the present constellation of specieswide characteristics that mark *Homo sapiens*. Their focus is not on behavior genetics, on how genes directly affect behavior, but on how evolution has influenced "phenotypic design," that is, the "psychological and physiological mechanisms" that underlie human behavior.[32]

There is no "gene for altruism," though human beings do possess a general emotional predisposition—based in but not determined by genes—to care more for close kin more than for others. People care more for close kin not because they consciously intend to promote their reproductive interests but because on a conscious level doing so is appropriate to the intense emotional bond within which it takes place. Specific psychological and emotional bonds are, in the jargon of evolutionary theory, a "proximate cause" of caregiving behavior that reflects the application of an adaptive emotional predisposition that has been shaped by natural selection, the "ultimate cause" of this behavior.[33]

Three further clarifications may prevent possible misunderstandings of my use of behavioral biology, and especially sociobiology. The first concerns the status of scientific arguments, the second the use of sociobiology, and the third determinism and human freedom.

First, it should be noted that I attempt to appropriate critically current scientific insights regarding human nature for matters fundamental to ethics and, because of my limited competence, I rely to a certain extent on arguments from scientific authorities. I have been trained as a theologian and ethicist, not as a biochemist, ethologist, or geneticist. Pertinent issues that are matters of scientific debate and yet require some kind of resolution for the purposes of this book are resolved in a provisional manner and with an appropriate acknowledgment of dependence on arguments from authority. By implication, nonscientific conclusions will be tentative to the extent that they rely on this kind of evidence.

The conclusions derived here will, moreover, reflect the incomplete character of scientific knowledge of human nature, sociality, and altruism. Behavioral biologists themselves often underscore the provisional, exploratory, and hypothetical nature of their investigations. I do not want to confuse speculative hypotheses with definitive explanations, and I take sociobiology in general to provide insights, not axiomatic truths, and, at times, only hypotheses to be used in an interpretation of recent Catholic literature on love. The conclusions I draw from this source, then, are modest in scope and open to revision in light of new information and theories concerning this subject matter.

A second caveat concerns the use of sociobiology, a notoriously controversial discipline, and sometimes for very good reasons. In this book I attempt to be both critical of the many errors of sociobiology, (particularly in chapter four), and, at the same time, cautiously appreciative of its insights into human nature. In human life, genetic influence and biological inclinations are always mediated, for example, through culture, intelligence, and personality. The behavior of individual human beings is marked by a very high degree of complexity and cannot be adequately described, let alone explained, in monocausal terms, whether biological, cultural, or existential.

Altruism provides a good example of this point. In other species, altruistic behavior can be accounted for in terms of "kin selection" theory according to which one organism assists others because doing so contrib-

utes to the former's inclusive reproductive fitness. For example, the dominant baboon males who defend their bands against external threats engage
in what is called "altruistic bravery." This behavioral tendency, primatolo-
gists tell us, evolved not because it is good for the band as a group but
because it is adaptive for the dominant male baboons; that is, the risk of
their being wounded or even killed is not greater than the reproductive
benefit that accrues from protecting their relatives, and therefore copies of
their own genes, from predation.[34] The same adaptive function—serving
the inclusive reproductive interests of the organism—is promoted by
other apparently "altruistic" kinds of behavior in the animal world, for
example, in the "altruistic" regurgitation of blood with which well-fed
vampire bats provide nourishment for other (genetically-related) bats
unable to secure their own sustenance.[35]

Human altruism, in contrast, is placed in a class by itself through
the intricate and highly complex workings of the human brain. Human
behavior is profoundly influenced by sociocultural structures, values,
norms, myths, customs, social institutions, and systems of beliefs, as well
as by a multitude of other factors—economic, political, and psychological. While the evolution of the human emotional preference for kin and
the capacity to internalize social norms of altruism can be explained by
sociobiology, the particular norms of altruism promoted by various cultures may or may not contribute to the inclusive reproductive success of
those individuals who are its members.[36]

Human intelligence is also reflected in intentionality. Certain kinds
of human behavior, of course, can be attributed to innate, highly complex, specialized biological mechanisms, for example, color perception.
Many important features of human life reflect in a powerful way the influence of genes, from eye coloration and blood type to sex determination
(the famous "Y" chromosome for males). Yet clearly human love, care,
and devotion reflect patterns of other-regarding affection, motivation, and
intention that cannot be explained in exclusively biological terms. This
general qualification having been registered, it is still the case that natural
selection is a process that has profoundly shaped the underlying nature of
every kind of organism, including that of *Homo sapiens.* "The nature of a
species," Midgley notes, "consists in a certain range of powers and tendencies, a repertoire, inherited and forming a fairly firm characteristic pattern, though conditions after birth may vary the details quite a lot."[37]

Human nature is the product of natural selection and this basic fact
has important implications, one of which is that human behavior is not
completely immune from the influences of the prevoluntary and the
prerational aspects of human nature. This influence can be detected in

certain invariant human behaviors, for example, facial expression,[38] but also on the deeper level of emotional predispositions. At its most interesting, at least in my perspective, behavioral biology offers an account of the evolution of the human emotional constitution. It needs to be noted, however, that behavioral biology offers a functional theory of the evolution of certain motivations and fundamental emotional predispositions basic to human nature, rather than a theory of these motivations and emotions themselves. Evolutionary theory points to certain basic motivations, often not fully conscious and usually not deliberate, underlying widespread forms of behavior that were originally shaped over the course of millions of years of natural selection because they provided adaptive responses to selective pressures presented by our hominid ancestors' environments.[39] Examples of such behavior include self-preservation, kin favoritism, parental altruism, incest avoidance, and alliance formation.

Evolutionary theorists argue that like all organisms, human beings possess certain specieswide characteristics that have been shaped by selective pressures. Unlike all other organisms, however, human beings have evolved to possess highly complex cognitive abilities expressed in culture and evidenced in the incredible diversity and malleability of human behavior. The evolution of human intelligence has been accompanied by a great plasticity of human behavior, and the influence of the human biological heritage is always in and through the culturally influenced particularities of concrete human social life. Biological predispositions assume various concrete forms in different cultural settings and are never expressed simpliciter, without cultural mediation. This book should not be taken as a naive effort to replace culture with biology, or nurture with nature. The need for nurture is part of human nature, and both biology and culture are essential to human behavior.

My third caveat regards the perennial problem of human freedom and determinism. Sociobiology, particularly in its early stages, was vehemently criticized for proposing various forms of "biological determinism."[40] While I cannot enter into an extended discussion of contemporary philosophers' highly refined and critical analyses of human freedom, determinism, and related issues,[41] it should be noted that I concur with earlier philosophical criticisms of sociobiological "hard determinism" and assume instead—without being able here to provide sufficient philosophical grounds—the general adequacy of the modest form of "soft determinism" and "compatibilism" defended by Midgely.[42]

Midgely distinguishes "determinism," which she defines as the broad assumption underlying modern science that nature is orderly and that human behavior exists within and is formed by a causal nexus, from "fatalism," the view that human effort is useless and freedom illusory. This kind of determinism is "soft" in that it is seen as a necessary condition of, but not as a replacement for, human freedom. Human choices are not free because they are idiosyncratic or arbitrary, but because they reflect the relatively unhindered expression of natural human capacities that ought not be stunted, suppressed, or disordered. Freedom involves the conscious, subjectively meaningful direction of wants, needs, and capacities that are themselves grounded in the natural human emotional constitution.[43]

This book accepts the biological basis of human love but rejects the fatalistic temptation seen in sociobiological reduction of human reason, will, and choices to the genetically controlled "neuronal machinery" of the brain. Yet it does accept the sociobiological claim that nature is orderly, that natural events are parts of causal sequences, that as members of the species *Homo sapiens,* we are not entirely exempt from the laws of biology, and that our biological and genetic substrates provide important material grounds for the exercise of human moral and emotional capacities. Recognition of the truth of these claims, of course, need not be accompanied by acceptance of sociobiological accounts, put however metaphorically, of human beings as really "survival machines—robot vehicles blindly programmed to preserve the selfish molecules known as genes."[44] Fortunately we need not accept this more comprehensive explanatory principle to learn something from sociobiology about human nature and social behavior.

The argument of this book proceeds on the basis of a reconciliationist approach to the freedom-determinism question; that is, I assume on the ground of philosophical arguments not rehearsed here that no strict contradiction exists between describing an act as determined, in the sense of affected by prior causes and not "free floating," and as also free, in the sense of reflecting an internal locus of control and resulting from neither external coercion nor internal compulsion. Those who reject this position on philosophical grounds will not find the treatment of human nature and love given here persuasive. My argument implicitly rejects both the "incompatibilism" of radical behaviorism and the libertarian view of freedom found in extreme individualism.[45]

Neither does it concur with those who reject what is labeled "mentalism" on the grounds that all notions must be able to be "operationalized" in order to be discussed in serious analyses of human nature.[46] As "evolutionary psychologist" Donald Symons correctly observes:

> Human action not only cannot be explained, it cannot even be *described* without referring—albeit implicitly—to the mind and its

goals. The point is not that we should pay more attention to what people think and feel than to what they do. It is rather that whatever our descriptions and characterizations of what people do are based on *effects* or *intentions* (which is virtually always), we are necessarily using mentalistic concepts. Evolutionists rightly assume that the mind has been designed by selection via mind's effects on behavior; nevertheless, their hypotheses about human affairs are ineluctably psychological.[47]

The soft determinism espoused here therefore by no means demands a complete rejection of recent Catholic appropriations of personalist, existentialist, and phenomenological descriptions of subjectivity and freedom. I do argue, however, that the latter ought to be more properly balanced with a greater appreciation of their biological limits, possibilities, conditions, and grounds.

Conclusion

Some readers will no doubt consider the attempt to join Catholic theology and behavioral biology in a common conversation about ethics, and especially the ethics of love, an exercise in futility. Love itself is an extremely complex reality, and, to a certain extent, irreducibly singular. As Robert Hinde points out, "an interpersonal relationship involves persons with individually specific constitutions and past histories, living in a particular social network in a particular culture. Multitudinous interacting variables thus affect its course."[48] Attempts to make generalizations must, in light of Hinde's statement, be made with a proper acknowledgment of provisionality and always with a sense of relevant exceptions. Yet if it is true that human beings share something called "humanity," and if this "humanity" has been significantly informed by the evolutionary process, then it seems reasonable enough to inquire into the constants and commonalities of human beings as well as into their particularities.

The examination of love from a theological and ethical perspective adds its own distinctive complications. Natural scientists and their intellectual allies often dismiss theology as metaphysical speculation based on superstitious and naive belief in an unverifiable realm of transcendence.[49] And moral theologians, while acknowledging the power of scientific methods in certain restricted domains, often proceed without considering the possibility that available scientific theories and information might be pertinent to their subject matter. A prime piece of evidence to this claim is that over the course of the last twenty years, evolutionary theorists have produced a vast body of literature that has to date never been examined by Catholic theologians or philosophers concerned with the ethics of love.

There is at present, then, a prominent and I think quite unfortunate intellectual divide separating theology, including moral theology, and the natural sciences. This book explores one way in which this gap might be narrowed, and if all the relevant concerns cannot be addressed, let alone exhaustively resolved, at least it sets the direction for future inquiry. The same modesty pertains to its central concern—the reexamination of the ordering of love in light of contemporary evolutionary theories of altruism. This book contributes some preliminary considerations for what actually constitutes a much larger project: a comprehensive and systematic theory of the ordering of love for contemporary Christian ethics. As preliminary and limited in scope, it is nonetheless significant and worthwhile.

NOTES

1.   Anders Nygren, *Agape and Eros*, trans. Philip S. Watson (Chicago and London: University of Chicago Press, 1982) (first Swedish edition, 1932, 1938, and 1939). Whether they agreed completely with his dualism or not (and most did not), no major Christian commentator on love, Catholic or Protestant, could avoid grappling with Nygren. Major Protestant responses to Nygren include Karl Barth, *Church Dogmatics*, IV, 2: *The Doctrine of Reconciliation*, trans. G. W. Bromiley (Edinburgh: T. and T. Clark, 1958), 727–840, especially 737ff.; Reinhold Neibuhr, *The Nature and Destiny of Man*, Vol 2: *Human Destiny* (New York: Charles Scribner's Sons, 1964 [1943]), esp. ch. 3; Paul Ramsey, *Basic Christian Ethics* (Chicago and London: University of Chicago Press, 1978 [1950]); Gene Outka, *Agape: An Ethical Analysis* (New Haven and London: Yale University Press, 1972).

Catholic responses include Robert O. Johann, S.J., *The Meaning of Love: An Essay towards a Metaphysics of Intersubjectivity* (Westminster, Maryland: Newman Press, 1959); Jules Toner, *The Experience of Love* (Washington/Cleveland: Corpus Books, 1968); M. C. D'Arcy, *The Mind and Heart of Love: Lion and Unicorn: A Study in Eros and Agape* (New York: Meridian Books, 1956). D'Arcy was also provoked by controversy over Pierre Rousselot's "Pour l'histoire du problème de l'amour au moyen âge," (Paris: J. Vrin, 1933); and Denis de Rougemont's *L'Amour et l'Occident*, translated as *Love in the Western World*, trans. Montgomery Belgion (New York: Harper and Row, 1956). Nygren has also influenced philosophical reflection on love. See, for example, Irving Singer, *The Nature of Love*, 3 vols., 2d. ed. (Chicago and London: University of Chicago, 1984), 1: 275–300. Not all progressive theology that preceded the council was primarily concerned with moral theology or specifically with retrieving the theme of love. But other streams of renewal (e.g., sacramental and liturgical theology) and other important concerns (e.g., aesthetics) are not discussed here.

2.   James M. Gustafson, *Ethics from a Theocentric Perspective*, 2 vols. (Chicago and London: University of Chicago Press, 1981, 84), 2: 164.

3.   See Stephen G. Post, *A Theory of Agape: On the Meaning of Christian Love* (Lewisburg: Bucknell University Press, 1990), chs. 1 and 6, esp. 97–101. Post's primary purpose is to critique and suggest a constructive alternative to the Kantian-based interpretation of *agape* as "equal regard," particularly as understood in Gene Outka's excellent and pervasively influential text, *Agape*. My attention in this book is confined to Catholic ethics, and my primary concern is to correct certain deficiencies that developed as a result of imbalanced appropriations of personalism, which is also influenced by Kant though not in a way that generates an impartialist understanding of *agape*.

4.   See, *inter alia*, Origin, *Hom. II. in Cantic.* on 2, 4, in PG 13, 64; Augustine, *De Doc. Christ.* I, 28 (PL 34,30); Peter Lombard, *Collectanea in epistulas Pauli*, on I Tim 1:1–5, PL 192, 329; Thomas Aquinas, *Summa Theologiae* II–II, 26 and *In III Sent.* d.29. See also John Calvin, *Institutes of the Christian Religion*, II, 8, 55.

5.   According to Rockefeller, "The growth of a large business is merely a survival of the fittest. . . . This is not an evil tendency in business. It is merely the working out of a law of nature and a law of God." Quoted in W. J. Ghent, *Our Benevolent Feudalism* (New York: Macmillan, 1902), 29.

6.   The pope did not endorse evolutionary theory, of course, but simply taught that the church does not forbid scientists to engage in research and scholarly discussion on the topic. See *Humani generis*, DS#419.

7.   Joseph T. C. Arnst, O.P., "Natural Law and Its History" in *Moral Problems and Christian Personalism, Concilium* 5, ed. Franz Bockle (New York: Paulist, 1965), 53.

8.   The pivotal distinction between the "person" and the "individual" was advanced by Jacques Maritain in his 1925 book, *Trois Réformateurs: Luther, Descartes, Rousseau*, and employed as the basis for the doctrine of rights in his more famous (and less vitriolic) 1942 text *Les Droits de l'homme et la loi naturelle*. Maritain and others were in turn criticized for implying that the soul merely dwells within the body rather than viewing the body as a constitutive component of the person. The personalists were thus criticized in Thomistic terms of developing a latent Platonism and Cartesianism that denies that the person is a *compositum humanum*. Because the personalists place the person above society, it was further argued, they undermine the common good and diminish the significance of political order and justice. For criticisms of the personalists, see P. Descoqs, "Individu et personne," *Archives de Philosophie* 14 (1938): 1–58; Charles de Koninck, *De la primauté du bien commun contre les Personnalistes. Le principe de l'ordre nouveau* (Québec: Univ. Laval, 1943); and Jules Baisnée, S.S., "Two Catholic Critiques of Personalism," *Modern Schoolman* 22 (1945): 59–75.

9.   For example, see Bruno Schüller, *Wholly Human: Essays on the Theory and Language of Morality*, trans. Peter Heinegg (Washington, D.C.: Georgetown University Press, 1986).

10.   Edward O. Wilson, *Sociobiology: The New Synthesis* (Cambridge, Massachusetts: Belknap Press, 1975), 595.

11.   Edward O. Wilson, *On Human Nature* (Cambridge, Massachusetts: Harvard University Press, 1978), 3.

12.   See Richard D. Alexander, *The Biology of Moral Systems* (New York: Aldine De Gruyter, 1987), 107–26.

13.   J. L. Mackie, "The Law of the Jungle," *Philosophy* 53 (1978): 464.

14.   Sigmund Freud, *Civilization and Its Discontents*, trans. James Strachey (New York and London: W. W. Norton, 1961), 64.

15.   Christopher Badcock, *Evolution and Individual Behavior: An Introduction to Human Sociobiology* (Cambridge, Massachusetts: Basil Blackwell, 1991), 114. See also Mary Maxwell, *Morality among Nations* (Albany, New York: State University of New York Press, 1990), 135.

16.   Mary Midgley, *Beast and Man: The Roots of Human Nature* (Ithaca: Cornell University Press, 1978), *xiii.*

17.   Critical doctrinal decrees on the goodness of the creation include the Council of Braga, Anathemas against the Priscillianists (561), DS#402, and the Decree for the Jacobites of the General Council of Florence (1442), DS#408. On sanctifying grace, see the Sixth Session of the Council of Trent (1547), ch. 7, DS#717, 719, 720.

18.   See R. A. Fisher, *The Genetical Theory of Natural Selection* (New York: Dover, 1930) and Theodore Dobzhansky, *Genetics and the Origin of Species*, 3d. ed. (New York: Columbia University Press, 1951).

19.   August Comte, *System of Positive Polity,* 2 vols. (London: Longmans Green, 1875), 1:556.

20.   See Jacqueline R. Macaulay and Leonard Berkowitz, ed., *Altruism and Helping Behavior* (New York: Academic Press, 1970), 3; see also Lauren G. Wispe, "Positive Forms of Social Behavior: An Overview," *Journal of Social Issues* 28 (1972): 1–19.

21.   See, for example, Alasdair MacIntyre, "Egoism and Altruism," in *The Encyclopedia of Philosophy,* ed. Paul Edwards (New York: Macmillan and The Free Press, 1967), 2:462–466; and Bernard Williams, "Egoism and Altruism," in his *Problems of the Self: Philosophical Papers 1956-72* (Cambridge: Cambridge University Press, 1973), 250–65.

22.   The phrase "altruistic suicide," originally coined by Durkheim, is a misnomer, since the intention of its agents is to save others rather than to destroy themselves. See Joseph A. Blake, "Death by Hand Grenade: Altruistic Suicide in Combat," *Suicide and Life Threatening Behavior* 8 (1978): 46–59.

23.   See Nechama Tec, *Dry Tears: The Story of a Lost Childhood* (New York: Oxford University Press, 1984). The altruistic rescue of Jews has been studied by sociologists Samuel P. Oliner and Pearl Oliner in *The Altruistic Personality: Rescuers of Jews in Nazi Europe* (New York: The Free Press, 1988).

24.   For example, according to Wilson, "When a person (or animal) increases the fitness of another at the expense of his own fitness, he can be said to have performed an act of altruism" (*Sociobiology*, 117). Mark Ridley and Richard Dawkins offer a virtually identical definition: "An altruistic act is one that has the *effect* of increasing the chance of survival (some would prefer to say 'reproductive success') of another organism at the expense of the altruist's," "The Natural Selection of Altruism" in *Altruism and Helping Behavior: Social, Personality, and Developmental Perspectives*, ed. J. Philippe Rushton and Richard M. Sorrentino (Hillsdale, New Jersey: Lawrence Erlbaum Associates, 1981], 19; authors' emphasis).

25.   Robert Trivers, *Social Evolution* (Menlo Park, California: Benjamin/Cummings, 1985), 41.

26.   David P. Barash, *Sociobiology and Behavior,* 2d. ed. (London: Hodder and Stoughton, 1982), 73.

27. See Trivers, *Social Evolution*, 42–43. "Phenotypical altruism" should not be confused with moral altruism. The term "phenotypical altruism" is employed by sociobiologists to refer to the self-sacrifice of individual biological fitness (or what is sometimes called "Darwinian fitness"), as distinct from "genotypical altruism," which detracts from inclusive fitness. The self-sacrificial behavior of "helpers at the nest" found in some bird species constitutes, for example, phenotypical but not genotypical altruism (on this example of phenotypical altruism, see Barash, *Sociobiology and Behavior*, 89–95). The major contribution of geneticist W. D. Hamilton was, as Barash points out, "to clarify how *phenotypic* altruism can actually evolve through behavior that is *genotypically* selfish and, hence, in conformity with the principle of natural selection" (ibid., 71).

28. Arnst, "Natural Law and Its History," 53

29. These rubrics are taken from James M. Gustafson, *Protestant and Roman Catholic Ethics: Prospects for Rapprochement* (Chicago: University of Chicago Press, 1978), ch. 5.

30. A. R. Radcliffe-Brown, "On the Concept of Function in Social Science," *American Anthropologist* 37 (1935): 397. Radcliffe-Brown's definition is specifically intended to describe sociological function but it covers conceptual function as well.

31. Mary Midgley, "Rival Fatalisms: The Hollowness of the Sociobiology Debate," in *Sociobiology Examined*, ed. Ashley Montagu (New York: Oxford University Press, 1980), 17.

32. The particular approach within neo-Darwinism that I find most attractive is called "evolutionary psychology" or "Darwinian psychology." The former expression is used in John Tooby and Leda Cosmides, "Evolutionary Psychology and the Generation of Culture, Part I," *Ethology and Sociobiology* 10 (1989): 29–49; the latter by Donald Symons in "A Critique of Darwinian Anthropology," *Ethology and Sociobiology* 10 (1089): 133. I interpret "evolutionary psychology" to maintain that discussion of evolutionary adaptive functions and heritable programs must be connected with more proximate accounts of specieswide psychological motivations and processes.

33. On proximate and ultimate causes, see Ernst Mayr, "Cause and Effect in Biology," *Science* 134 (1961): 1501–06.

34. See, for example, Hans Krummer, *Primate Societies* (Chicago: Aldine-Atherton, 1971).

35. See G. Wilkinson, "Reciprocal Food Sharing in the Vampire Bat," *Nature* 201 (1964): 1145–47.

36. I do not provide here a description of how sociobiology accounts for kin preference and the capacity to internalize norms. See a very helpful paper by Jerome H. Barkow, "Social Norms, the Self, and Sociobiology: Building on the Ideas of A. I. Hallowell," *Current Anthropology* 19 (1978): 99–103.

37. Midgley, *Beast and Man*, 58. Note that the contemporary philosophy of science is the scene of intense and prolonged debates over the validity of the notion of "species." See, for example, Michael Ruse, ed., *What the Philosophy of Biology Is: Essays Dedicated to David Hull* (Dordrecht, Boston, and London: Kluwer Academic Publishers, 1989) and Elliott Sober, ed., *Conceptual Issues in Evolutionary Biology: An Anthology* (Cambridge, Mass.: MIT Press, 1984) pp. 529–703. My position assumes the general lines developed by Midgley on this matter, particularly as presented in *Beast and Man*.

38.   See Paul Ekman, *Darwin and Facial Expression: A Century of Research in Review* (New York: Academic Press, 1973). Facial expression of course is also susceptible to cultural interpretation.

39.   See, *inter alia*, Owen Lovejoy, "The Origin of Man," *Science* 211 (1981): 341–50.

40.   See, for example, Stephen Jay Gould, "Biological Potential vs. Biological Determinism," *Natural History Magazine*, May 1976, 12–22, and R. C. Lewontin, Steven Rose, and Leon J. Kamin, *Not in Our Genes: Biology, Ideology, and Human Nature* (New York: Random House, 1984).

41.   See, *inter alia*, Sidney Hook, ed., *Determinism and Freedom in the Age of Modern Science* (New York: Collier Books, 1961); Bernard Berofsky, ed., *Free Will and Determinism* (New York: Harper & Row, 1966); and John Martin Fischer, ed., *Moral Responsibility* (Ithaca and London: Cornell, 1986).

42.   See Midgley, "Rival Fatalisms"; see also idem, *Beast and Man*, 51–82, and *Wickedness: A Philosophical Essay* (New York: Routledge and Kegan Paul, 1984), 93–112.

43.   See Midgley, *Beast and Man*, 51–82 and 321–44.

44.   Richard Dawkins, *The Selfish Gene* (New York: Oxford, 1976), ix.

45.   See Midgely, *Beast and Man*, 322–63.

46.   This objection is registered by Jeffrey Kurland in his criticism of Barkow's use of evolutionary theory in the latter's "Social Norms, the Self, and Sociobiology." See *Current Anthropology* 19 (1978): 107–8.

47.   Donald Symons, "If We're All Darwinians, What's the Fuss About?" in *Sociobiology and Psychology: Ideas, Issues and Applications*, ed. Charles Crawford, Martin Smith, and Dennis Krebs (Hillsdale, New Jersey: Lawrence Erlbaum Associates, 1987), 137; author's emphases.

48.   Robert A. Hinde, *Towards Understanding Relationships* (New York and London: Academic Press, 1979), 8.

49.   This assumption, for instance, pervades Wilson's discussion of religion and his endorsement of scientific materialism in ch. 8 of *On Human Nature*.

1

Recent Catholic Ethics of Love

The most distinctive characteristic of Catholic moral theology in the last forty years has been its gradual shift of focus from human nature and the natural law to the human person and human experience. A massive shift in emphasis has taken place, from obedience to the moral law to interpersonal love as the central motif of the Christian moral life. Indeed two general perspectives have come to dominate the Catholic ethics of love in the post-conciliar period: the first is personalism/existentialism; the second, liberation theology.[1] The former has clearly assumed the dominant perspective in moral theology, at least since the Second Vatican Council; the latter has emerged more recently but constitutes an increasingly influential source of reflection on the social dimension of love, particularly in pastoral circles. Notwithstanding their distinctive features and the contributions they make to Catholic ethics, these perspectives share certain common deficiencies that require correction.

Personalism

Roman Catholic ethics from the mid-1950s to the present must be understood in the context of the neo-Thomistic "manuals" that are used to teach moral theology to seminarians. The manuals were intended to provide clear guidance to confessors who needed to identify the precise nature of various sins to assign the appropriate penances. Although they provided clear, precise, and authoritative moral guidance, the manuals also suffered from certain weaknesses, most notably legalism, a focus on law rather than love, minimalism, a concentration on avoiding guilt rather than doing good, and individualism, a primary concern with individual moral purity rather than on meeting the needs of the neighbor.[2]

Love in the manuals tended to be conceived as an act of benevolence that issues from the intellectual appetite, or will,[3] and charity as supernatural love commanded by God.[4] In Father Anthony Koch's much used five-volume *A Handbook of Moral Theology*, adapted and edited in 1933 by Arthur Preuss, the topic of interpersonal ethics—"Man's Duties to his Fellow Man"—was only taken up in the fifth and last volume of the handbook, after exhaustive discussion of the objective moral law, duties to God, and duties to the self. Neighbor love was clearly not the central organizing virtue of moral theology.[5]

Before the Second Vatican Council, a number of prominent theologians in the 1950s criticized Catholic moral theology for its unbalanced emphasis on the moral law, excessively narrow concern with meeting minimum moral obligations, and stingy preoccupation with avoiding sin rather than doing good. Gerard Gilleman's seminal text, *The Primacy of Charity in Moral Theology*,[6] argued that love rather than law is the primary *motif* of Christian morality, both in its biblical and authentically Thomistic senses. In the manuals, he charged, Christian charity was simply one chapter among others, and did not appear as the "nourishing substance" of all the virtues, as it did in the ethics of Thomas Aquinas.[7] The moral manuals, he lamented, "overstress the objective and individualistic bearings of moral theology; they keep harping, with a casuistic bias, on minimum obligation and sin."[8]

Gilleman claimed even more critically that the manuals in fact represent the antithesis of true Christian morality: "Law rather than love is their dominant theme. Where there should be a spiritual impulse, we find a fixed body of doctrine. Even inspiration and liberty are precisely codified."[9] System replaced vitality, philosophy outweighed revelation, casuistry supplanted theology, and extrinsicism, minimalism, and individualism smothered traditional emphasis on the virtues.[10] Authentic Christian life, on the contrary, is essentially a *"Nachfolge Christi,"* an imitation of Christ, a phrase Gilleman adopted from Fritz Tillmann, whose biblical theology was one of the early attempts to move moral theology away from "legal minimalism."[11]

The programmatic intention of Gilleman's *The Primacy of Charity* was thus to bring charity back into the center of the enterprise of moral theology, as its "inner soul" and "nourishing substance."[12] He pursued this agenda by selectively appropriating insights from existentialism and personalism and by retrieving Thomas Aquinas's notion of charity as the "form of the virtues." From this perspective, all traditional virtues and the moral norms associated with them could be placed within the context of charity and reinterpreted in a more theologically insightful and pastorally helpful manner.

Bernard Häring, arguably the most influential Catholic moralist of the century, attempted what at the time was a daring revision of moral theology in his groundbreaking three-volume text, *The Law of Christ: Moral Theology for Priests and Laity*.[13] Häring's center of attention was clear: "Our life above all must be a life in Christ,"[14] he wrote, and conformity to Christ consists in responsible love. Previous attempts by the manualists to give love a central place in the moral life were regarded as seriously flawed by Häring because they continued to understand love primarily as a duty, an externally imposed command, rather than as a personal, dynamic, and affective response of the person to the neighbor and God.[15] This juridical emphasis lead to a preoccupation with the moral correctness of one's own behavior rather than with responsiveness to the needs of others.

According to Häring, an ethic based fundamentally in the gospel recognizes the primacy of love, the gift of human freedom, and especially the moral centrality of personal responsibility:

> The more the Christian grows to maturity in the liberty of God's children, the more does the law of God unfold itself to him as a living safeguard of love. . . . Only those who possess the liberty of the children of God have real insight into the true nature of law, which in its depths is loving dialogue with God.[16]

Häring accentuated the creative and immanent dimensions of the divine, an emphasis coordinated with a sense of grace as inviting and eliciting love.

The use of existentialism and personalism brought freedom and intersubjective relationships into the center of Catholic moral reflection. Freedom was construed not simply as "free choice" (*liberum arbitrium*) but as the existential self-definition of the person. Human beings could thus be regarded as free subjects possessing unfathomable depth and as connected to one another in an ongoing dialogue intrinsically ordered toward interpersonal communion. Regard for the neighbor could be given primacy over adherence to law and conformity to the moral order, abstractly conceived. Questions in special moral theology could thus be considered in a more open, reasonable, and pastoral manner. Sexual behavior, for example, could be evaluated from its emotional and psychological impact on both parties and on other people. Immoral sexual behavior could be identified as exploitation and irresponsibility, rather than as violation of a moral law or the illicit use of sexual "faculties."[17]

The focus on interpersonal dialogue and responsiveness found in the writings of Martin Buber, and most notably in his *I and Thou*,[18] were particularly important to many Catholic thinkers in this period. And though Buber never offered a clear presentation of the meaning of love or its ethical implications, Catholic moralists in this period were profoundly attracted by his image of the "I-Thou" dialogue. According to Buber, authentic responsiveness attends to particularity and engages in empathic identification. Responsiveness, as he put it, is "a bold swinging . . . into the life of the other."[19] Reverence for the unique identity of "the other"—and, indeed, the "otherness of the other"—replaced the tendency to regard "objects" of charity as a means to the self's final end. Häring's ethics of responsibility drew on Buber's conviction that a genuine sense of responsiveness takes the perspective of "the other" rather than regarding him or her as one to whom the agent is obligated through the moral law or a common desire for eternal salvation. Both Gilleman and Häring suggested that love be understood on the model of interpersonal dialogue as distinct from mere benevolence, that is, willing the good to another person. Whereas the manuals categorized individuals and their acts in "third party" terms, from an abstracting distance and as exemplifications of universal categories, authentic responsiveness was said to appreciate the absolute uniqueness of each person.

The church assimilated the insights of personalism in many quarters. The modification of natural law ethics with personalism is exemplified in the claim of *Gaudium et spes* that objective moral standards must be based on "the nature of the human person and his acts,"[20] a belief that was later cited by theologians who dissented from Pope Paul VI's prohibition of artificial birth control in the 1967 encyclical *Humanae vitae*. More recently, the significance of the personalist shift is clearly felt in John Paul II's writings, for example, his apostolic exhortation *On the Family*, which advances a personalist argument for the prohibition of artificial birth control, a moral norm that had been defended previously on "physicalist" grounds.[21]

Gilleman and Häring, along with other theologians, had a powerful impact on the renewal of moral theology, but ultimately their work was transitional. They intended to move out of neo-Thomism but never quite completed a full methodological or substantive renovation of moral theology. Even their writings on love, though begun in a personalist and existentialist mode, did not develop in a systematic and comprehensive manner; the final chapters of their major texts sound in fact very like the manuals that they had originally criticized.

The same year that Gilleman published the English translation of *The Primacy of Charity* (1959), a clearer and more systematic analysis of love appeared in philosopher Robert Johann's seminal text, *The Meaning of Love: An Essay towards a Metaphysics of Intersubjectivity.*[22] This book, written in part to offer an alternative to Nygren's dualistic opposition of *eros* and *agape*, argued that the integration of "desire" (*eros*) and "direct love" (*agape*) occurs in the ontological dynamism of the love of relative being for Absolute Being as a participation in God's own self-love.[23] *The Meaning of Love* was written primarily, however, to correct in Catholic thought what Joseph de Finance had termed the "objectification of the existential,"[24] and its major innovation was to offer a more dynamic anthropology, informed by insights from phenomenology and personalism, as a corrective to the excessive abstractions of neo-Thomism.[25]

Johann's main contention was that a greater awareness of the mystery of intersubjectivity would lead to a more profound understanding of the "love of friendship" (*amor amicitiae*) than was currently available in standard neo-Thomism. He established the meaning of love through metaphysical analysis rather than dogmatic or moral theology, and he consistently appealed to the conscious experience of direct, interior self-inspection. This focus was grounded in his personalist view of the self as a "subsistent plenitude revealed to itself in its own immanent activity, a generous abundance of being open to itself . . . as affirmed and attained in the act by which it poses itself."[26] Accent was clearly placed on consciousness, subjectivity, interiority, freedom, originality, and personal singularity.

The strongest contrast to human love is, Johann maintained, presumably on the basis of common sense and ordinary observation, the instinctively-driven attraction of animals. Unlike "animal love," which regards its objects as no more than means to self-gratification, human love regards others as ends in themselves. Johann's attentiveness to animal love served to underscore human love's recognition of the dignity and irreplaceable individuality of each person and "regard for the other as other." Only the radical evolutionists, Johann argued, maintain that human love is only an extension of animal sociality.[27]

Johann's central distinction was between "direct love" and "desire." Desire grasps the other for the benefit it provides to the self, whereas direct love views the beloved not as an object or a mere instantiation of a generic nature but as a subject with its own irreplaceable and unfathomable depths of inner mystery. Direct love is hierarchically superior to desire and therefore requires examination on its own terms; the former cannot be reduced to the latter. True human love, Johann argued, is "an extension of the inward presence of being to itself. . . . Hence any theory of love which examines that reality only from *outside*, which treats both lover and beloved merely as objects brought into relation with one another in a certain way is doomed to failure from the start."[28]

Though individual variations can be noted, similar ways of construing love can be identified in other recent Catholic authors. For Karl Rahner, phenomenological reflection on natural human sociality and natural human relatedness provide the broad anthropological grounds for regarding the properly human world not only as personal but as *inter*personal and, as such, intrinsically oriented to mutuality.[29] As concrete, embodied, and particular, the human person cannot be absolutely solitary, Rahner argued; on the contrary, "the embodied spirit that man is exists necessarily in relation to a Thou."[30] By establishing a relationship with another person, a "Thou," the self is able to attain a proper relation with itself, the "I."[31] More important, transcendental experience of the eternal Thou is made possible through categorical encounters with concrete, individual human "Thous."

The hallmark of personhood for Rahner is freedom, and not simply freedom of choice but the more important freedom of "self-disposal," "the capacity of the one subject to decide about himself in his single totality"[32] vis-à-vis God. For Rahner, the divine-human relationship is analogous to friendship: through free and forgiving self-communication, he wrote, God becomes "a 'partner' in a personal and direct relationship between himself and man."[33] This friendship is made possible through the human person's free acceptance of God's offer of love. Sounding very much the existentialist, Rahner claimed that freedom is not simply the "capacity to do this or that but (formally) a *self*-disposing into finality; the subject (from a formal point of view) is always concerned with itself."[34] Freedom, in other words, regards not simply what one does but also what one becomes, not merely one's external actions but one's identity and character.

Each and every truly free human act constitutes a response not only to the self's immediate categorical object, for example, this or that person, but also, at least implicitly, to God, the person's "unthematic" transcendental horizon.[35] Or as moral theologian Josef Fuchs puts it, "love of neighbor is *the* absolute value of every human morality."[36] Interpersonal love in Rahner's perspective is the focal point of the transcendental affirmation of God. Indeed, one implication of this position is that the characteristic act of charity is direct love of neighbor. Genuine Christian love does not regard "the other" as a means to the agent's own salvation or as an object loved in an "overflow" from the more primary direct love for God. As a "Thou," the "other" is a mystery worthy of direct love in his or her own right.

Rahner did not phenomenologically differentiate among different concrete forms of love but maintained more generally that in a transcendental way, all concrete forms of neighbor love act as mediations of the love for God. The radical experience of God, he maintained, "can be made only in an always already going-out into the world which, understood as the whole of man, is primarily the people *with whom* he lives."[37] Though it applies to all human relations, Rahner's ethics of love gives particular emphasis to proximate relations, that is, to "our turning towards the people we live with, and . . . our explicit communication with them."[38] In this perspective, Rahner regarded with utmost seriousness the biblical claim that he paraphrased when he wrote, that "whoever does not love the brother that he 'sees', [sic] also cannot love God whom he does not see, and . . . [that] one can love God whom one does not see only by loving one's visible brother lovingly" (I John 4:7, 11).[39]

This personalist understanding of love, at least in its general lines, has been replicated and further developed more recently in feminist authors. Margret Farley's *Personal Commitments*, for example, treats love as properly fulfilled in mutuality based on equal respect and justice.[40] She conceives love, following Jules Toner, as an affective affirmation of another person in and for him or herself.[41] Her focus on commitment reveals existential concerns and a heightened awareness of the moral responsibility that always attends human freedom. Her position is in many ways broadly similar to the personalists, though perhaps with less direct use of continental philosophy as the major interpretive key to human experience. Her account of love coheres with feminism, including its affirmation of the dignity of all human beings, women as well as men; its appreciation of embodiment, a sense of the inseparability of self from body and of the body's goodness; and its endorsement of an egalitarian rather than hierarchical model of human relations.

Farley's perspective is distinctive in its balance. While some liberal feminists advocate autonomy as their central moral value, she consistently coordinates a sense of the value of independence with an appreciation of the significance of human interdependence. And unlike some personalists, she integrates an awareness of the uniqueness of individuals with a sense of fundamental human commonality. Nevertheless, in her focus on freedom, intersubjectivity, commitment, and mutuality, she can be broadly identified with the personalists and existentialists.

In all of these authors, a personalist anthropology supports a dynamic view of love—a view more adequate to human experience than the excessively impersonal, abstract, and extrinsic treatments of love found in neo-Thomistic circles. For these writers, love exists only where there is an existential presence to, and an affective union with, a unique other; it is by no means reducible to mere good will based on common humanity. Love is most adequately conceived in terms of interpersonal mutuality, and not, as Rahner characterized the manualists' views, a "duty, a heartless fulfillment of commandments, and a sheer act of the will."[42] Catholic thinkers have learned from the personalists to appreciate relationality— the fact that we are not primarily isolated individual entities but beings constituted in relationship with others—as an intrinsic dimension of human existence. The philosophy of dialogue provided an antidote to the individualism of the manuals by encouraging a deeper recognition of the dignity of the human person and the importance of communication and language, and therefore, at least implicitly, to the significance of community, as constitutive of interpersonal life.

Liberation Theology

Whereas personalists gave a great deal of attention to interpersonal dialogue and its attendant qualities, such as openness, trust, and availability, liberation theologians understand love primarily in terms of solidarity with the poor. Rahner acknowledged "political love" as an important component of neighbor love, and in this he attempted to avoid, at least in his mature writings, the narrowing temptations of personalism and existentialism, or what Johann Baptist Metz calls the "privatizing tendency" found in the emphasis on "the 'closed circuit' of the I-Thou relation."[43] While an improvement over earlier personalism, however, his reflections on the social implications of neighbor love were occasional and partial. None of the previously discussed writers attend to the connection of love and social justice as much as they do to the various traits, for example, trust and availability, that characterize interpersonal love.

Whereas personalism takes its point of departure with the general experience of intersubjectivity and interpersonal relations, Peruvian Gustavo Gutiérrez, the most prominent liberation theologian, begins with the particular experience of the poor and oppressed.[44] Christian love generates a critical assessment of the broad social, political, and economic oppression of the poor. Theological and moral concerns are interpreted in tandem with, rather than hermetically isolated from, social analysis. As Enrique Dussel puts it, when considering sin, for instance, liberation theology does not begin with the "relationship of the solitary self with another individual self but considers the structure in which the sin of the world conditions our own personal sin."[45] The same point applies to neighbor love.

Nothing better captures Gutiérrez's understanding of Christian love than the kinds of questions he takes most seriously: "How are we to live evangelical charity in the midst of this situation? How can we reconcile the universality of charity and a preferential solidarity with the poor who belong to marginalized cultures, exploited social classes, and despised racial groups?"[46] Gutiérrez expresses the evangelical task of liberation theology simply: "The question is how to tell the nonperson, the nonhuman, that God is love, and that this love makes us all brothers and sisters."[47]

Agape inspires a response to the plight of the needy neighbor that is practical rather than theoretical: the commitment to solidarity and social transformation, that is, the "preferential option for the poor." The preferential option is religiously grounded in at least three mutually complementary ways: theologically, in that the God revealed in the Bible has a special love for the poor and "sides with them" in their struggle for justice;[48] christologically, in that Jesus himself, the "poor Christ," sided with the poor and outcasts in his teaching, ministry, death, and resurrection;[49] ecclesiologically, in that the true church is the "church of the poor," called to welcome into communion and spiritually support all the faithful and not just the wealthy and powerful.[50]

Several important features of Gutiérrez's interpretation of love are relevant to the topic of this study. First, in striking contrast to the personalists, he takes solidarity with the poor to be the fundamental expression of Christian love. Love is communal, neither purely individual nor exclusively interpersonal. The evangelical and pastoral task mentioned above—announcing to the oppressed that God is love—is pursued ecclesially, not only through individual conversion but by building a community within which God's love can be experienced, shared, and promoted. Interpersonal love is thus always considered in the context of communal love and never simply within the setting of two dialoguing individuals in the closed circuit of "I-Thou" relations.

Second, Gutiérrez interprets love in an explicitly pastoral manner, and particularly as an expression of the Christian imperative of service. Direct appropriation of biblical material is more central to his enterprise than it was for the personalists and results in a clear emphasis on service, generosity, and self-denial as critically important aspects of love. As one might expect, the cross plays a much greater role here than in the philosophy of dialogue. Much less attention is given to themes like responsiveness, availability, trust, and intimacy, though these could be interpreted in terms of solidarity as responsiveness to the suffering of the poor, or availability to those in need.

Interpreting openness to the "other" in the context of solidarity with the poor heightens the connection between the preferential option and what Gutiérrez depicts as the unexpected "reversal" worked by *agape*.[51] A love that imitates the Christ who associated with prostitutes, tax collectors, and other outcasts, is more likely to be committed to solidarity with the nonperson than one that loves strictly in proportion to the goodness of its object or its closeness to the subject, the two criteria of love in Thomas and the manuals. The preferential option thus provides a powerful corrective to both the individualism of the manuals and the tempting parochialism of the personalists.

Third, love is conceived in a profoundly proactive manner. As Gutiérrez explains in his interpretation of the parable of the good Samaritan, *agape* does not stay on its own "front porch" but actively seeks out the "other":

> As long as I define my neighbor as the person next door, the one I meet on *my* way, the one who comes to me for help, my world will remain the same. All spirit of individual "aid and assistance," all social reformism, is a "love" that stays on its own front porch. ("If you love those who love you, what thanks can you expect?"—Luke 6:32). But if, on the contrary, I define my neighbor as the one whose way *I* take, the person afar off whom I approach ("Which of these three, do you think, proved himself a neighbor to the man who fell into the brigands' hands?"—Luke 10:36), if I define my neighbor as the one I must go out to look for, on the highways and byways, in the factories and slums, on the farms and in the mines— then my world changes. This is what is happening with the "option for the poor," for in the gospel it is the poor person who is the neighbor par excellence.[52]

This interpretation of the parable about neighbor love is problematic in some ways. The author of Luke does not indicate that the Samaritan was actively seeking someone to help, only that he happened to come across the man on his journey. Moreover, the "neighbor" in this parable is not the victim, whom Gutiérrez likens to the poor, but the Samaritan, who acts as "neighbor."[53] Finally, Jesus employs the parable to illustrate the meaning of neighbor love and he does not speak to the issue of how the character ("the world") of the agent, that is, the Samaritan, is transformed when he encounters "the other." This may of course be a valid interpretation of the preferential option, but it is not integral to this particular parable.[54]

Be this as it may, Gutiérrez's call to "go out to look for" the oppressed and poor neighbor suggests a much more expansive, proactive ethic than one finds in the conventional Catholic morality that he criticizes or in the moral theology of the manuals, which held that charity addresses individuals whom one happens to encounter and that one is only morally obligated to love and care for those particular individuals to whom one is bound in some kind of friendship—professional, civic, or familial.[55] Gutiérrez underscores to an unusual degree the Christian obligation to seek out the poor person, the neighbor—"the one whose way I take, the person far off whom I approach."

Fourth, Christian love inspires, in some sense, a kind of partiality. Solidarity involves "taking sides" with the poor over and against their oppressors and giving priority to the "underclass" in contrast to the preference traditionally given by the church, either actively or by default, to the dominant classes.[56] Gutiérrez maintains that God has a preferential love for the poor and yet that God "loves all human beings in an equal fashion."[57] *Agape* encompasses all people, he explains, first "the poor and dispossessed, and then through them . . . all human beings."[58]

Gutiérrez clearly recognizes that *agape* includes love of enemies, though not in a sentimental way that pledges a false apolitical neutrality, effectively ignores ongoing de facto social conflict, and permits exploitation to continue in the name of Christian love. *Agape* in this context refers to the refusal to exclude the enemy from love, not to "warm affection" (let alone unconditional acceptance). It clearly involves respect for the humanity of the enemy while allowing for a realistic acknowledgment of the objective evil entailed in the behavior of the oppressor. Love of enemies thus issues in a genuine identification with the true good of the oppressor, in spite of the latter's corruption, and therefore it works for the enemy's transformation.[59] Conversion of the enemy into a friend is the most perfect expression of charity, though one that is, regrettably, difficult to affect in practice.

Christian love as solidarity respects the humanity of the enemy but gives the strongest "moral pull" to the poor and oppressed. Precisely as "preferential," it suggests a "reversal" of the usual priority system whereby primary attention is given to family, friends, and peers, and the "remainder" to those who are more remote. Though God loves all people, the poor are loved with priority not because they possess some kind of moral superiority but, Gutiérrez writes, "because God is God, in whose eyes 'the last are first.'"[60] His explanation of this synthesis of apparently contradictory beliefs—equality vs. preference—is, however, far from crystal clear.

Perhaps the distinctiveness of the preferential option for the poor can be underscored by contrasting it with the neo-Thomistic treatment of charitable giving. The manuals generally regarded almsgiving as an expression of charity rather than justice. They maintained, however, that amassing wealth with utter disregard for the poor was mortally sinful, and they also held that Christians have a positive moral duty to give alms to the poor out of their "superfluities," out of whatever goods are left over after one has provided the things needed to care for one's family and to maintain one's "station in life." According to Noldin, for example, a wealthy banker cannot be required to give away his resources to such an extent that he would be reduced to living in the manner of a small merchant.[61] At the same time, the manuals held that one must give out of one's "necessities" (in the sense of social amenities appropriate to one's station in life, not the goods indispensable for one's own life or one's family) to another person who is in "extreme necessity" (as distinguished from "grave necessity" and "common necessity"). In other cases, almsgiving was considered supererogatory, that is, morally praiseworthy but not mandatory.

Given these principles, the manualists debated over what percentage of one's annual income ought to be devoted to alms. The majority of the manuals, following Alphonsus Ligouri, maintained that no one is morally obligated, on pain of mortal sin, to donate more than the "fiftieth portion," or two percent, of superfluous income, unless he or she is extremely wealthy.[62] Dissenters from this particular percentage argued, as one would expect, that two percent of one's superfluous income is too lenient and (some proposed an alternative of five to seven percent).[63] Still others, to use our language, argued that it is unjustly "regressive" to demand the same percentage of income from all people regardless of financial status, and that the very notion of "superfluities" is excessively vague. Yet the focus of these discussions was on the almsgiver's strict obligations rather than on the needs of others. Sparing the wealthy person "qualms of conscience" appears to have been of greater concern than relieving the suffering of the poor.[64]

Häring criticized this approach to alms for its uncritical acceptance of the prevailing standard of living among the affluent classes and insisted that "superfluities" be assessed in light of the needs of the poor rather than simply in terms of conventional social expectations. He rejected the practice of offering mathematical formulas for the percentage of superfluous income that must, in strict justice, be given to the poor, focusing instead on the "magnanimity" generated by true love of neighbor. According to Häring, "true Christian life is not to be judged by its conformity to the special privileges or prerogatives of a station in life, but rather by conformity to the teaching and example of Christ."[65] In this sense he was closer to Gutiérrez, who would no doubt regard attempts to calculate the exact minimal requirement of almsgiving as missing entirely the point of the parable about the good Samaritan.

Häring identified some of the difficulties with the manualists' assessments of almsdeeds that would later exercise Gutiérrez, including their tendency to focus on the bare minimum that had to be provided as a matter of precept and their distance from the biblical and particularly christocentric inspiration for solidarity with the poor. Yet Häring qualified his criticism by arguing that in spite of these difficulties, "there is a correct sense in which one may use the term, 'station in life'."[66] Gutiérrez exceeds Häring in his unequivocal rejection of the paternalistic assumptions of almsgiving and in his affirmation of the fundamental equality of all Christians regardless of social status.

Gutiérrez is influenced by personalism, but he interprets interpersonal dialogue in a more profoundly corporate context. He employs the personalist "I-Thou" metaphor, for example, but his very specific "Thou" is the poor: "our partners in dialogue are the poor, those who are 'nonpersons'."[67] Whereas almsdeeds involve the donation of surplus possessions to the poor, solidarity involves giving of the self to the poor. Indeed, a number of liberation theologians argue that the preferential option involves becoming poor in a material rather than figurative sense.[68] The fullness of love resides in communion, and the distinctive character of Christian love is solidarity with the poor and outcast, those with whom Christ himself developed a special friendship.[69] Gutiérrez thus emphasizes solidarity with the poor whatever their connection to the agent, and indeed, the preferential option creates special connections and friendships with the poor if they do not exist already.[70]

Common Themes

In spite of various differences, these recent Catholic authors have certain themes in common. First, they all construe *agape* or *caritas* primarily in terms of love for neighbor rather than direct love for God. This construction includes a deliberate move away from loving the neighbor on the basis of certain qualities or for extrinsic reasons, including love "for God's sake," toward affirming the neighbor as a unique individual to be loved for his or her own sake. Loving the neighbor "in God" or for the neighbor's own sake are not necessarily conflicting interpretations, but the emphasis in recent Catholic ethics is clearly on the "horizontal" direction, just as the "vertical" was accentuated earlier in the century. Love is regarded as radically particular rather than primarily universal, that is, as affirming the special value of particular individuals in their uniqueness rather than focusing on the generic value of all human beings qua human beings. A person is to be loved for what he or she is actually, not for what he or she can become or once was. Using the language of "the other," a common usage in thinkers as diverse as Johann and Gutiérrez, underscores the particularity of the neighbor, of that which is different from the self.

Second, these writers regard love primarily as an affection rather than an attitude, that is, as rooted fundamentally in human emotional life rather than in an act of the will, as we saw in the manuals.[71] None of them understands love as simple *bene velle*. They accentuate responsiveness to "the other" as an end in himself or herself. Love includes qualities like responsiveness, copresence, participation in the being of the other, or as Jules Toner puts it, a profound "conscious affective identification with the beloved as a person."[72] Gutiérrez stresses Christian conversion giving rise to compassion, a profoundly affective term. "The Samaritan approached the injured man on the side of the road," he writes, "not because of some cold religious obligation, but because 'his heart was melting' (this is literally what the verb *splankhnizein* means in Luke 10:33; cf. Luke 1:7, 8; 7:13; 15:20), because his love for that man was made flesh in him."[73]

The personalists recognize that particular affection in and of itself does not accommodate the full scope of *agape*. As a result, they strive to extend their accounts of love to all human beings, including strangers, but this effort strains against the fully affective and particularistic sense of love that they usually employ. None of them, it seems to me, fully coordinates love as a particularistic affection with love as an ethical attitude of universal care, concern, respect, or related notions. The personalist understanding of love as a positive affective engagement of another person in light of concrete experience and personal knowledge makes it awkward to claim that care for a complete stranger is a genuine expression of love in the full personalist sense of the term.[74]

Fourth, they all utterly reject neo-Thomistic "legal minimalism." One is hard pressed, moreover, to find even the slightest endorsement of the traditional distinction between commands and counsels, that is, between strict obligations, the violation of which places one in a state of sin, and striving for perfection. Not a single writer is concerned with the danger of love placing excessive demands on the Christian conscience, and, with the exception of Farley, none even alludes to the need to coordinate interpersonal love with commutative justice.

Fifth, these authors view mutuality as the culmination of love, its interpersonal fruition and proper fulfillment. Love implies a consonant presence, agreement, balance of selves, and interpersonal harmony; it is a liberation from the confines of "one's own egoistic isolation."[75] Some of these authors are divided over the appropriate emphasis or the proper objects of love, for example, liberationist solidarity with the poor as distinct from interpersonal communion, but all regard mutuality as the heart of Christian love.[76] All, in other words, employ some version of the "I-Thou" model of relationality as constitutive of love.

Lastly, all of these authors in various ways reflect the influence of Thomas Aquinas. For example, Johann's distinction between "direct love" and "desire" presents a variation on Thomas's "love of friendship" (*amor amicitiae*) and "love of concupiscence" (*amor concupiscentia*). And further, these authors all display varying degrees of coherence with what Nygren called the "caritas-synthesis,"[77] particularly regarding the complementary relation between natural love and Christian love or charity, the positive value of reciprocal love, the value of proper self-love in addition to neighbor love, and the integration of love for God, love for self, and love for neighbor. All of these positions display a fundamental affinity with the classical Catholic view that grace perfects nature.

Critical Assessment

I would now call attention to some of the characteristic weaknesses that can be found in this literature. My central criticism is that in general recent Catholic ethics fails to address sufficiently the traditional question of the ordering of love. I begin by discussing two related oversights regarding the perceived scope of human interaction and the fundamental inclinations of human nature.

My first criticism is that recent Catholic ethicists assume a context of human love that is excessively narrow. It is true that they reject the individualistic framework of the manuals that was concerned only with the agent and his or her individual acts. For their part, the personalists cannot be accused of "individualism" because they clearly view individual human beings as constituted in and by their interpersonal relations rather than as self-enclosed substances. This important qualification notwithstanding, the personalists restrict excessively the assumed sphere of human interaction to the interpersonal. Indeed, at times the perceived sphere of human interaction seems to be narrowed down to an "I-Thou" conversation between two adults found on the set of an existentialist play. The sphere of moral responsibility is similarly constricted, and therefore the personalist understanding of love can be fairly criticized as a kind of *égoisme à deux* that narrowly collapses moral concern into immediate interpersonal relations. The wider context of other kinds of relations, including family, associates, and role relations are ignored, as is the wider communal setting and responsibility for the common good.

The larger setting assumed by liberationist theologians like Gutiérrez is a vast improvement over this personalist truncation of the moral life. Gutiérrez recognizes the communal context of human interaction rather than simply its intersubjective matrix. Yet the liberationist depiction of the human context shares with the personalists a complete abstraction of human relations from their wider natural setting. According to Gutiérrez, for example, Christianity is inherently oriented to history rather than nature: "Other religions think in terms of cosmos and nature; Christianity, rooted in Biblical sources, thinks in terms of history."[78] This seems to me to impose a false dichotomy between creation and redemption, analogous to that proposed by those who maintain that human behavior reflects culture but not biology, or vice versa. As a result, features of human nature that are not purely intersubjective or historical are dismissed. Human nature—including the basic inclinations, desires, needs, and other aspects shared by all or most members of the species *Homo sapiens*—tends to be ignored.

Recent Catholic authors thus unnecessarily separate the human person from human nature and the wider natural world. Typical in this regard is Johann's statement that the self has a nature but is a person.[79] Though nature cannot be equated with body, this kind of statement leads to what some feminists like Farley would regard, properly in my judgment, as a "disembodied" anthropology. Johann suffered from an unfortunate tendency to dismiss the "object" as merely incidental to the "subject." He argued, for example, that any theory of love which "examines that reality [i.e., love] only from *outside*, which treats both lover and beloved merely as objects brought into relation with one another in a certain way is doomed to failure from the start."[80] In my judgment, however, the appropriation of information and theories regarding the social or biological order need not involve an examination of interpersonal love "only from outside." It need not be "only" because other methods can be employed in the study of human behavior without being used in a single-mindedly reductionistic manner. It need not be "from outside" because social and biological ordering is intrinsic to the human person, not only because human beings are embodied, and therefore biological beings, but also in the sense that human beings are required by their own biological constitution to be formed by culture, to undergo socialization, and to learn from their social and natural surroundings.

On closer examination one can recognize that Johann did in fact attend to human nature, but under the exclusive guise of intersubjectivity, relationality, responsiveness, and freedom. Similarly, Rahner's view of human nature concentrated almost exclusively on human freedom. These interpretations of human nature as revealed most clearly in the context of unique self-conscious subjects in dialogue with other equally unique self-conscious subjects relegates both less intimate human relations and nonpersonal social institutions to the periphery of the moral life—indeed, it excludes them altogether.

Disregard for human nature in all its dimensions seems to be accompanied in these authors with a disregard for the place of humanity within the wider natural world. The "turn to the subject" of modern philosophy has been accompanied by a shift from nature to the self as the primary locus of the experience of transcendence. Thus, whereas classical Greek thought was oriented to nature, modernity is anthropocentric.[81] Christianity is at least partially responsible for the modern technological subjugation of nature because it disconnected God from the elemental powers and processes of the natural world.[82] In the Incarnation, Rahner argued, human beings became God's own history; therefore, Christians regard human beings as standing "over against" other creatures "on the side of God," as their steward and God's "deputy" on earth.[83] Given this "anthropology" and an understanding of matter as essentially a limit to the human spirit, it is no wonder that the prerational, prevoluntary inclinations flowing from within human nature do not receive any attention from Rahner.[84]

Gutiérrez shows similar proclivities, though with his own distinctive emphases. He is strongly impressed with the development of modern technological capacities to exploit nature for the benefit of humankind.

His acceptance of the modern Baconian notion of "nature" as mere passive material subject to human dominance lends support to his belief that we are increasingly to control nature, thereby creating progressively better living conditions for human beings. An intense awareness of historicity no doubt provides Gutiérrez with certain advantages, not the least of which is a heightened sense of both the conflictual elements within and the transformative possibilities of history. One would certainly not expect and indeed one does not find any sense that ethics involves conformity to a given moral order in this theological and philosophical context.

Gutiérrez understands the person as fundamentally dynamic and historical, oriented to the future and not defined by the past. Contrary to static essentialism, he argues, history is not "the development of potentialities preexistent in human nature," but the creation of "new, qualitatively different ways of being a human person in order to achieve an ever more total and complete fulfillment of the individual in solidarity with all humankind."[85] Thus, the goal of liberative solidarity is not simply to raise the quality of life of the poor but to make possible the "creation of a *new humanity*"[86] and the "creation of a wholly new way for men and women to be human."[87]

One criticism of this position that anticipates my own alternative is Midgley's comment that "We are not free to create or annihilate wants, either by private invention of by culture. . . . Wants are not random impulses. They are articulated, recognizable aspects of life; they are the deepest structural constituents of our characters."[88]

Johann's emphasis on intersubjectivity, Rahner's exclusive focus on freedom, and Gutiérrez's radical historicism all share a common neglect of human beings as parts of nature. It is no surprise that they also share the habit of ignoring current scientific and empirical information and theories regarding natural human sociality. Gutiérrez proposes a theory of solidarity, for example, without attending to empirical studies of sociality and allied behavior such as cooperation, altruism, and group bonding—studies which highlight the preferential nature of human behavior that ought to be addressed by proponents of the preferential option for the poor.

A further criticism of these authors is that their excessively narrow understanding of the context and content of human nature has contributed to a serious neglect of the major issues surrounding the ordering of love. They have failed, in other words, to respond to the pervasive human need to establish, in spite of enormous complexities and the impossibility of attaining either comprehensive clarity or complete emotional satisfaction, a reasonable and ethically justifiable ordering of moral and affective priorities.

Most recent Catholic authors tacitly accept the traditional pattern of ordering love for self, properly understood, as prior to love for neighbor. "Properly understood" indicates that appropriate self-love is fully compatible with, and indeed requires, a self-transcending love that issues in significant degrees of self-denial in the service of the neighbor. Farley, more than the other authors, emphasizes self-denial: "Agape, of course, has a normative meaning which in general repudiates loving ourselves more than others and which in a powerful sense calls for loving others more than ourselves."[89] At the same time, she sees the dangers of a one-sided understanding of *agape* as self-sacrifice, particularly in the case of women, who have often been expected to be more self-sacrificing than men. She attempts to reconcile self-denial with self-regard by developing an account of self-transcending love as the basis for the authentically unitive love that constitutes human happiness in its full sense. However, beyond ruling out choices that imply servility or self-destruction, Farley explains neither the moral status of natural self-love within this position, nor whether, or on what grounds, individuals might legitimately choose to advance their own good rather than promote the good of others. In fact, none of these authors offers a careful moral analysis of natural self-love or discusses sufficiently the moral status of the natural tendency to ascribe priority to self vis-à-vis neighbor.

This may reflect a general turn from preoccupation with obligations to greater freedom, a hesitancy to view love as morally required rather than spontaneously evoked. Or it may reflect an emphasis of virtue ethics on the obligation of the subject to cultivate certain dispositions, for example, trust and responsiveness, rather than to be concerned with the status of certain individuals as objects of obligatory love. The latter coheres with a theory of love as an act of the intellectual appetite, less so in affectively centered theories. All of our authors seem more interested in expounding on the radical generosity of love at its least inhibited than on its observance of duties. Neglect of the order of love in current authors is probably in part a healthy reaction against minimalism and the tacit authoritative sanction the manuals gave for not going beyond the strict duties owed to others. Rather than compassionate caring for the neighbor in need, the manualists' order of love provided the theoretical apparatus for evading actions that could be deemed as not morally binding because merely supererogatory. Some of the kinds of questions that the *ordo amoris* addressed in the past do engage moralists today, for example, regarding moral responsibility for elderly parents,[90] but they are taken up in the course of specialized debates in bioethics rather than in the major Catholic literature devoted to love.

Personalist preoccupation with interpersonal dyads, that is, one-to-one relations, tends to obscure or at least ignore the multiplicity of relations within which the ethic of love is applied in the concrete moral life. It oversimplifies very complex kinds of relations and the range of considerations that are relevant to their proper ordering. It tends to ignore the inherent limits and the possibilities for conflict that at times accompany love for multiple objects. They are completely unclear how the needs of various objects of care are weighed, or according to what scale, or how the obligations due to primary relationships are placed in relation to obligations due to other people in need.

Farley is the one exception to this omission. Her sensitive reading of concrete human experience leads her to be acutely aware of the many possibilities for conflict built into human affectivity. She recognizes that conflict between obligations owed to different people is a steady feature of the moral life, and that some ordering is necessary. After introducing the two central criteria of priority in the tradition—need and proximity—she highlights the ambiguities attending their application in concrete decisions and underscores the need for moral discernment. Like the other authors examined in this chapter, however, she does not provide a sufficiently developed set of warrants for the general moral priority she gives to primary relations.

The juxtaposition of different kinds of relationships poses the question of the order of love in a particularly acute fashion. Rather than narrowly focusing on the love between two communicating, mature adults, we need to attend to the multitude of interacting relations within which we are immersed. Human love is not only simple and dyadic, but also complex and multiple; it involves existential encounters, and relationships extended over time. We need to attend to the "moral pull" of relationships that evoke great love, care, and loyalty despite the fact that they exist prior to free choice, full knowledge, and complete self-disclosure. We need to develop, in other words, a greater attunement to the ways in which we are embedded in a social network, in what feminists refer to as a "web of relations,"[91] a network of love and attachment, rather than simply moving between various unconnected, self-contained two-party relationships. This confinement is very unrealistic, since any person's relation to another is constrained and affected by all the other human relations within which he or she is involved.

The personalists tacitly assume that our responsibility to primary relationships differs in kind from our responsibility to strangers, and that bonds to family and friends engender heightened degrees of loyalty, empathy, self-sacrifice, and devotion. However, they often simply assume the validity of the preferential and selective implications of mutuality without providing their ethical justification or explicating their significance for the moral life. The personalists wish to retain the centrality of natural priorities without also retaining its traditional foundation in human nature—an awkward position that suggests absent or at least insufficient ethical justification.

Johann is a case in point. He recognizes the fact of ontological finitude but has little sense of the kind of natural limitations imposed on love. He views love as the direct effect of free choice, and it is true that fully human love does reflect the ongoing option to love. At the same time, however, human beings are often called on to love others who do not in themselves spontaneously evoke from them a desire to engage in dialogue or "reciprocity of consciousness."[92]

Most of these authors omit from consideration the complications that attend many ordinary human relationships. Emphasis on freedom and on the dyadic context of intersubjective relationships tends to exclude natural interdependencies and responsibilities existing prior to free choices, for example, the claims made by aging parents on their grown children or on siblings by one another. It is sometimes suggested that humans are individuals first who then consciously and deliberately choose to enter into relationships and social ties. In many social contexts the person is presented with objects of love with whom love will never be mutual. These relationships are established with consent, to be sure, but they are given to the agent without prior free choice. As Farley points out, some relations are established prior to free choice, that, for example, "some roles that we fill or relationships in which we participate entail commitments, but they become ours without an original choice on our part."[93] Of course, even these "given" roles must be ratified in personal freedom, at least implicitly, if they are to be real to the agent.[94]

Emphasis on free decisions based on love as the key to moral obligation might be taken to imply that duties result only from an act of the will and that binding obligations exist only when freely chosen. The voluntary basis of many special obligations is apparent. Yet it seems to me that some if by no means all obligations to affirm particular people affectively arise organically within ordinary social life and that people are obliged to love others prior to their own deliberate decision to do so. A case can be made that people are morally obliged to love in a particular way those with whom they have some kind of an interpersonal relationship, including those to whom they are connected through family ties or work association.[95] Farley correctly claims that people obligate themselves through explicit promises in order to strengthen themselves in the face of human frailty and weakness. At the same time, bonds sometimes exist prior to free choices and they can be said to place a claim on human freedom, prior to autonomous choice, to love and care.

The most poignant example of these kind of relations is provided in the familial context, where interpersonal relations are often placed in a broader and more complex context than that which obtains between two free and independent centers of self-consciousness. One does not freely choose one's parents, children, or siblings, yet these people and the relations they involve one in are, for most people, absolutely fundamental to human love and therefore to the Christian moral life. The personalist description of the self as "a free initiative ready to engage in dialogue"[96] applies paradigmatically to love between friends and spouses, yet not to the parent-infant bond, which is a different love than that found in mutuality and one that generates its own distinct if not completely unique virtues and obligations.

Indeed, the kinds of capacities for interpersonal dialogue, reciprocal affective attachment, and mutual long-term commitment presupposed by the personalists do not characterize the parent-child relation, at least not when very young children are involved. Interpersonal virtues are initially formed within the family, primarily through the nurturance of loving parents, whose existence the personalists take for granted. Why do these parents care for their children the way they do? Certainly not because their children, especially when very young and most demanding, engage in mature and self-conscious "I-Thou" dialogues with their parents. If the possibility of mutuality were the necessary condition for all human love, one can safely guess that the species would never have survived. In some way, the details of which will be explored in a later chapter, human beings possess an elemental natural orientation to love and care for their children that is subsequently shaped, but not created *ex nihilo*, by human freedom and intelligence. The natural basis of love that is at the root of many primary human bonds needs to be given moral recognition.

It should also be noted at this point that recent Catholic authors have expended little or no effort on coherently relating particular attachments to universal concerns. The affective-centered view of love found in these thinkers is affirmed alongside a universalist attitude-centered view without any reconciliation or coordination. Rahner and Johann attempted to relate love as interpersonal to the more universal "love of neighbor" owed to all human beings. And Gutiérrez obviously places great importance on care for the needy flowing from the universality of *agape*, but he never discusses how the preferential option is to be coherently related to the natural human priority for the primary relations of family and friendship. Indeed, the latter are given no status whatsoever in Gutiérrez's his account of Christian love.

Dickens provides a literary critique of the failure to properly order love in *Bleak House*. Mrs. Jellyby is said to possess "telescopic philanthropy" because she could see nothing nearer than Africa, while her own children went dirty, hungry, and generally neglected—a condition that made them, as Dickens put it, "absolutely ferocious with discontent."[97] That injustice can be wrecked in the absence of a proper ordering of love has been illustrated more recently by a grown child's criticism of her "committee mother" in psychologist Lillian Breslow Rubin's, *Worlds of Pain*:

> My mother was always busy—too busy for us. At least that's the way it felt when I was little. She was always out doing her thing—worrying about the poor people or the black people and on one damn committee to save the world or another. I used to be jealous of those people because she didn't seem to spend nearly as much time worrying about me or caring that I felt lonely or scared.[98]

Gutiérrez regards concern for the poor and oppressed as the focal point of *agape*, a position that underscores the need for radical conversion. He often calls for a global, comprehensive conversion, a "radical break," or "complete renunciation," but not every Christian can or ought to renounce his or her present state in life and its opportunities for good, if only because doing so would entail neglect and betrayal of one's deepest and most serious moral responsibilities. Of course, the "reversal" Gutiérrez speaks about should obviously not be interpreted in a literal sense, such that those who are now close to us should become oppressed and remote. Rather, it constitutes a commitment to the transformation of social structures that result in the exclusion and oppression of others, a transformation of the social order—not a simple rearrangement of the individuals or classes within this order.

In fairness it should be noted that Gutiérrez seems to recognize that love requires an appropriate ordering of priorities. He never suggests that the preferential option eliminates all ordinary human forms of love, or that Christians should be concerned for the poor instead of their family and friends. Nevertheless, he ignores the role of natural love within the

Christian life and nowhere relates its demands to those of the preferential option for the poor.

Conclusion

The authors discussed here fail to deal with, and, in many cases, even to recognize, the need to discriminate between various objects of love and to prioritize the moral responsibilities attending various relationships. They obviously recognize that love issues in devotion to, self-denial for, and care for the beloved in need, yet they never explain how the needs of various objects of care are prioritized, or according to what standards, or how the duties owed to primary relationships are set in relation to duties to other people. This omission reflects an insufficient attentiveness to the natural basis of the ordering of love, a deficiency that is not found in the ethics of Thomas Aquinas.

NOTES

1.   The sources discussed in this chapter have been selected from among a large body of books on love by Catholic authors in the last half-century, and have been chosen primarily on the basis of their representativeness, relative clarity, and influence. Full justice cannot be given to the argument of each of the texts cited here. References must be understood as illustrative rather than demonstrative. Other major treatments of love include Martin C. D'Arcy, *Mind and Heart of Love*; Jules Toner, *Experience of Love*; Maurice Nédoncelle, *Vers une philosophie de l'amour et de la personnne* (Paris: Aubier Editions Montaigne, 1957); Jean Guitton, *Essays on Human Love*, trans. Melville Chaning-Pearce (New York: Philosophical Library, 1951); John Burnaby, *Amor Dei* (London: Hodder and Stoughton, 1947); John Cowburn, S.J., *The Person and Love: Philosophy and Theology of Love* (New York: Alba House, 1967); Dietrich von Hildebrand, *Ethics* (Chicago: Franciscan Herald, 1953); John Cowburn, S.J., *The Person and Love* (N.Y.: Alba House, 1967); Bernard J. F. Lonergan, S.J., *Method in Theology* (New York: Herder and Herder, 1972), 101–24, 237–44.

2.   A helpful discussion of historical background to the manuals is found in John Mahoney, *The Making of Moral Theology: A Study of the Roman Catholic Tradition* (Oxford: Clarendon Press, 1987), ch. 1; and John A. Gallagher, *Time Past, Time Future: An Historical Study of Catholic Moral Theology* (New York: Paulist Press, 1990).

3.   See, e.g., Thomas Slater, *Manual of Moral Theology* 1:115–116. The definition of love as benevolence can be supported by certain passages in Thomas (e.g., *Summa Theologiae*, I.II.27.3 [hereafter ST]) but is at odds with Thomas's explicit statement that benevolence is a necessary but not sufficient condition of charity (II.II.27.2).

4.   Slater, Ibid., 4:74–75; 5:17–18.

5.   Anthony Koch, *A Handbook of Moral Theology*, ed. Arthur Pruess, 3d. revised ed., 5 vols. (St. Louis, Missouri: B. Herder, 1933). Koch/Preuss' treatise represents the themes criticized by personalist theologians and is used here for illustrative purposes. Not all manualists reflect the same understanding of these matters, for example, Davis, while still adhering to the legal model of ethics, understood charity much more in terms of friendship than did Koch/Preuss. Contrast Davis, *Moral and Pastoral Theology*, 1:304–6, with Koch, *Handbook of Moral Theology*, 5:15f.

6.   Gérard Gilleman, S.J., *Le primat de charité en théologie morale* (Brussels-Paris: Desclée De Brouwer, 1954). English Translation, *The Primacy of Charity in Moral Theology*, trans. William F. Ryan, S. J., and André Vachon, S. J. (Westminster, Maryland: The Newman Press, 1961).

7.   Ibid., *xxxi*.

8.   Ibid., *xxxiii*.

9.   Ibid., *xxviii–xxix*.

10.   Ibid., *xxvi*.

11.   Ibid., 31–32. The reference is to Fritz Tillmann, *Handbuch der katholischen Sittenlehre*, vol. III: *Die Idee der Nachfolge Christi*. 2d ed. Düsseldorf 1940. Vol. IV, 1 and 2: *Die Verwirklichung der Nachfolge Christi*. 3d. ed. Düsseldorf, 1947.

12.   Ibid., *xxxi*.

13.   Bernard Häring, C.S.S.R., *The Law of Christ*, trans. Edwin G. Kaiser, C.PP.S., 3 vols. (Westminster, Maryland: The Newman Press, 1963), 1:31. Originally *Das Gesetz Christi* (Freiburg im Breisgau, Germany: Erich Wewel Verlag, 1959). Häring's mature thought is found in *Free and Faithful in Christ*, 3 vols. (New York: Seabury, 1978, 1979, 1981).

14.   Ibid., *vii*.

15.   Ibid., p. 31. Häring is referring to Otto Schilling, *Moraltheologie*, 1922; 2d. ed, 1952.

16.   Ibid., 1:103.

17.   Recall Pius XII's judgment that the obtaining of semen by masturbation was "wholly unlawful" on the grounds that is constitutes a direct abuse of the "generative faculty." In an allocution of May 19, 1956, to a congress on fertility and sterility, Pius XII stated: "Eiusmodi procuratio humani seminis, per masterbationem effecta, ad nihil aliud directe spectat, nisi ad naturalem in homine generandi facultatem plene exercendam; quod quidem plenum exercitium, extra coniugalem copulam peractum, secum fert directum et indebite usurpatam eiusdem facultatis usum. In hoc eiusmodi indebito facultatis usu propie sita est intrinseca regulae morum violatio" (*A.A.S.*, XLVIII [1956], 472).

18.   Martin Buber, *I and Thou* (New York: Charles Scribner's Sons, 1937). It might be noted that Buber also profoundly influenced Protestant theology as well as Catholic. See, for example, Emil Brunner, *Man in Revolt: A Christian Anthropology*, trans. Olive Wyon [from *Der Mensch im Widerspruch: Die christliche Lehre vom wahren und vom wirklichen Menschen*, published in 1937] (Philadelphia: Westminster Press, 1939), 22–24.

19.   Ibid., 81. Buber's insistence that we enter into the life of the other does not suggest that we simply imagine ourselves in the other person's place, but that we imagine what the other person feels in his or her place. The latter is akin to Scheler's "fellow feeling" (see Max Scheler, *The Nature of Sympathy*, trans. Peter Heath [London: Routledge and Kegan Paul, 1954], 39–40).

20.   Second Vatican Council, *Pastoral Constitution on the Church in the Modern World (Gaudium et spes)* no. 51, in Joseph Gremillion, ed., *The Gospel of Peace and Justice: Catholic Social Teaching Since Pope John* (Maryknoll, New York: Orbis Press, 1976), 288. See also the *Declaration on Religious Freedom (Dignitatis humanae)* no. 1: "A sense of the dignity of the human person has been impressing itself more and more deeply on the consciousness of contemporary man" (ibid., 337). See also the Vatican *Declaration on Certain Questions Concerning Sexual Ethics*, no. 3: "The people of our time are more and more convinced that the human person's dignity and vocation demand that they should discover, by the light of their own intelligence, the values innate in their nature, that they should ceaselessly develop these values and realize them in their lives, in order to achieve an ever greater development" (*L'Osservatore Romano*, January 22, 1976, 300). Whether the document as a whole, particularly its treatment of moral norms, was entirely consistent with this personalism was a matter of subsequent debate.

21.   See John Paul II, *Familiaris consortio*, ET: *On the Family* (Washington, D.C.: United States Catholic Conference, 1982), 32, 28–29. In this document the pope argues that artificial birth control is "intrinsically immoral" because by its very nature it constitutes a refusal to engage in the "total self-giving" that is the essence of proper interpersonal conjugal love between husband and wife. In the same text the pope also argues, in language reminiscent of the manuals, that married people ought to respect "the structure and finalities of the conjugal act which expresses that love" (ibid., 35, 34). See also the Congregation for the Doctrine of the Faith, "Instruction on Respect for Human Life in Its Origins and on the Dignity of Procreation: Replies to Certain Questions of the Day" (Braintree, Massachusetts: Pope John XXIII Center, 1987). The pope continues to resist identification with "physicalism" in *Veritatis Splendor* No. 48.

22.   Johann's reflection on questions of human nature and love continued to develop beyond that presented in *Meaning of Love*. Johann's later writings, most notably *Building the Human* (New York: Herder and Herder, 1968), drew upon American pragmatism, but not in a way that seriously addresses the critique developed here.

23.   Johann, *Meaning of Love*, 71.

24.   Ibid., 15 and 64. Johann's reference is to Joseph de Finance, *Etre et Agir dans la Philosophie de Saint Thomas* (Paris: Vitte, 1945), 324, n.2.

25.   Ibid., 11–18. The following texts were central to Johann's project: Gabriel Marcel, *Being and Having: An Existentialist Diary*, trans. K. Farrer (Boston: Beacon, 1951); *Homo Viator: Introduction to a Metaphysic of Hope*, trans. Emma Crawford (London: Victor Gollancz, 1951); *Journal métaphysique* (Paris: N.R.F., 1935); Louis Lavelle, *De l'acte* (Paris: Aubier, 1946); Maurice Nedoncelle, *Love and the Person*, trans. Sr. Ruth Adelaide, S.C. (New York: Sheed and Ward, 1966); and M. Madinier, *Conscience et amour: Essai sur le "nous"* (Paris: Alcan, 1938).

26.   Ibid., 41–42.

27.   Ibid., 46.

28.   Ibid., 14.

29.   Karl Rahner, *Love of Jesus, Love of Neighbor*, trans. Robert Barr (New York: Crossroad, 1983), 20–21.

30.   Karl Rahner, *Theological Investigations* 1 (New York: Seabury, 1961), 287.

31.   Karl Rahner, "Why and How Can We Venerate the Saints?" *Theological Investigations* 8 (New York: Herder and Herder, 1971), 13. For the most comprehensive

discussion see Karl Rahner, *Foundations of the Christian Faith: An Introduction to the Idea of Christianity*, trans. William V. Dych (New York: Seabury, 1978), 1–137.

32.   Rahner, *Foundations*, 94; see also "Theology of Freedom," *Theological Investigations* 6 (New York: Seabury, 1969), 178–96.

33.   Rahner, "Unity," 245.

34.   Rahner, *Foundations*, 240.

35.   Karl Rahner, "Reflections on the Unity of the Love of God and Love of Neighbor," *Theological Investigations* 6 (New York: Seabury, 1969), 239. See also Karl Rahner, "The 'Commandment' of Love in Relation to the Other Commandments," *Theological Investigations* 5 (New York: Crossroads, 1966), 439–59. It should be noted that Rahner's early writings, particularly *Spirit in the World* and *Hearers of the Word*, did not display the concern with interpersonal that came to be a characteristic mark of his more mature writings.

36.   Josef Fuchs, S.J., *Human Values and Christian Morality*, trans. M. H. Heelan, Maeve McRedmond, Erika Young, and Gerard Watson (Dublin: Gill and Macmillan Ltd., 1970), 123.

37.   Rahner, "Unity," 246; my emphasis.

38.   Ibid.

39.   Ibid., 247.

40.   Margret A. Farley, *Personal Commitments: Making, Keeping, and Breaking* (San Francisco: Harper and Row, 1986); see also her, "Feminist Theology and Bioethics," in Barbara Hilkert Andolesen, Christine E. Gudorf, Mary D. Pellauer, eds., *Women's Consciousness, Women's Conscience: A Reader in Feminist Ethics* (San Francisco: Harper and Row, 1987), 285–305. There are of course many forms of feminist theology, including liberal, socialist, and radical varieties. Farley is a fine representative of the movement but not its only major figure. Her understanding of mutuality has affinities with Barbara Hilkert Andolesen, "Agape in Feminist Ethics," *Journal of Religious Ethics* 9 (1981): 69–85 and Christine E. Gudorf, "Parenting, Mutual Love, and Sacrifice," in Andolsen, Gudorf, and Pellauer, eds., *Women's Consciousness, Women's Conscience*, 175–91.

41.   See Toner, *Experience of Love*, esp. 183.

42.   Rahner, "Unity," 244.

43.   Johannes B. Metz, *Theology of the World*, trans. William Glen-Doepel (New York: Seabury, 1973), 109–10. Rahner recognized that the universality of *agape*, and particularly concern for the most needy neighbors, must not be neglected. He noted, for example, that rather than simple sympathy or pity for the poor, *agape* generates transformation of the long-term structural causes of poverty. See Karl Rahner, "The Unreadiness of the Church's Members to Accept Poverty," *Theological Investigations* 14 (New York: Seabury, 1976), 271–72. He also noted the danger that interpersonal love can become "a most sublime form of egoism" and that neighbor love must include "political" love as well. See Karl Rahner, "Christian Humanism," *Theological Investigations* 9 (New York: Seabury, n.d.), 188. Finally, it might also be suggested that Rahner provides a partial corrective to the dangers of the "closed circuit" of the "I-Thou" relation in an interesting article entitled, "Marriage as a Christian Sacrament," *Theological Investigations* 10.

44.   Gutiérrez is discussed here but other liberation theologians could be adduced to illustrate the same themes, for example, Jon Sobrino, S.J., Leonardo Boff, and Juan Segundo. An interesting secondary source on some of this material is John

O'Brien, *Theology and the Option for the Poor* (Collegeville, Minnesota: Liturgical Press, 1992).

45.   Enrique Dussel, *Ethics and the Theology of Liberation* (Maryknoll, N.Y.: Orbis, 1978), 2.

46.   Gustavo Gutiérrez, *A Theology of Liberation: History, Politics, and Salvation*, 15th. Anniversary Edition, trans. Sister Caridad Inda ad John Eagleson (Maryknoll, N.Y.: Orbis, 1988), 156.

47.   Gustavo Gutiérrez, *The Power of the Poor in History: Selected Writings*, trans. Robert R. Barr (Maryknoll, New York: Orbis, 1979), 193.

48.   Gutiérrez, *Theology of Liberation*, *xxvii*. John Paul II proclaimed the poor to be "God's favorites" in his address in the barrio of Santa Cecilia, a neighborhood of Guadalajara. Cited by Gutiérrez in *Theology of Liberation*, 138.

49.   Gutiérrez, *Power of the Poor*, 142–43. Gutiérrez cites Puebla no. 1142. As the second Vatican Instruction puts it, human misery "elicited the compassion of Christ our Savior, who willed to take it on himself and to identify with the very least of his brothers and sisters (Mt. 25:40–45)." In *Origins* 15, 723, no. 68.

50.   The phrase "Church of the poor" was originally coined by Pope John XXIII in his Radio Message of September 11, 1962. See *The Pope Speaks* 8, no. 4 (Spring 1963): 396.

51.   The "reversal" motif is found in Gutiérrez, *Theology of Liberation*, *xxviii* and *Power of the Poor*, 141.

52.   Gutiérrez, *Power of the Poor*, 44; author's emphases.

53.   See Joseph A. Fitzmyer, S.J., *The Gospel According to Luke (X-XXIV)*, Anchor Bible (New York: Doubleday, 1985), 884.

54.   See also Victor Paul Furnish, *The Love Command in the New Testament* (Nashville and New York: Abingdon, 1972), 34–45; John R. Donahue, S.J., "Who Is My Enemy? The Parable of the Good Samaritan and the Love of Enemies," in *The Love of Enemy and Nonretaliation in the New Testament*, ed. William M. Swartley (Louisville, Kentucky: Westminster/John Knox, 1992), 137–56.

55.   See, for instance, Koch/Preuss, *Handbook of Moral Theology* 5:25.

56.   The Vatican *Instruction on Christian Freedom and Liberation* also affirms the special love of God for the poor in I, 22, p. 717, of the Church for the poor in IV, 68, 723, and of individual Christians for the poor in III, 50, 720 (citing *Libertas nuntius* IV.9 on Mt 25:31–46). For a more focused discussion of "partiality" in Gutiérrez see Stephen J. Pope, "Proper and Improper Partiality and the Preferential Option for the Poor," *Theological Studies* 54 (1993): 242–71.

57.   Gutiérrez, *Power of the Poor*, 19.

58.   Gustavo Gutiérrez, *The Truth Shall Make You Free: Confrontations*, trans. Matthew J. O'Connell (Maryknoll, N.Y: Orbis Books, 1990), 100.

59.   Gutiérrez, *Theology of Liberation*, 160.

60.   Ibid., *xxviii*.

61.   H. Noldin, S.J. and A. Schmitt, S.J., *Summa Theologiae Moralis*, 2 vols., 27th ed. (Oeniponte: Sumptibus et Typis Feliciani Rauch, 1940), 2:104.

62.   See Koch/Preuss, *Handbook of Moral Theology* 5:177; Davis, *Moral and Pastoral Theology*, 1:325. Alphonsus Liguori, *Theologia moralis*, ed. L. Gaudé (Rome: Vatican Press, 1905) 1. II, n.31–33, 326. The notion of "superfluities," or superfluous material possessions, was employed by Augustine to indicate that while all who are able

are morally bound to give alms, each must do so according to his or her means. See *Enarrationes in Psalmum* 147, 12 (Migne, PL, 37, 1922); and Augustine, *Sermo* 61 (PL 38, 413). On Thomas, see ST II.II.118.4ad2.

63. Francis J. Connell, *Outlines of Moral Theology*, 2d. ed. (Milwaukee: Bruce, 1958), 91.

64. See, for example, Koch/Preuss, ibid., 177–178, n.18. Preoccupation with the benefactor rather than recipient has been a classic criticism of almsgiving. See, for example, Sidney and Beatrice Webb, *English Local Government. Poor Law in History*, 2 vols. (London, 1927, 1929) 1:4–5. A response is provided by Brian Tierney, *Medieval Poor Law: A Sketch of Canonical Theory and Its Application in England* (Berkeley and Los Angeles: University of California Press, 1959), ch. 3. The Webbs targeted the "unenlightened" practices of medieval poor relief, but these general lines of criticism have been applied to modern almsgiving as well.

65. Haring, *Law of Christ*, 2:401.

66. Ibid.

67. Gutiérrez, *Theology of Liberation*, xxix.

68. See O'Brien, *Theology and the Option for the Poor*, 80–83.

69. See, *inter alia*, Jacques Dupont, O.S.B., "The Poor and Poverty in the Gospels and Acts," in *Gospel Poverty: Essays in Biblical Theology*, ed. Augustin George, S.M. et al. (Chicago: Franciscan Herald Press, 1977), 25–52; Robert C. Tannehill, *The Narrative Unity of Luke-Acts: A Literary Interpretation*, 2 vols. (Philadelphia: Fortress, 1986), 1:103–39.

70. Ibid., *xxxi.*

71. I assume without argument that "love" in the Christian tradition has been employed in both affective and attitudinal ways. Many of its major figures have regarded complacency, desire, delight, and intimacy, for example as central components of love (e.g., Augustine, Bonaventure, Thomas Aquinas, and Jonathan Edwards); others have understood love primarily in terms of disinterested duty, a command to regard the neighbor in certain ways and a settled disposition to act accordingly (e.g. Kierkegaard and Bultmann). Bultmann argued, for example, that "in reality, the love which is based on emotions of sympathy, or affection, is self-love; for it is a love of preference, of choice, and the standard of the preference and choice is the self" (in Rudolf Bultmann, *Jesus and the Word*, trans. Louise Pettibone Smith and Erminie Huntress Lantero [New York: Charles Scribner's Sons, 1958], 117). One must be alert to the dangers of drawing excessively strict dichotomies between affective and attitudinal approaches to love, particularly as interpreted by figures as complex as these. Both Thomas and Edwards understood love as including "disinterested" as well as "preferential" dimensions. It seems to me, however, the tradition's inclusion of both attitudinal and affective uses of "love" warrants the criticism that it sponsors a falsely inclusive use of the term "love." The perdurance of this usage, even though it has been the scene of many unresolved debates in theological ethics, reflects in part the complexity and pluriformity of biblical usage. This dual use will no doubt be a permanent feature of Christian discussions of *agape* or *caritas*, but it seems to me that at the very least ethicists ought to employ more specific terms when possible, for example, respect, forgiveness, care, and solidarity.

72. Toner, *Experience of Love*, 134.

73. Gutiérrez, *Theology of Liberation*, 114.

74. For example, Toner, *Experience of Love*, 104.

75.   Rahner, "Christian Humanism," 188. According to Toner, love frees one from "affective solipsism" (*Experience of Love*, 98). See also Farley, *Personal Commitments*, 119–20

76.   Toner distinguishes love from mutuality; he argues that the former can exist without the latter but that mutuality is the consummation of love (see *Experience of Love*, ch. 9). Johann, on the other hand, identifies the two. There are some exceptions in the wider literature that are not analyzed here. One example is Louis Janssens, "Norms and Priorities in a Love Ethics," *Louvain Studies* 6 (1977): 207–38. According to Janssens, for example, echoing Outka, "love of neighbor is impartial. It is fundamentally an equal regard for every person, because it applies to each neighbor qua human being. . . . Being impartial, agape is independent of our personal feelings of sympathy (no favoritism) or aversion" (ibid., 219). According to Janssens, primary relations of family and friendship deserve a special place in the ordo caritatis because they contribute to personal development of self and others in an unparalleled way (ibid., 222). I do not discuss Janssens at length because his position was never sufficiently developed into a book-length explication.

77.   Nygren, *Agape and Eros*, 692.

78.   Gutiérrez, *Theology of Liberation*, 102. See also ch. 10: "Encountering God in History."

79.   Johann, *Meaning of Love*, 70.

80.   Ibid., 14.

81.   See Karl Rahner, "Christology in the Setting of Modern Man's Understanding of Himself and of His World," *Theological Investigations* 11 (New York: Seabury, 1974), 215–29, esp. 221–25.

82.   Karl Rahner, "The Man of Today and Religion," *Theological Investigations* 6 (New York: Seabury, 1974), 10.

83.   Ibid., 10.

84.   See Karl Rahner, "The Theological Concept of Concupiscentia," *Theological Investigations* 1:346–82. Rahner's position was highly complex and can by no means be captured adequately in the claim that matter is simply a limit to spirit. Matter also provides possibilities for spirit that would not otherwise obtain; concupiscence is not to be simply identified with sinfulness. Rahner also argued that conversion includes the interpenetration of sense with spirit. Yet it seems to me that he tended to depict nature, that "sluggish mass of . . . natural material in man" (ibid., 366), as fundamentally resisting spirit. Spirit ought to have dominion over matter and the person ought to penetrate nature, but due to the intransigence of nature this process is never complete. As a result, human existence is marked by what Rahner calls a "dualism" between these two poles. The result, in my judgment, is a relative devaluation of nature.

85.   Gutiérrez, *Theology of Liberation*, 21–22.

86.   Ibid., 81; author's emphasis.

87.   Ibid., 29.

88.   Midgley, *Beast and Man*, 182–83.

89.   Farley, *Personal Commitments*, 104. The author regards it as unnecessary to make an argument for the priority of other-regard in this sense, and presumably she would offer biblical resources to support her position (e.g., Matt 20:26–28; 23:11; Mark 9:35; 10:42–45). Yet her assumption runs against the grain of a number of major figures in the tradition, including, as she is well aware, its two greatest theologians, Augustine

and Thomas Aquinas, both of whom maintained the ultimate priority of self-love, properly understood, to neighbor love. See, *inter alia*, Augustine, *De Doc. Christ.* I, 23, 22; Thomas Aquinas, ST II.II.26.4. See also Ambrose, *De Officiis*, quoted in *Glossa Ordinaria*, 42 c.2; Peter Lombard, *Collectanea in epistulas Pauli*, on I Tim 1:1–5, PL 192, 329; Bonaventure, III Sent.d.29q.3.

90.   See Daniel Callahan, "What Do Children Owe Elderly Parents?" *Hastings Center Report* 15 (1985): 32–37.

91.   See Diane M. Yeager, "The Web of Relationship: Feminists and Christians," *Soundings: An Interdisciplinary Journal* 71 (1988):485–513. Yeager attributes this phrase to Hannah Arendt but she provides no supporting documentation.

92.   It should be noted that a later essay, "Love and Justice" (in *Ethics and Society: Original Essays on Contemporary Moral Problems*, ed. Richard T. DeGeorge [Garden City, New York: Doubleday, 1966], 25–47), reflects a movement in Johann's thought toward a recognition of the significance of the human community as the context of interpersonal love. He also sketches here a notion of "universal love" that seems to be at odds with the more restricted interpersonal meaning developed in *Meaning of Love*.

93.   Farley, *Personal Commitments*, 15, and chs. 4–5.

94.   See ibid., 16.

95.   This is noted by Farley in *ibid.*, 83, but it seems to me that this acknowledgment stands in need of further explication and development.

96.   Ibid., 47.

97.   Charles Dickens, *Bleak House* (New York: Penguin, 1971), 151.

98.   Lillian Breslow Rubin, *Worlds of Pain: Life in the Working-Class Family* (New York: Basic Books, 1976), 26.

2

The "Order of Love" According to Thomas Aquinas

In some fundamental ways Thomas Aquinas stands in stark contrast to the figures examined in the previous chapter. For obvious historical reasons one cannot say that Thomas deliberately avoided the weaknesses of personalism or liberation theology per se, but it can be argued that his incorporation of nature enabled him to develop a comprehensive view of love that avoided the narrowing temptations that characterize Catholic ethics at the present time. The thesis of this chapter, then, is that Thomas's account of the order of love includes important features of human nature that must be considered by any adequate contemporary ethics of love. The examination of ways in which Thomas's ethics of love are superior to current alternatives contributes to the larger argument of the book, namely, that substantive considerations of natural human sociality, based on empirical studies, can contribute to a more comprehensive account of the ordering of love.

Human Nature

The major difference separating Thomas from the personalists and liberation theologians is his deliberate attempt to ground his notion of love in a developed, scientifically grounded theory of human nature. His interpretation of "nature" relied, of course, on Aristotle, according to whom nature was the intrinsic principle of motion and rest, a process of "becoming and growing" that proceeds from the intrinsic directives that constitute a being's form.[1] In Aristotelian perspective, the person is more than his or her network of relationships, freedom, and historical location. To be a person is to be a member of a species and to have an integral place in the organically natural world.[2] For Aristotle and Thomas, the collective activities of all individual substances harmoniously interlock and coordinate to comprise a hierarchically ordered universe. The created world is pervaded by "order," by which Thomas meant that things are, in some way, before or after one another and related to some higher principle.[3] Order includes three elements: a plurality of distinct objects; a principle or source of order (a *ratio ordinis* according to which things are arranged in a particular way); and an arrangement of these objects according to their relation to the principle (the *ratio prius et posterioris*).

Thomas takes "order" to denote two kinds of relation: the internal order of an object to its proper end, and the external order of various objects to one another. The external order of parts in relation to one another serves, and is subordinate to, the internal order of the whole toward its proper end. God's ordering activity, observed in the regularity of nature, directs all finite beings to their own proximate ends and relates all beings to one another in ways appropriate to the harmony and unity of the order of creation. Thus, to use examples Thomas drew from Aristotle, the various parts of an army are arranged for the purpose of the whole as determined by its general and the well-laid out home reflects the arranger's plan.[4] Thomas's focus on God's objective ordering of life in the world differs markedly from recent emphases on subjectivity, just as emphasis on the order of being differs from that on interpersonal freedom.

Thomas's "hylomorphic" view of human nature, which maintained that the rational soul is the form of the body, clearly recognized the moral significance of the animal, the vegetal, and material aspects of the person. Sensitive appetite is subordinate to the rational, but both must be balanced and coordinated for the health of the whole.[5] Biological nature is an essential component of this psychophysical unity, and for this reason Thomas claimed in the *Summa contra Gentiles*, against a Platonizing anthropology, that the soul is not "in" the body as a sailor is "in" a ship.[6] "It is of a man's nature to be in matter, and so a man without matter is impossible," he wrote.[7] For this reason Kenneth E. Kirk maintains that Thomas was "perhaps the first Christian philosopher to take the corporeal character of human existence calmly."[8]

An important discussion of the order of nature is found in Thomas's treatment of the natural law in the *Prima secundae*. Practical reason apprehends the good as "that which all things seek after," to which the first principle of practical reason, "good is to be done and pursued, and evil is to be avoided," orients all human actions.[9] Applied to ethics, the moral life of one who respects the natural law flows from within (*ab intrinseco*); it is connatural to his or her own nature as a human being. Thus, natural law theory is not, as philosopher Jeffrie Murphy charges, an obscurantist form of divine command ethics.[10]

The threefold order of the natural inclinations provides the objects ordered by the precepts of the natural law. The natural inclination to the good of survival common to all substances is related to one set of precepts regarding self-preservation, and the natural inclination to goods shared with all animals, such as sexual intercourse and reproduction, is related to a second set of precepts. A third and more distinctively human level of natural inclination, to live in society and to know the truth about God, accords with human nature as rational and provides the basis for a third set of precepts. All three levels are critically important for the human good in its full and proper sense.

The natural law is related to these inclinations in its primary and secondary precepts. The natural inclination to self-preservation common to all creatures is immediately recognized in human experience generally and can be easily observed in animal life (its analogous extension to inorganic matter can be set to the side for now). This inclination is coordinated with a precept regarding the general moral obligation to preserve life, which has been formulated in various ways. Maritain's interpretation of this claim is identified with the preservation of life: "to take a man's life is not like taking another animal's life."[11] R. A. Armstrong's rendering focuses on preservation of life in general: "while recognizing that not all beings have equal value in the world of creation, one ought to respect and preserve not only human life, but where possible, all life."[12] Interestingly, each of these formulations has its own particular difficulties. For example, Armstrong's general "respect for life" contrasts with Thomas's position that life be preserved for human use.[13] Yet these formulations also have a common tendency to ignore Thomas's explicit formulation of the precept, that "because of this inclination, whatever is a means of preserving human life, and hampers its obstacles, belongs to the natural law."[14]

It is unfortunate that Thomas did not elaborate on the meaning and specific moral implications of this primary precept, but it does appear elsewhere, for example, in his ethical justification of killing in self-defense, an act obviously flowing from the natural inclination to self-preservation,[15] and in his condemnation of suicide, an act categorized as mortally sinful and strictly prohibited on the grounds that it directly contravenes this same natural inclination.[16] Presumably different cultures might interpret the meaning of "preserving life" and "warding off its obstacles" somewhat differently in detailed applications, for example, regarding infanticide. At the same time, all cultures consider the protection of innocent human life, however interpreted, as having great moral significance.

The second set of natural inclinations pertain to those shared by all animals for sexual intercourse and the begetting of offspring. Maritain formulates the precept governing sexual behavior in the following way: "sexual intercourse has to be contained within given limitations."[17] Armstrong is more prolix regarding the regulation of sexual conduct: "all people, when they are aware that it is through sexual intercourse that children come into existence, cannot help but see that the action in question has a dignity and significance which renders it entirely different from other pleasures of life which may without harm be casually indulged in."[18]

Maritain coordinates the natural inclination to bear offspring with the precept that, "the family group has to comply with some fixed pattern,"[19] and Armstrong concurs, maintaining that family arrangements must be orderly if children are to be properly cared for and educated. This primary precept is distinguishable from its specific culturally defined application in secondary precepts, for example, monogamy or polygyny as the proper marital context for the care of children. Thomas resolved the medieval debate over the polygamy of the patriarchs by arguing that it violated the secondary precepts of the natural law by compromising the secondary good of marriage, partnership; however, it did not violate the primary precept, which promotes the primary good of marriage, namely, procreation.[20] At the same time, Thomas maintained that polyandry, the affiliation of many husbands to one wife, does violate the primary precept of marriage because it destroys the ability of fathers to identify their offspring, a principle of some interest to evolutionary theorists, as we will see in the following chapter.

The third set of natural inclinations are those proper to human beings, including the desire to know the truth about God and to live in society. Maritain formulated the precept corresponding to the former inclination, somewhat awkwardly, as the requirement that "we are bound to look at the Invisible."[21] According to Armstrong, Thomas's suggestion that there is a natural desire to know God was mistaken, and therefore no formulation of this precept is offered.[22]

Thomas also identified in human beings a natural inclination to live in society. Maritain's formulation of this precept is that "we are bound to live together under certain rules and prohibitions."[23] Armstrong's is similar: "we ought to live together in obedience to certain rules."[24] Anything pertaining to this third level of human inclination also pertains to the natural law, for example, "to avoid ignorance and to offend one's associates."[25]

The primary precepts are exceptionless but highly indefinite, providing no specific description of actions that are prohibited or enjoined. They are universally known but expressed with a high level of generality. Thomas regarded secondary precepts as more specific but less universally recognized; thus, he maintained that moral norms can be driven from the conscience of vicious individuals and that among some cultures theft and sexual vices are not regarded as sinful.[26] Thomas assumed that deviations from the secondary principles held by the church are sinful, whereas many people in our day would tend, barring the most egregious cases of human oppression (e.g., murder for cannibalism or human sacrifice), to speak more neutrally of cultural variability.

The comprehensiveness of Thomas's approach to natural inclinations can be underscored. He maintained that the natural law is grounded in the nature humans share with other animals ("generic nature") and in human reason ("specific nature"). The former emphasis reflects his deference to the authority of the Roman lawyer Ulpian, who is said to have defined the natural law as that "which nature has taught to all animals."[27] Yet it is sometimes forgotten that only rational animals are subject to the natural law in Thomas's sense of the term. Humans do not, strictly speaking, share the natural law with animals, but only the natural inclinations toward various natural goods to which correspond certain appropriate precepts of the natural law. In his discussion of the "original state" of the human race, Thomas argued that what makes us like the animals in sexual intercourse is not the experience of intense pleasure but the inability of reason to curtail the immoderate influence of such pleasure on human behavior.[28] Indeed, acting in the manner of animals was taken as evidence of fallen human nature.

Thomas's use of Ulpian did not lead him to encourage a simple imitation of animal behavior but to recognize that humans, like other animals, experience the divine governance through the promptings of certain natural inclinations as well as through the exigencies of human reason. Essential human inclinations are to be both fulfilled and transformed in light of human intelligence. It is the former emphasis, of course, that puts Thomas's thought at considerable distance from that of the authors analyzed in the previous chapter. Whereas the order of nature is regarded by Thomas as providentially designed, contemporary authors like Rahner and Gutiérrez understand nature as matter subject to rational control and use in the satisfaction of human desires.

Love

Given the centrality of nature in Thomas's thought, it comes as no surprise that his interpretation of love in the *Summa Theologiae* begins not with a direct inspection of human subjectivity, as it does for Johann and

Rahner, but with a theory of natural appetency. Thomas defines love in language quite different from the language of contemporary Catholic ethics, namely, as the first movement of the will, and, indeed, of every appetite.[29] Every natural being is ordered to seek its own good and so is marked by "appetency," a natural desire of a being toward its proper end.[30] The classic example of the acorn becoming an oak tree illustrates Thomas's belief that natural "appetite" is displayed in the organic structure of the plant to grow into a fully developed tree. He did not of course believe that the acorn consciously "desired" to become an oak tree. By "appetite" Thomas indicated a natural inclination to develop in certain ways under certain ordinary conditions, for example, of sunlight, moisture, and soil. By "end" in this case Thomas meant simply the termination of its natural developmental sequence. Unless we keep this qualification in mind when considering his statements regarding "natural" and "sensitive" love, we will inevitably caricature Thomas as naively anthropomorphic.

Thomas employed a variety of terms to describe "love." Among the most important are (1) *coaptatio*, adaptation;[31] (2) *complacentia*, affective consent;[32] and (3) *connaturalitas*, connaturality.[33] Philosopher Eric D'Arcy translates these terms, respectively, as "a sense of affinity with some object, a feeling of its attractiveness, a sense that it and oneself are naturally fitted for each other."[34] According to Thomas, human love is not, as it is for Johann, exclusively the product of human rationality and freedom. Love corresponds to appetite, rational as well as irrational, and appetite precedes the "reciprocal consciousness" of "I-Thou" relations.

"Natural love," the principle of movement of the natural appetite, is the natural orientation and innate affinity of a finite being for the good pertaining to its own nature. Natural love is not identified with the human experience of spontaneous interpersonal caring or affection. Natural love for Thomas was much broader: it characterizes all inanimate objects in that they are ordered to their proper acts by natural necessity, that is, by the author of their nature rather than by their own choices based on a rational grasp of their good.[35] The character of natural love as a "weight of nature" (*pondus naturae*) is illustrated in a simple physical event like a stone falling to the ground, which Thomas described as the "connaturalness" of a heavy body for the earth by reason of its weight.[36] Natural love is not restricted to inanimate objects, but precedes and supports both sensitive and rational love. It is found, Thomas wrote, in all powers of the soul, all parts of the body, and indeed, in all things, since everything that exists has a connaturalness with that to which it is naturally suited.[37] Natural love is, as Thomas Gilby explains, "the foundation of all activity, the underlying principle of every movement, the striving of something imperfect for completion without."[38]

Sensitive love, similarly, is the connaturality of the sensitive appetite to its own proper good. In irrational animals sensitive love follows of necessity on the sensible apprehension of a concrete, singular appetible object; it is thus "elicited" rather than "innate." The modification of the sensitive appetite by the appetible object (or, more precisely, by the "sensory cognitive form") is known as a "passion" (*passio*).[39] As a metaphysical term, passion denotes the receptivity of an object to being moved from potency to act. As a biological and psychological term, passion refers to the change wrought in the sensitive appetite as a material, corporeal entity, and, as such, it always includes a sensory, bodily effect.

Thomas identified five basic passions or emotions: love, desire, pleasure, hope, and fear.[40] The passions are essentially felt responses to actions on the agent; thus, they include a physiological component, but cannot be regarded as purely irrational because their arousal implies an interpretation of the experience and therefore includes a cognitive component. They can be intentionally shaped by training and habituation to play an important role in the life of virtue. The moral challenge is how to order properly love and its opposite, hate, so that one relates properly to others, to the self, and to God. The same is true of all the passions and their opposites. Thus, as odd as it may sound to some readers, from a Thomistic standpoint, one can distinguish proper from improper hate. It is wrong to feel hate toward the wrong object, or for the wrong reason, or in the wrong mode, but at the same time, it may also be wrong *not* to feel hate for the object that deserves it, or to feel it with insufficient intensity. The same is true of desire and aversion, pleasure and sadness, hope and despair, fear and courage, and anger.

The controlling Thomistic model of all the passions, including love, is that of local motion (*motus*). In local motion, an agent is related to a patient in three ways. First, the agent gives the patient an "inclination or aptitude to tend to the mover [i.e., the object]"; second, the agent gives the patient any required movement toward the mover; and third, the agent gives the patient rest in its term.[41]   These three distinguishable stages of motion correspond to love (complacency, or connaturality) for the object as such, desire for the absent or distant object, and joy in the object attained.[42] This connaturalness of the appetite to the good is the ground of Pierre Rousselot's "physical" or "Greco-Thomistic" concept of love.[43] While prior to "concern," love as complacency connotes receptivity, appreciation, and affective consent.[44]

Thomas's treatment of natural and sensitive love is best understood as a prelude to his more elaborate analysis of properly human love. The latter, it should be emphasized, builds on the former—a point frequently overlooked by theologians who attend only to the uniquely human features of love. Properly human love always involves the will, but reflects the influence of both rationality and animality. It consists in a complacency of the will that follows the intellectual apprehension of an object that is perceived by the agent as good in some way. Unlike animal love (*amor animalis*), human love is necessitated only by the universal good (the *bonum in communi*) and therefore in the concrete results from a choice among various appetible objects. This choice is based on the intellect's grasp of the *ratio* of the object's appetibility, that is, the object's relation to the universal good, and for this reason Thomas referred to properly human love as dilection (*dilectio*), which adds to the notion of love (*amor*) an implicit reference to an antecedent choice (*electio*).[45] Fully human love always reflects human intelligence and freedom.

At the same time, it must be remembered that human love as a conscious, free act is only possible because of the prior connaturality of the will to its good, which in turn is based on the sensitive and natural appetite. Human love differs from angelic love because it is based on the sensitive appetite, yet it differs from animal love in that the passions are subject to reason. With Aristotle, Thomas affirmed the value of moderately expressed passions, and therefore he respectfully dissented from the Stoic moral ideal of *apatheia*. With Augustine, Thomas held that virtue is rightly ordered love: rightly ordered passions are good, and wrongly ordered passions are vicious.[46]

Moreover, Thomas argued that it is better that a person be bent on what is good, not only with the will, but also with the desires of the senses.[47] The ideal of love, then, is not that of moral duty overcoming natural inclinations, as Kant thought,[48] but that of an integral personal response *ordering* and *incorporating* the appetites as well as the intellect. Thus, while Thomas claimed that an act of charity is more meritorious when performed from deliberate choice than simply from a feeling of pity, he also argued that passion positively increases the moral goodness of an act when it follows the guidance of reason.[49]

Rationality enables human beings, unlike irrational animals, to have a "love of friendship" for one another. Properly human love has two objects: the good that is willed, and the person for whom it is wanted. Thomas, clearly drawing on Aristotle's notion of friendship, identified the former as the "love of concupiscence" (*amor concupiscentiae*) and the latter as the "love of friendship" (*amor amicitiae*), and within this context he appropriated Aristotle's celebrated definition of love as "wanting good things for someone" (*velle alicui bonum*).[50] The "love of friendship" consists of complacency in its object for its own sake; the "love of concupiscence," on the other hand, tends to its object "not simply and for itself" but for the sake of something else.[51] Thomas argued that human beings naturally tend to love one another on the basis of their common humanity, and that the golden rule, "Thou shalt love thy friend as thyself" (Lv 19:18), is a fundamental expression of the core content of the natural law.[52] By implication, all the precepts of the natural law are expressions of the golden rule.

Thomas accepted Aristotle's principle that similarity is a cause of love,[53] a claim, it might be noted, that is supported in some sense both by common sense and contemporary research on prosocial behavior.[54] This "principle of similitude" is observed, for instance, in the natural union between animals of the same species and commonly experienced in interpersonal relations, but it reflects a deeper metaphysical truth: everything that exists loves what is one with itself in some manner or other and in so doing tends to communicate its form to the object of its love.[55] This principle provided the metaphysical basis for Thomas's description of human beings as social animals who flourish through political association, assistance, cooperation, and friendship, as "parts" of the larger social "whole," and as beings who naturally care for one another.[56] As Thomas observed in the *Summa contra Gentiles*, natural human sociality is evidenced in the fact that one person will help another, even a total stranger, who happens to be in need, for example, lost or fallen down. In so doing people act as if they were the friends of everyone.[57]

Charity and Its Order: Foundations

The heart of the Christian moral life is charity, the friendship of the human person with God that Thomas associated with the words of Jesus as depicted by Gospel of John: "I will not now call you servants . . . but my friends" (John 15:15).[58] Thomas's interpretation of charity followed from the fundamental theological axiom that grace perfects, and does not destroy, nature.[59] One important implication of this principle is, in Thomas's theological perspective, that charity *retains* natural love, though the latter is given a new animating principle.[60] Another is that the objects of charity—God, self, neighbor, and body—are *materially identical* with, though *formally distinct* from, the objects of love. Charity first loves God and secondly loves all other people as capable of sharing in eternal fellowship with God. Self-love is embedded in human nature by God. The human person, like everything that exists, naturally loves its own being, that is, desires its own good, and this love, too, is perfected in charity.[61]

For Thomas, the key distinction in this regard was not between self-love and neighbor love as such but between proper and improper self-love and proper and improper neighbor love. Both could be disordered for a multitude of reasons and both need to be properly ordered by charity. Even Jesus' commands regarding the love of sinners and enemies, which many theologians have understood to be distinctively Christian,[62] were characteristically taken by Thomas to be part of the natural law, and by implication included in the cardinal virtue of justice.[63] (Whether his account accords with biblical perspective is, of course, another matter.) Thus, all neighbors are loved with the same love of charity insofar as they are referred to one common good, that is, God.[64]

The *ordo amoris* is the natural basis of the *ordo caritatis*. The former naturally begins with the first principle of creation and orders all other beings according to the ways in which they are "before" or "after" one another in relation to God. Thomas understood natural love to share the orderly nature of the created world, as evidently intended by its author.[65] The same is true of sensitive and rational love. Thus charity, like love, is ordered according to two principles: first, to God and those who are objectively nearer to God (the *meliores*); and second, to those who are nearer to the agent in particular ways (the *conjunctiores*). While Thomas was not always clear about the relation between these two principles, he appreciated the special character of natural human love and attempted to incorporate it into the heart of the love of charity. One important implication is that charity does not require the Christian to imitate strictly the priority observed in God's love for those who are more virtuous (the *meliores*).[66] Natural human bonds based on various forms of proximity are thus incorporated into the Christian moral life, neither relegated to afterthought nor evacuated from it altogether.

In this connection, it should be noted that Thomas's appetency theory of love, in conjunction with his interpretation of the perfective relation of grace to nature, did not allow a "pure love" position in which all reference to the self is eliminated, or, still less, one in which the self is held in contempt.[67] In contrast to modern egoistic accounts of human nature,[68] however, Thomas did not assume that the welfare of one person can be pursued essentially in competition with and opposition to that of others: self-love and neighbor love are ultimately complementary, not mutually exclusive. The difference is registered in Thomas's use of the teleological term "love," which implies an appreciation of that which is outside the self, in contrast to the more egoist term "interest," which suggests arbitrary preferences.[69]

Some studies in contemporary psychology seem to confirm Thomas's position regarding the interconnection between self-love and neighbor love.[70] The priority of self over neighbor love goes against the grain of much contemporary moral philosophy, as illustrated in Thomas Nagel's claim that the essence of morality is to "regard oneself as merely one individual among many."[71] Thomas's belief that charity for the self, following the natural order of love, *precedes* charity for the neighbor is similarly at odds with trends in contemporary Christian ethics.[72]

Thomas argued for the priority of self-love in two ways, both of which drew on purely natural considerations. In the first, the golden rule was taken by Thomas to imply that a normative love for self is the paradigm for the love of others. Just as the "model exceeds the copy," so ought the love for self exceed the love for neighbor.[73] The second argument proceeded from the familiar Aristotelian notion of friendship as a union based on shared good: God is loved out of charity as the principal good, the self is loved as "partaker" in that good, and the neighbor is loved as a lesser "partner" in that good.[74]

Self-love, properly understood, ought to precede neighbor love, according to Thomas. Despite the "ecstatic" or self-transcending effect of love, he argued, the agent does not will the good of a friend *more than* his or her own good and cannot be obliged to love another more than the self.[75] As a general principle, the connection of unity surpasses that of union, so the unity one has with one's own participation in the divine good surpasses the union one has with another who shares in the divine good.[76] Thomas thus believed that the "as" in "love your neighbor *as* yourself" (Matt 22: 39) involved not strict equality but likeness, that is, as commanding: love your neighbor like yourself but not in strict equality to yourself,[77] and he interpreted I John 3:16, that "we ought to lay down our lives for our brethren," to mean that one ought to love the neighbor more than one's own body.[78]

What is true of natural love is also true of charity. Love of charity for the self refers first to one's spiritual nature: one is not to commit sin even if by so doing one were able to free the neighbor from sin. Yet charity gives rise to very important forms of self-denial. Indeed, the welfare of the neighbor's soul takes priority over concern for one's own body, since the neighbor's soul is closer to one's own soul than is one's soul to one's own body.[79] Thus, one ought to bear bodily injury, suffering, and even death for one's friend. In this sense, Thomas can be said to concur with Farley's claim that "agape, of course has a normative meaning which in general repudiates loving ourselves more than others and which in a powerful sense calls for loving others more than ourselves."[80] This self-denial is not pure sacrifice, however. On the contrary, it a form of profound self-love because on a deeper level, it exhibits the perfection of virtue, which is a good of the soul.[81] In this way Thomas attempted to coordinate biblical self-sacrificial themes with the received eudaemonism of Aristotle and Augustine.

Though, it may have its weaknesses from a contemporary stand-point, clearly Thomas's account of charity does not fit neatly into the ste-reotype of Christian ethics given scornfully by philosopher Michael Ruse, that is that a true Christian should "give without reservation or limit to others, without discrimination to relative, friend, foe, or stranger, and continue, no matter what harm befalls [one's self]."[82] Ruse's depiction and implied criticism of Christian ethics as unworkable and unnaturally idealistic, might seem appropriate to Gutiérrez's interpretation of *agape* but it clearly does not pertain to Thomas's. The essential difference between these positions, it should be clear by now, lies in Thomas's appro-priation of natural love within his account of the ordering of charity.

Order of Love among Particular Neighbors

Thomas's discussion of the primary order of charity in question 26, "the order of charity," was complemented by an extended analysis of the order of charity for various neighbors, a topic which, as we have seen, has been regularly omitted from consideration in contemporary accounts of love. Thomas understood the terms of the question, "Whether one neigh-bor ought to be loved more than another?"[83] in the context of an unnamed position (but on terms remarkably similar to Augustine's), namely, that one ought to love all people equally, but since one cannot do good to all, one ought to apportion beneficence according to proximity.[84] He depicted the position counter to his as claiming that the Christian ought to love all people with equal affection but not with equal action or beneficence. In this position, acts of charity are channeled in a preferential way to those to whom the agent is connected in some way or other, yet this preference does not extend to the deeper inward affections, which ought to be given equally to all people, including one's enemies, regardless of particular connections.[85]

Against this position, Thomas argued that the affections produced by charity ought to be as orderly as the affections springing from nature, since both inclinations flow from divine wisdom. In the natural world, inner tendencies accord with external actions suited to the natures of things; so also in human life the inner affections, whether of grace or nature, correspond with the external actions that they produce. The order of charity requires not only greater beneficence but also more intense affection toward those nearest to the agent.[86]

Thomas graded the objects of charity in direct proportion to their nearness to God or the self. The first principle of order inclines the agent to love those nearest to God, for example, holy men and women, because of their goodness; the second principle of order inclines the agent to love more those who are closest to the self. Charity is universally benevolent insofar as it desires salvation for all people, but it is partial in its intensity and in its beneficence, its actual doing good for others.[87] The presence of two principles has the effect of making Thomas's interpretation of the order of charity more complex, and at times more ambiguous, than it would have been if only one principle were involved. At the same time, it carries the advantage of attending to the contingencies of personal and natural loyalties while recognizing God as the principal object of charity.[88]

Thomas's more extended treatment of natural priorities was based on the principle that every action ought to be proportioned both to its object and to the agent producing it, the object providing its species, and agent furnishing its degree of intensity.[89] Thus, a person ought to love those closest to him or her and to will them good more intensely than he or she loves those who are morally better and for whom a greater good is willed. This treatment provides a theoretical basis for giving a central place to natural priorities, family, and friends in the moral life—a fact given short shrift in recent Catholic ethics, as we have seen. Scriptural corroboration for Thomas's position is found in I Tim 5:8: "If anyone does not take care of his own, and especially those of his household, he has denied the faith and is worse than an infidel."[90]

Natural relations are given a general priority over all other kinds of union by Thomas, for two reasons: first, they are more stable and permanent than other bonds; second, they coincide with other bonds that together offer more reasons for loving. In his argumentation, Thomas advanced the strictly natural claim that the connection of biological origin is prior to and more stable than other kinds of connections, a claim reminiscent of his other statements regarding the order of nature. Whereas virtue and even sanctity can "progress and recede, wax and wane," natural origin and its connections concern the very substance of the human person and consequently, Thomas inferred, the friendship of blood relatives is more stable than others.

Thomas also justified the priority of natural relations by arguing that people tend to love family members in more ways than they love others, that is, love within a family is based not only on simple biological ties but also on various kinds of shared goods, and these complex and interconnected bonds provide a stronger basis for love than one based exclusively on charity.[91] For Thomas, all friendships are referred to charity; therefore, the multiple forms of friendship shared (at least ideally) by members of a family are also taken up within the life of charity. The love of natural relations is informed and indeed commanded, rather than replaced, by charity.

Yet what about Jesus' apparent rejection of the primacy of blood loyalties and, more strongly, his command to forsake family ties? "Whoever comes to me and does not hate father and mother, wife and children, brothers and sisters, yes, and even life itself, he cannot be my disciple" (Luke 14:26 N.R.S.V.). In this as in other sayings, Jesus apparently even condemned love for the self. Thomas was, of course, well aware of Luke 14:26 and similar passages (e.g., Matt 10:37ff. and Luke 9:59-62), and he interpreted them as requiring, not an abolition of love of family and self simpliciter, but their false and improper counterfeits. Whereas *caritas* subordinates love of self to love for God, *cupiditas* reverses this order. Charity by implication respects a parallel distinction between ordered and disordered kin loyalties.[92] Just as improper love of self amounts in fact to "hatred" of self,[93] so, by implication, disordered love of family entails a de facto "hatred" of family, a disordered attachment that frustrates and undermines its own true good.[94] As the "form of the virtues,"[95] charity actually intensifies, perfects, and elevates (rather than obliterates or abandons) the moral virtues, especially justice, that govern domestic life. Presumably the distinction between proper and improper love provides a principle for interpreting and reconciling other biblical passages relevant to the ordering of love, such as I Cor 10:24: "Let *no* one seek his *own* good but the good of his neighbor," and Phil 2:4: "Look to each other's interest and *not merely* to your own" (my emphases).

However strong the bonds of "blood ties," natural relations do not minimize friendships based on other kinds of union, nor are other kinds of friendship mere surreptitious means to self-interest. Other friendships are good in and of themselves and possess relative authority in their own spheres; in fact, Thomas noted that other friendships can be stronger in what is proper to each of them. Just as kindred ought to be given preference in matters pertaining to nature, so civic friends ought to be given priority in matters concerning civil society, and fellow soldiers in matters pertaining to military affairs.[96] In many areas of life, the pursuit of goods associated with kinship ties is thus subordinated to the promotion of other goods. The family was regarded as the scene of the most basic and inescapable moral responsibilities, if not always and necessarily the sphere of the most exalted human goods.

Thomas did not view the order of charity as a simple system of concentric circles (somewhat like the system of concentric spheres that marked the medieval *cosmos*), in which family and members of one's own household come first, next close friends, neighbors and associates, and finally others in an outwardly radiating gradation of various relations to the self (though this scheme is often adopted by philosophers, moralists, and, of late, sociobiologists). This simple scheme would only be appropriate if Thomas recognized one ultimate good and one basis for friendship, whereas in fact he had a more realistic sense of the pluralism of human goods and friendships. His interpretation of the order of charity recognized the importance of different spheres of life and acknowledged the need for different schemes of priority, depending on the various matters that are the basis of the different connections people share.[97] Claims of kinship for Thomas were not assigned absolute priority, and only "trump" other claims in the arena of basic material well-being—and even here they have priority only when the degree of need is roughly comparable.

The special priority of natural relations "in matters pertaining to nature" in no way entails a narrow particularism. Beneficence for all is encouraged insofar as possible. People ought to care for the needy and assist those to whom they are closely connected. The general principle that we ought to do good first to those who are most closely connected with us is modified with the proviso, other things being equal (*ceteris paribus*).[98] Thus, in a particular case because of their greater need, strangers may have a greater claim to be assisted than one's family members, as in the case of a person who is bound to give aid to a stranger in extreme need rather than to his or her own parent who does not happen to be in such dire straits.[99] Cases of conflict are adjudicated through the exercise of the cardinal virtue of prudence, which carefully weighs degrees of need and connection.[100] True charity observes the mean[101] and follows the dictates of reason[102]—virtue is, after all, in the venerable words of Augustine, simply "the ordering of love."[103] Universally valid laws for the concrete ordering of love cannot be given because of the complexity of "contingent singulars"[104] and therefore Thomas was content to indicate the general lines of virtue in these matters, along with some judgments of cases which yield clear resolution.[105]

Biological Connections and the Order of Love

Thomas's most distinctive treatment of the order of love is found in his analysis of the order of natural relations. Articles nine through eleven of Question 26 of the *Secunda secundae* developed distinctions among these natural priorities with a kind of precision, grounded in a reading of the natural order, that is foreign to contemporary authors like Johann, Farley, and Gutiérrez. The question that Thomas addressed in these articles is the following: Granted that relations grounded in biological ties ought to be given preference in comparison to other relations (at least regarding "matters pertaining to nature"), what kind of moral priorities can be established *among* these natural relations? Thomas's specific conclusions are not as important for us as his general approach, which explicitly incorporates Aristotelian biology into an account of the natural relations between family members. This methodological commitment enables Aristotelian science to function within Thomas's ethics in a way that allowed him to avoid the kind of deficiencies that plague contemporary Catholic analyses of love.

Explicit reliance on biological nature is displayed in article ten of Question 26, which asks whether a person (Thomas uses *homo*, not *vir*) ought to love his or her mother more than his or her father? The normal reaction to this question in contemporary circles is incredulity. Relations between parents and children are so affected by the particularities of family history that uniform and ahistorical blueprints based on human biology seem to be completely irrelevant. Approaching this issue from the standpoint of natural ties strikes many contemporaries as quaint (if not perverse), but, in fairness to Thomas, it should be noted that he realized that biological origin is only one of many bonds that unite parents and their children. Moreover, he did not propose a rigid and universal ranking of love based only on biological connection. This question pertains to the proper relation between family members understood strictly per se, that is, whether a father, precisely as father, ought to be loved more than a mother precisely as a mother. Thomas gave this caveat because he recog-

nized realistically that the virtues and vices of individuals can deeply mod-
ify—either negatively or positively—the moral status of a relationship
partially based on biological connections.

This having been said, Thomas proceeded to affirm that speaking
per se, it is one's father who ought to be loved more than one's mother.
The argument supporting this claim depended heavily on Aristotle's theory of biological generation, which maintained that while both parents are
loved as principles of one's being, one's father, whose semen provides the
"active principle" of one's generation, is the source of being in a higher
way than one's mother, who Aristotle thought supplies only the "passive
and material element."[106] A biological father makes a contribution that is
"more excellent" than a biological mother, and therefore the former claims
an honor and respect not due the latter.

Given the premise that only God, not the biological father, creates
the human soul, the form of the body,[107] should not Thomas have argued
that a greater love be given to one's mother for at least producing the
"formless matter" out of which our bodies are made? Thomas claimed in
response to this objection that in human generation, the "formless matter" supplied by the mother is completely unformed until it receives its
form by means of the power contained in the father's semen.[108] Thus
though God alone creates the rational soul, the human father nevertheless
prepares the matter of the body to receive its proper form.[109]

Several other objections to Thomas's position seem valid, however.
A mother would seem to deserve greater love since it is she who suffers the
pains of childbearing and, at least in the family structure assumed by Thomas, it is she who exhausts herself on the daily tasks of rearing and educat-
ing the children. Thomas accepted Aristotle's claim that mothers love
their children more than do fathers,[110] and he believed that a just love is
reciprocal. It seems only fair therefore for Thomas to have maintained
that children ought to love their mothers more than their fathers. Thomas's response to these objections reiterated the distinction between the
kind of honor owed by a child to his or her parent strictly in light of biological generation and the many other kinds of friendship found in that
relationship.[111] The gratitude and respect owed to a parent devoted to the
growth and happiness of his or her children is not deduced from reproductive origins but is the natural human response to years of maternal
love.

In answering the question in article eleven of Question 26, whether
a man ought to love his wife more than his father and his mother, Thomas
built on the already established claim that objectively one's parents, as the

natural principles of one's generation, take precedence over all other persons with regard to honor and respect. Yet while parents are the most exalted good, and so are more due the love of honor than one's spouse, the spouse, Thomas argued, is due priority in the love of intimacy. In terms of intimate union rather than objective good, in other words, one's wife is to be loved more than one's parents because union with the former is that of "one flesh."[112] This position is reinforced by the *Summa contra Gentiles*, which claimed that the love of marriage is the greatest natural friendship.[113] Thomas maintained, reasonably enough, that the intensity of love is proportioned to the degree of intimacy and on this ground concluded that a man ought to love his wife more intensely than others but ought to show greater reverence for his parents.[114]

Thomas's treatment of "how much" one ought to love various people actually turns out to have been concerned with the fact that one relates to different kinds of people with different kinds of love and that different kinds of love (here, those of intensity and reverence, respectively) ought to be given priority within their respective spheres. Marriage is both a natural institution and a Christian sacrament, and it is attended by a wide range of moral obligations. At the same time, it does not abrogate obligations deriving from prior natural bonds. Ties of natural origin are permanent and therefore, the most stable of all. Thus, a man is not required to utterly desert his parents for the sake of his wife, Thomas argued, and in certain cases a man ought to care for his parents rather than his wife.[115] The order of the affections thus becomes more complicated with the love and commitments of marriage, but it retains the objects of natural loyalty developed in the original familial setting—though in a differently structured context.

Thomas and the Contemporary Ethics of Love

Thomas's ethics of love clearly managed to avoid the deficiencies that afflict contemporary Catholic ethics. In a broad sense, of course, this outcome was facilitated by the simple historical fact that Thomas preceded the modern philosophical movements represented by Bacon, Descartes, and Kant, among others, whose influence significantly contributes to the defects (as well as certain strengths) found in contemporary Catholic ethics. The strength of Thomas's position is in no small part due to his willingness to employ interpretations of biological dimensions of human nature within his understanding of the order of love.

Thomas's interpretation of charity and its order is formulated in terms of what he took to be the known "facts" of human nature. He was thus able to understand the complexities and diversity of human love in a way that is not generally found in contemporary Catholic ethics. Thomas employed knowledge of the biological constituents of human nature in a variety of ways, from the most general to the very specific. His understanding of the human person as a unified composite of matter and form encouraged a general attentiveness to biological aspects of human nature, for example, the natural inclinations, the sensitive appetite and the passions, and the proper love for the body. In principle, his ethics acknowledged embodiment in a more complete way than either Johann or Rahner. Human love was understood by Thomas to be rooted in human generic nature, that is, as a passion rooted in the sensitive appetite and involving somatic aspects of the person. He recognized that true human happiness is not that of angels, but includes natural goods such as bodily health, friendship, and a modicum of temporal goods.[117] Properly ordered natural inclinations and desires contribute to human flourishing in a substantial and irreplacable way.

Charity incorporates the tendencies and needs of natural love. Though self-denial plays an indispensable role in Christian morality, the life of charity does not altogether transcend ordinary human needs or require self-immolation. Physical needs, either those of the self or the neighbor, are not perceived as insignificant or trivial, and therefore, at times, for example, corporeal alms take precedence over spiritual.[118] On this point Thomas and recent Catholic ethicists concur.

One interesting indication of the inadequacy of the pre-Vatican II manuals of moral theology was their tendency to retain Thomas's order of love while jettisoning its original scientific backing, Aristotelian biology, without any new scientific evidence to take its place. The typical manualist treatment of the order of charity simply enumerated a list of moral conclusions without supplying the kinds of supporting empirical evidence that Thomas had provided.[119] Behind Thomas's focus on the natural order and his attentiveness to empirical aspects of human nature lay the theological claim that God governs human life through its intrinsic ordering to certain goods. The neo-Thomistic formal acceptance of this theological principle in the modern age was not accompanied by an openness to relevant data and insights from the sciences.

In Thomas's analysis of the order of love, Aristotle's theory of the biological father as the active principle of a child's conception was taken as the decisive evidence supporting the argument that one's father should be naturally loved more than one's mother. Thomas's repeated use of this biological principle, in this and a variety of other contexts, coupled with his evident respect for what he interpreted as the order of nature and natural design, indicates that he was not using it as a "proof text" (as biological evidence taken out of context and used in a purely supplementary way). Rather, evidence appropriated from biology provided indications of the larger ordering of nature, and indeed as disclosing the ordering will of God. This larger context requires a conceptualization of "nature" omitted in most contemporary approaches. Further, this understanding of the relation between God and nature is at some distance from Rahner's emphasis on God as present in interpersonal experience and Gutiérrez's focus on God as acting in liberating praxis and solidarity.

By contemporary standards, of course, Thomas's "order of love" is overdetermined. On biological grounds alone, for example, we can no longer maintain that one's father must be loved more than one's mother. James M. Gustafson rightly points to Thomas's "classicism" when he argues that the latter's "effort to develop an 'order of charity' implants on the dynamism of human nature a rigidity that violates it."[116] Thus Gustafson speaks correctly of dynamic patterns and processes of love's ordering rather than of a static order. We must consciously deliberate on the ordering of love and its concomitant moral priorities, and live our lives accordingly, yet we do not do so in an anthropological vacuum or with the existentialist's unhindered radical freedom. Emotional predispositions, of course, incline the agent to establish and maintain particular affective bonds, but they do not determine them. Yet some of the most important human affective ties have emerged out of deep biological needs and drives. We are naturally oriented to some form of ordering these relationships.

In summary, Thomas's attentiveness to the biological aspects of human nature, despite various weaknesses from a contemporary standpoint and in conjunction with other important features of his thought, enabled him to avoid the difficulties found in contemporary treatments of love. First, it supported an appreciation of the dependence of the human on the natural world. Thomas' interpretation of human nature highlighted rationality but did not ignore aspects of significant human continuity with the rest of the animal world.

Second, it recognized that human love is rooted in natural "passions" and is an act of the whole person—sensitive as well as rational, passionate as well as intellectual. Third, it supported an attentiveness to the problem of moral ordering and the need to make certain kinds of distinctions among multiple objects of love. Moreover, and this point is most important, it provided a basis for this order by attending to the moral centrality of primary bonds of marriage and consanguinity as understood in available scientifically based sources. Other forms of friendship are given their due, but primary relations are never merely taken for granted, let alone minimized.

These advantages of Thomas's position having been noted, we can now consider whether contemporary evolutionary accounts of natural ordering might be able to function within contemporary Catholic ethics to overcome its characteristic deficiencies.

NOTES

1.   Aristotle, *Metaphysics*, trans. W. D. Ross, in *The Basic Works of Aristotle*, ed. Richard McKeon (New York: Random House, 1941), 1015a13–19, 756.

2.   In *The Spirit of Medieval Philosophy*, trans. A. H. C. Downes (New York: Charles Scribner's Sons, 1936), Etienne Gilson parts ways with those Thomists, and especially Pierre Rousselot, who, he believed, gave undue significance to the part-whole argument, suspecting that it leads to a failure to recognize both the special dignity of the person and the transcendence of God. Gilson interpreted the part-whole model as an illustrative metaphor that is properly understood only in light of the nature of the human person as *imago Dei*. Disinterested love for God is the love of the image of God for its original. Gilson argued that, "it is impossible to love the image without at the same time loving the original, and if we know, as we do know, that the image is only an image, it is impossible to love it without preferring the original" (ibid., 286). For criticism of Gilson's position, see D'Arcy, *Mind and Heart of Love*, 111–12, and Dom Gregory Stevens, O.S.B., "The Disinterested Love of God According to St. Thomas and Some of His Modern Interpreters," *The Thomist* 16 (1953):315–17.

3.   ST II.II.26.1.

4.   ST I.103.1; see also I.2.3.

5.   Thomas ranked the intellect as more noble than either the rational or sensitive appetites and, moreover, as "not constituted out of matter" (ST I.76.2 ad 1). While the latter position may suggest a latent dualism, it must be noted that Thomas frequently and unequivocally affirms the corporeal basis of the human composite. It is not claimed in this chapter that there are no strains of dualism in Thomas's thought, for clearly he at times leans in that direction. Whatever the influence of Augustine and Neoplatonism in this regard, this chapter maintains that the positive evaluations of matter, nature, the human body, and the passions reflect the dominant anti-Manichean direction of Thomas's thought.

6.   *Summa contra Gentiles* (hereafter SCG) II.68.2. The Platonic understanding of the body as a "tomb" for the soul can be found in Gorgias 193a and Phaedrus 250c.

7.   ST I.44.3ad2; "non potest inveniri homo sine materia." See also I.76.1ad6; I.75.6c and 7c.

8.   Kenneth E. Kirk, *The Vision of God: The Christian Doctrine of the Summum Bonum* (New York: Longmans, Green and Co., 1931), 157.

9.   ST I.II.94.2: "Hoc est ergo primum praeceptum legis, quod bonum est faciendum et prosequendum et malum vitandum."

10.   Jeffrie Murphy, *Evolution, Morality, and the Meaning of Life* (Totowa, New Jersey: Rowman and Littlefield, 1982), 62.

11.   Jacques Maritain, *On the Philosophy of History*, ed. Joseph Evans (New York: Charles Scribner's Sons, 1957), 85.

12.   R. A. Armstrong, *Primary and Secondary Precepts in Thomistic Natural Law Teaching* (The Hague: Martinus Nijhoff, 1966), 48.

13.   ST II.II.64.1.

14.   ST I.II.94.2: "Et secundam hanc inclinationem, pertinent ad legem naturalem ea per quae vita hominis conservatur, et contrarium impeditur."

15.   ST II.II.64.7.

16.   ST II.II.64.5.

17.   Maritain, *On the Philosophy of History*, 85.

18.   Armstrong, *Primary and Secondary Precepts*, 48–49.

19.   Maritain, *On the Philosophy of History*, 85.

20.   ST Suppl. 65.2. See also SCG III.124.

21.   Maritain, *On the Philosophy of History*, 85.

22.   Armstrong, *Primary and Secondary Precepts*, 48–49.

23.   Maritain, *On the Philosophy of History*, 85.

24.   Armstrong, *Primary and Secondary Precepts*, 50.

25.   See ST I.II.94.2. "utpote quod homo ignorantiam vitet, quod alios non offendat cum quibus debet conversari, et cetera huiusmodi quae ad spectant."

26.   ST I.II.94.6.

27.   ST I.II.94.2: "jus naturale est quod natura omnia animalia docuit." See Michael Bertram Crowe, "St. Thomas and Ulpian's Natural Law," *St. Thomas Aquinas 1274-1974 Commemorative Studies* (Toronto: Pontifical Institute of Medieval Studies, 1974), 261–82. On the relation of natural inclinations to the natural law, and the centrality of "nature matérielle" in Thomas's natural law theory, see Félicien Rousseau, *La croissance solidaire des droits de l'homme: Un retour aux sources de l'éthique* (Tournai: Descleé & Cie, 1982), ch. 3.

28.   ST I.98.2ad3.

29.   ST I.20.1

30.   ST I.II.8.1

31.   ST I.II.26.1; I.II.28.1ad2.

32.   ST I.II.25.2.

33.   ST I.II.23.4; I.II.26.1.

34.   Eric D'Arcy, "Introduction," *Summa Theologiae*, vol. 16, I–II, 1–5 (New York: McGraw Hill Book Co., 1963–69), *xxxi*. The best secondary source on Thomas's notion of complacency is Fredrick E. Crowe, "Complacency and Concern in the Thought of St. Thomas," *Theological Studies* 20 (1959): 1–40, 198–231, 343–96.

35.   ST I.II.26.1; see also I.6.1ad2; I.103.1ad2; I.103.3.

36.   ST I.II.26.2.

37. ST I.II.26.1ad3.

38. Thomas Gilby, *Poetic Experience* (London: Sheed and Ward, 1934), 81. Unless otherwise indicated, "natural love" in this book takes the broader sense of natural that includes natural, sensitive, and rational love. All are "natural" in that they belong to human nature, and are not the result of God's grace (supernatural love).

39. The relevant Latin terms, *passiones animae*, *passiones*, and *passio* present various problems for translation. The two candidates for English translations, "passions" and "emotions," both carry unfelicitous connotations. The first seems too narrow for Thomas's *passiones*, the second tends to obscure the crucial element of passivity. Both terms will be used here, as seems appropriate.

40. ST I.II.22–54.

41. ST I.II.23.4.

42. ST I.II.23.4; I.II.25.2.

43. Pierre Rousselot, *Pour l'historie du problème de l'amour au moyen âge* (Paris: J. Vrin, 1933).

44. The *motus* model also provides a framework for interpreting the order of the passions. The passions of the "concupiscible appetite," which inclines to the good as such, are divided into three pairs corresponding to the three stages of the model: love and its contrary, hate, correspond to inclination; desire and its opposite, aversion, correspond to movement; and joy and its contrary, sorrow, correspond to rest (ST I.II.23.4;-I.II.25.2). The passions of the "irascible appetite," which intends the good as arduous, follow the same pattern. In the order of execution, love is the first of the concupiscible powers: love precedes desire, and desire precedes joy (ST I.II.25.2). The order of intention is the reverse.

45. ST I.II.26.3.

46. ST I.II.24.1. For Augustine, see *De Civ. Dei*, XIV,7.

47. ST I.II.24.3. D'Arcy renders the Latin words *appetitus* and *appetitiva* as "orexis" and "orectic" because of the misleading connotations of the English word "appetite" and the affective and conative emphases of "orexis" in contemporary psychology. See Thomas Aquinas, *Summa Theologiae*, vol. 19, trans. D'Arcy, "Introduction," *xxiv–xxv.*

48. See Immanuel Kant, *Foundations of the Metaphysics of Morals*, trans. Lewis White Beck (Indianapolis, In.: Bobbs-Merrill, 1959), "First Section: Transition from the Common Rational Knowledge of Morals to the Philosophical," esp. 9–18.

49. ST I.II.24.3.

50. ST I.II.26.4. Also SCG I.91; III.90. For Aristotle, *Rhetoric*, II, 4, 1380b35, 1386–88. Thomas incorporated Aristotle's maxim without viewing it as a sufficient definition of love. Thomas treated benevolence as one of the three components of love but not the whole of love in ST II.II.23.1.

51. ST I.II.26.4. Love of concupiscence, it should be noted, is not to be confused with concupiscence itself, nor identified with egocentrism. Properly ordered love tends to rational creatures with a love of friendship and to other objects with the love of concupiscence.

52. ST II.II.25.4.

53. I.II.28.3. H. D. Simonin, O.P., explores this theme in the seminal article, "Autour de la solution thomiste du problème de l'amour," in *Archives d'histoire doctrinale et littéraire du moyen âge* 6 (1931): 174–276.

54. Preference for those who are similar has been studied by, *inter alia*, Ervin Staub, *Positive Social Behavior and Morality: Social and Personal Influences*, 2 vols. (New York: Academic Press, 1978), 1:313–333; Mary B. Harris and Hortensia Baudin, "The Language of Altruism: The Effects of Language, Dress, and Ethnic Group," *Journal of Social Psychology* 91 (1973): 37–41. According to Dennis Krebs, "Perception of similarity increases the disposition to imagine how one would feel in another's place." ("Empathy and Altruism," *Journal of Personality and Social Psychology* 32 [1975]:1143.)

55. ST I.60.4.

56. See ST Suppl.41.1 (political association); I.II.27.3 (friendship); I.60.5 ("parts" of a social "whole"); II.II.114.1ad2 ("general love" for other people).

57. SCG III.117. Thomas's theological ethics abound with references to human nature as social. To mention a few examples: (1) sociality and truthfulness, ST II.II.109.3ad1; (2) friendliness, II.II.114.2ad1; (3) trust, II.II.129.6ad1; (4) priority of the common good, I.II.90.2, and II.II.26.3; and (5) mutual assistance, SCG III.117. Regarding individuals as parts of a larger social whole, see ST I.II.90.2; II.II.58.5; II.II.61.1. See also Aristotle's *Politics*, I, 2, 1253a20.

58. ST II.II.23.1: "Iam non dicam vos servos, sed amicos meos."

59. ST I.1.8: "gratia perficit naturam non destruit."

60. See ST II.II.23.2.

61. ST I.60.3.

62. For example, Reinhold Neibuhr, *An Interpretation of Christian Ethics* (New York: Crossroad, 1979), ch. 2, "The Ethic of Jesus."

63. See ST II.II.25.9. On the relation of *caritas* to the natural law, see J. M. Aubert, "La spécifité de la morale chrétienne selon saint Thomas," *Le Supplément* 92 (1970): 55–73. According to Thomas, enemies are not to be loved as such, for this would be a perversion of both nature and charity, "because it means loving evil in another" (ST II.II.25.8). Enemies are naturally contrary to one as enemies but not as human beings capable of eternal happiness, and, as Thomas argued, it is precisely as such that one is bound to love them (ST II.II.25.8ad2). His further distinctions of general and special acts of love for enemies and their inward and outward expressions, were based on this conviction. See also ST II.II.25.6 on the love of sinners.

64. ST II.II.25.1ad2.

65. ST I.60.1ad3.

66. ST II.II.26.7ad2.

67. This chapter cannot examine in detail the perennial problems surrounding the relation between self-love and the disinterested love for God. Only the basic lines of Thomas's position can be given here. These issues are most often associated with the Bossuet-Fénelon conflict but clearly have medieval precursors, as evidenced in Rousselot's groundbreaking work, *Pour l'histoire du problème de l'amour*. Gilson attempts to rebut Rousselot's dichotomization of "ecstatic" and "physical" theories of love in *Spirit of Medieval Philosophy*, ch. 14 and Appendix. The most comprehensive historical survey from an Anglo-Catholic perspective remains Kirk's *Vision of God*. Nygren's monumental *Agape and Eros* represents the landmark twentieth-century assault on the reconciliation of *eros* and *agape* in the "caritas synthesis."

68. John Stuart Mill writes, for example, that, "Of the social virtues it is almost superfluous to speak; so completely is it the verdict of all experience that selfishness is natural." In "Three Essays on Religion," in *Essays on Ethics, Religion, and Society*,

vol. 10 of *Collected Works of John Stuart Mill*, ed. J. M. Robson (Toronto: University of Toronto Press, 1969), 394.

69.   See Stephen J. Pope, "Expressive Individualism and True Self-Love: A Thomistic Perspective," *Journal of Religion* 71 (1991): 384–99.

70.   Reinforcing Thomas's claim that self-love is the model of neighbor love, psychologist Ervin Staub argues, in the converse case, that, a "poor self-concept makes it more difficult to extend the boundaries of the self in benevolent ways." In Ervin Staub, "A Conception of the Determinants and Development of Altruism and Aggression: Motives, the Self, and the Environment," in *Altruism and Aggression: Biological and Social Origins*, ed. Carolyn Zahn-Waxler, E. Mark Cummings, and Ronald Iannotti (Cambridge, England: Cambridge University Press, 1986), 142.

71.   Thomas Nagel, *The Possibility of Altruism* (Princeton, New Jersey: Princeton University Press, 1970), 3.

72.   See, *inter alia*, Garth Hallett in *Five Theories of Neighbor-Love: An Assessment of Six Rival Versions* (Washington, D.C.: Georgetown University Press, 1989), which throughout advocates the position of subordination of self to others, and Joseph L. Allen, *Love and Conflict: A Covenantal Model of Christian Ethics* (Nashville, Tennessee: Abingdon, 1984), 116–30. Influential preceding texts expressing priority of the neighbor include Niebuhr, *The Nature and Destiny of Man*, vol. 2, ch. 3 and Paul Ramsey, *Basic Christian Ethics* (New York: Charles Scribner's Sons, 1957), 92–103, 147–52.

73.   ST II.II.26.4.

74.   Ibid. These arguments are subject to certain objections articulated by Hallett in *Five Theories of Neighbor-Love*, 64–69. My intention is not defend every position taken by Thomas but rather to display the natural basis of his account of the ordering of love.

75.   ST I.II.28.3ad3.

76.   ST II.II.26.4.

77.   ST I.60.4ad2. Also II.II.44.7; *In III Sententiarum*, dist.29,a.5; *Commentum in evangelium s. Mattaei*, chap.22,n.4.

78.   ST II.II.44.8ad2.

79.   ST II.II.26.5.

80.   Farley, *Personal Commitments*, 104.

81.   ST II.II.26.4ad2.

82.   Michael Ruse, "The Morality of the Gene," *The Monist* 67 (1985): 178. Ruse could obviously appeal to a straightforward reading of certain Biblical texts for his characterization of Christian love (e.g., "in humility regard others as better than yourselves"; [Phil 2:3, N.R.S.V.], and others, e.g., I John 3:16 and 1 Cor 10:24), but Thomas made theoretical distinctions that allowed him to reconcile biblical imperatives with the law of God inscribed in human nature, and in the natural order of love.

83.   ST II.II.26.6: "Utrum unus proximus sit magis diligendus quam alius?"

84.   See ST II.II.26.6ob1. See also *III Sentences* 29,2.

85.   See ST II.II.26.6.

86.   Ibid.

87.   ST II.II.26.6ad1.

88.   As one would expect Thomas assigned a high priority to beneficence for special relations. His treatment of q.31, a.3, "Utrum sit magis benefaciendum his qui

sunt nobis magis conjuncti," is consistent with what had been established previously. It affirmed, first, that grace and virtue reflect the order of nature that has been established by divine wisdom and, second, that in the order of nature each natural agent acts first and most effectively on things that are nearest to it. The order of beneficence accords with the order of nature, and thus, Thomas argued, the closer one is to another person, the more good one should do for him or her (ibid.). At the same time, Thomas did not understand the priority of natural relations to diminish or minimize other connections. On the contrary, he maintained that beneficence ought to reflect the various goods that bind people more closely together and that ties of kinship are only one such bond. A soldier on the battlefield ought then, to assist a fellow soldier who is a stranger rather than a kinsman who is an enemy (ST II.II.33.3ad2; also II.II.26.8).

89. ST II.II.26.7.

90. ST II.II.26.7, sed contra: "Si quis suorum, et maxime domesticorum curam non habet, fidem negavit et est infideli deterior."

91. ST II.II.26.7.

92. See ST II.II.26.2.

93. ST II.II.25.7; also I.II.77.4ad1.

94. See ST II.II.26.7ad1.

95. ST II.II.23.8

96. ST II.II.26.8

97. ST II.II.31.3.

98. ST II.II.31.3ad1.

99. ST II.II.31.3

100. ST II.II.31.3ad1.

101. ST I.II.64.

102. ST I.II.59.1ad3.

103. *De mor. eccl.* I,15, cited in S.T.I. II.55.1.

104. ST II.II.47.9ad2; II.II.185.7ad1.

105. ST II.II.31.3ad3; also IIII.185.7.

106. ST II.II.26.10. See Aristotle, *De Generatione Animalium* I.20. 729a10; see also II.4 738b23. For a helpful secondary source, see Allan Gotthelf and James G. Lennox, eds., *Philosophical Issues in Aristotle's Biology* (Cambridge: Cambridge University Press, 1987).

107. ST I.90.2; I.118.2.

108. See ST I.90.2c and 3c.

109. ST II.II.26.10ad1.

110. See *Nic. Ethic.* IX, 7, 1168a25.

111. ST II.II.26.10ad2.

112. ST II.II.26.11; citing Matt 19:6.

113. See SCG III.123.6.

114. ST II.II.26.11.

115. ST II.II.26.11ad1.

116. Gustafson, *Ethics from a Theocentric Perspective* 1:312; see also his "Nature: Its Status in Theological Ethics," *Logos* 3 (1982): 5–23.

117. ST I.II.41.6.

118. ST II.II.32.3

119.   See, for example, Thomas Slater, *Manual of Moral Theology* 1:91 or Davis, *Moral and Pastoral Theology*, 1:319–321. This is not to suggest that argument is completely absent, but only that the kinds of arguments given—biblical, common sense, Thomistic axioms—do not display the careful use of current scientific information of the sort employed by Thomas.

3

Thomas's "Order of Love" and Evolutionary Theories of Altruism

The previous chapter sketched the significant features of Thomas's ethics of love which enabled him to avoid the deficiencies that afflict contemporary Catholic ethics. This chapter relates Thomas's ethics to evolutionary theory, with an eye to using the latter critically as a corrective to the deficiencies of recent treatments of love by Rahner, Johann, and Gutiérrez, among others. To avoid misunderstanding, I should say unequivocally at this point that no simple synthesis of Thomas's ethics with evolutionary theory is possible. No simple and direct one-to-one correspondences exist between Thomas's order of love and contemporary evolutionary accounts of human sociality, and I do not argue that the latter are simply replicated with genetic backing in the former.

This chapter establishes only that certain features of evolutionary theory can act as functional equivalences to aspects of Thomas's account of the order of love. Functional equivalences in ethology are interesting and fruitful precisely because they do not simply posit identical organs performing identical functions, for example, a human jaw and chimpanzee's jaw; rather, they examine ways in which dissimilar, entities sometimes highly dissimilar, entities can perform similar functions, for example, an elephant's trunk and a human hand. The distinction between functional similarity or "analogy" and substantive resemblances based on common descent or "homology"[1] allows ethologists to avoid drawing dubious analogies between human and animal traits, for example, regarding "aggression," "infanticide," "dominance hierarchies," "territoriality," and "communication." It can also allow Catholic ethics to avoid drawing similarly dubious analogies between Thomism and evolutionary thought.

In this chapter, I introduce these functional equivalences; then, in chapter four, I will offer a more developed interpretation and assessment of evolutionary theories of altruism.

The Natural Order

The most obvious place to begin comparing Thomas Aquinas and evolutionary theory is in the attention both sources give to the ordering of nature, in which "order" is considered to refer to the intelligible relation of "parts" of nature to one another and to various "wholes." Thomas, as we have seen, understood nature to be orderly, not haphazard, capricious, or random, and to be composed of relations essentially comprehensible to human reason. His belief in the lawlike consistency of nature cohered with his metaphysical conviction regarding the foundation of the intelligibility of the order of being in the divine wisdom. Natural science, particularly as provided by Aristotle, was taken to yield accurate insights into aspects of the intrinsic teleological ordering of each individual substance and the much broader order of the whole of nature.

Contemporary biology also obviously concerns itself with natural ordering. Genetics, cell biology, and embryology, for example, provide insights into the orderly processes of ontogeny, the genetically programmed formation of appropriate organs at certain fixed times in the sequence of normal embryological development. Ethologists attend to the ways in which various species have been phylogenetically ordered to develop certain "releasing mechanisms" that respond to certain stimulus situations and not others.[2] Ecologists, similarly, study systems of ordered interaction between various particular organisms and their habitats. Behavioral ecologists account for the patterns of ordering observed between various organisms and their environment in terms of natural selection, an ordering that covers a spectrum from the genetically fixed, "hard-wired" behavior of less intelligent species, for example, the "waggle dance" by which the honeybee communicates the location of food stores to other members of its hive;[3] to the various kinds of more complex natural ordering seen in the social organization of primates and other mammals.

Evolutionary theorists view "human nature" itself as ordered biologically, as dependent on and participating in the natural world, and as located within a vastly enlarged time and space framework.[4] We are part of the animal kingdom, the mammal class, and the primate order. "Human nature," Midgley writes, should be viewed in the context of "the long evolutionary perspective" within which it "fall[s] into place as one remarkable variation among many others on a vast but coherent evolutionary range."[5] Evolutionary biologists teach us, Midgley says, that "we are not just rather like animals; we *are* animals."[6] The human species, like others, "consists in a certain range of powers and tendencies, a repertoire, inherited and forming a fairly firm characteristic pattern."[7]

Sociality

Thomas held that we have a natural prompting to will good to others, in virtue of our common humanity, and to spontaneously assist others in need.[8] Both sources—Thomas and evolutionary theory—recognize that we need to curb natural tendencies that pose a threat to human love, and that positive coexistence (both personal and social) does not come spontaneously but must be carefully crafted by wise human decisions. Human beings are ordered by nature to live with one another and to participate in political community.[9] We naturally desire to belong, to form bonds of friendship, to cooperate in day-to-day social life, and to attain fulfillment in communion with others. The human person develops and flourishes within and through interpersonal and communal ties rather than simply over against them.

In contemporary evolutionary terms, "sociality" includes a vast array of behavior found in the interaction of conspecifics, from mutual grooming and feeding to "alarm calls" and "mating coalitions." Sociality involves living in groups and interacting with group members, communication, developing alliances with other individuals, and mating and rearing offspring. For humans it includes particularly complex kinds of behavioral traits and emotional predispositions, including a desire for acceptance by other individuals and social approval, participation in moral systems, political activity, and other forms of communal life. According to evolutionary theory, natural human affective and social capacities did not simply appear without precedent, with the first emergence of *Homo sapiens*, but have been selected by millions of years of hominid evolution.

Attachment theorists argue that the patterns of interaction that lead to emotional bonding between newborns and caregivers are not arbitrary, but powerfully directed genetically based predispositions that have been shaped by the evolutionary process.[10] The elemental inclination to form and maintain strong affectional bonds provides an obvious selective advantage to members of the species by supporting the extended parental caregiving needed during the human infant's prolonged dependency and complex process of physical, cognitive, and psychological maturation. Attachment theorists shed light on the earliest glimmerings of our natural sociality by tracing ways in which infants are directed by complex innate physiological processes to seek out and become attached to one or at most several permanent caretakers. They have drawn on ethological analyses of "releasers," such as eye contact, clinging, and smiling, by which newborns spontaneously evoke cherishing behavior in their caregivers and thereby encourage and strengthen parental bonding.[11]

In contrast to Freud's view that infants are completely egoistic,[12] attachment theorists have developed a more complex view of early sociality that recognizes rudimentary precursors of prosocial concern and altruism in "empathic distress" (a response to the experience of another child's crying) and "helping behavior."[13] A number of converging sources from the social sciences indicate that altruism is a component of human nature. As sociologists Jane Allyn Piliavin and Hong-Wen Chang observe, "People do have 'other-regarding sentiments,' they do contribute to public goods from which they benefit little, they do sacrifice for their children and even for others to whom they are not related.[14] "Later childhood concern and caring for others (e.g., sharing, comforting, helping) are developed on the basis of innate prosocial biological predispositions, not purely and exclusively the result of socialization and learning. Assistance-giving is said to be "caused" not by culture or genes alone but to reflect the influence of both these as well as other factors such as personality and history.

Prosocial inclinations are included in the repertoire of the human emotional constitution. Neo-Darwinians, like Darwin himself, claim that the "evolutionary process of our species has produced in most of us an assortment of inborn tendencies to form emotional attachments with others, in some contexts a concentrated and intense attachment with one or two others or a very few, in other contexts a very diffuse attachment with many."[15] Spontaneous empathy, rather than a one-track calculation of reproductive profitability or other forms of self-interest,[16] is one of the emotional predispositions produced by our evolutionary heritage.[17]

As Ruse explains:

> As part of our biology, we have feelings of sympathy and caring for others. We do desire the well-being—the happiness—of others, as well as of ourselves, and judge that this desire is a good thing. That is one of the key conclusions of modern evolutionary biology.[18]

Philosopher Peter Singer makes the same point regarding reciprocity, namely, that there is "an evolutionary advantage in being genuinely altruistic instead of making reciprocal exchanges on the basis of calculated self-interest."[19] Midgley argues, similarly, that sociobiology itself, though often mistakenly accused of social Darwinism, "shows plainly that there is no reason at all why creatures need be unmitigatingly selfish and deliberately competitive in order to succeed in evolution."[20] The general shape of this natural ordering is succinctly summarized by Ruse: "Biologically, our major concern has to be towards our own kin, then to those in at least some sort of relationship to us (not necessarily a blood relationship), and only finally to complete strangers."[21]

Self-love

Evolutionary theory claims, as Thomas did, that self-love is based in human nature. According to Thomas, all love of others is grounded in self-love.[22] Nature teaches all beings to seek their own good; even things completely lacking in intellect tend by nature to procure the good for themselves. So too rational creatures naturally seek their own good and perfection can be said to love themselves.[23] Put in this way one can understand that self-love is neither good nor bad, neither a virtue nor a vice, but simply an expression of human nature, and therefore capable of displaying either adherence to, or departure from, right reason. Self-love is virtuous when it properly relates one to the good, vicious when its distorts this relation.

Behavioral biology explains the rudiments of self-concern in terms of the innate tendency of all individual organisms, from the simplest amoeba to human beings, to seek their own safety and to reproduce, a fundamental biological ground out of which develops in human beings the infinitely more complex, fully self-conscious experience of self-love.[24] Sociobiologists generally understand the unit of selection to be proximately the individual organism and ultimately the gene, not the group or the species.[25] Organisms obviously can only persist when equipped with behavior traits that promote their own survival and reproduction or that of their relatives (or at least this is the case with all higher animals, unlike the social insects).

Genes successful in self-replication cannot incline their individual organisms (or "carriers") to act consistently against their own reproductive self-interest (or that of their "replicators") for the simple reason that individual organisms that consistently put the reproductive interests of other organisms ahead of their own will tend not to live long enough to successfully reproduce. In human beings, elemental self-regard is the basis for what we recognize as fully developed self-love. Self-concern is a deeply rooted human motivation, and, indeed, it is so strong that it can undermine the agent's genes in some sense. According to sociobiologist Pierre van den Berghe:

> We have been programmed to love ourselves, directly, and indirectly in our children and relatives, because that is how our constituent genes were selected in the first place. Genes that had this effect in their carriers were selected for. But human consciousness now turns that self-love against the genes. We use the proximate mechanisms of genetic selection, including sexual behavior, not only as means to the end of gene reproduction, but as ends in themselves. We proclaim, in effect, that we love the entire assemblage of genes we call "me" better than our genes taken separately, and that therefore we are going, in some circumstances, to gratify that "me," even at the expense of reproducing our genes.[26]

Kinship

As we have seen, Thomas accorded a central role to family within the *ordo amoris*. According to Thomas, people are naturally drawn to love their own parents, offspring, and siblings more than others. Though friends may be loved more than family members in respect to certain goods (e.g., as soldiers love their comrades in arms), in the necessities of life, one's family members are primary. Thomas maintained that one's own children are "part of oneself" in a way not true of other human beings, including one's spouse. This kind of interpretation of familial connections, including their biological components, provided a certain backing for his ethical prescriptions, though not without remainder.

Contemporary evolutionary theory also regards kinship as indirect self-love and as the elemental human connection. "Altruism," according to the sociobiologists, is behavior that reduces one organism's own fitness in favor of that of another.[27] One common example of such "altruism" is the "alarm calls" given off by prairie dogs (and many other species as well) that warn fellow members of their group of an approaching coyote. Such calls may help others to escape at the risk of the caller's own detection and possible predation.[28] Other well-known examples include female lions that suckle cubs of other lionesses,[29] the "self-sacrifice" of soldier aphids, who forgo their own reproduction in the interests of the clone mates,[30] and primates who engage in "grooming" behavior to rid members of their troop of parasites.[31] "Altruism" is widespread in the animal world, from parental care, mutual defense, and rescue behavior to cooperation in hunting and food sharing. In each of these and a multitude of other behaviors one individual organism contributes to the fitness of another at some cost to its own individual fitness, however marginal it may seem, for example, the measure of energy expended in grooming might have been expended elsewhere.

A major question is posed by the fact of altruism to evolutionary theory: how could "altruism," which by definition reduces personal fitness, have evolved through the process of natural selection? It would seem that "altruistic" individuals, that is, those that contribute to the fitness of others and reduce their own fitness, can over the long haul neither survive nor reproduce (the occasional "altruist" is here regarded as statistically insignificant). Nature would seem to select against "altruistic" behavior, yet altruism seems to abound in nature.

Kin selection theory provides the solution to this apparent difficulty by explaining "self-sacrificial" behavior in terms of "payoffs" made to genetic kin. In Wilson's terms, "if the genes causing the altruism are shared by two organisms because of common descent, and if the altruistic act by one organism increases the joint contribution of these genes to the next generation, the propensity to altruism will spread through the gene pool."[32]

In this succinct quotation, Wilson has summarized the conclusion of the theory that many sociobiologists take to be their most well-established contribution to current interpretations of assistance-giving, the theory of "kin selection."[33] The investigation of kin selection did not begin with human evolution but was initiated by W. D. Hamilton in his pioneering research on the behavior of sterile female workers among Hymenoptera insects (ants, bees, and wasps).[34] Hamilton proposed that genes responsible for the apparent "altruism" of these insects—which consists of sterile workers devoting energy not to their own offspring but to those of the queen—are selected when it results in differential reproduction. Hamilton discovered that altruism in the Hymenoptera is proportioned according to the "coefficient of relationship" (the degree of genetic relatedness) between the "altruist" and its beneficiary; that is, an individual hymenopteran is more inclined to assist a sister than its own progeny because as a member of a "haploid" species (which have not two but only one set of chromosomes) it would share copies of approximately seventy-five percent of its genes with the former.[35] Further empirical research has repeatedly confirmed Hamilton's findings and extended his lines of thought to account for the "altruistic" behavior of other social species, including the human.[36]

It is important to underscore the fact that the theory of kin selection considers not only individual Darwinian fitness but also "inclusive fitness," which Wilson defines as "the sum of an individual's own fitness plus the sum of all the effects it causes to the related parts of the fitness of all its relatives."[37] According to inclusive fitness theory, individuals are selected to tend to maximize representation of their own genes in the next generation and they do so primarily by distributing assistance in proportion to degrees of genetic relatedness. Nature does not work through a relentless pursuit of exclusively self-interested behavior, in other words, but primarily by inclining organisms to assist kin.

Inclusive fitness theory has replaced individual fitness in current evolutionary theory. According to sociobiologist Robert Trivers, "natural selection does not favor the traits of the individual who maximizes her reproductive success but rather the traits of the one who maximizes her inclusive fitness."[38] Traditional Darwinian fitness encompasses only the survival and reproduction of the organism and its direct descendants; inclusive fitness encompasses direct descendents but also the survival and reproduction of collateral relatives, that is, any other individuals to whom one is genetically related.

What is critical for kin selection theory is that an act that detracts from the organism's own individual fitness may at the same time contribute to the fitness of the organism's genetic relatives, including especially direct descendents. Because the latter carry copies of the organism's own genes, the precise proportion of which is called "coefficient of relatedness," sacrifice of the organism for its relatives can be described as phenotypically "altruistic" but genotypically "egoistic." "Altruism" directed toward kin, and especially direct offspring, is the prime example of behavior that is phenotypically "altruistic" but genotypically "egoistic."[39]

In this way sociobiologists argue that over the long haul nature selects genes that promote their own survival and reproduction without necessarily implying that genes themselves are "selfish" in any literal sense.[40] Kin selection theory, as noted above, has been scientifically verified in a multitude of empirical biological studies across a wide variety of species, and even the staunchest critics of sociobiology concede that it clearly applies to nonhuman animals. A great deal of sociobiological research has gone into testing and verifying predictions made on the basis of inclusive fitness hypotheses.[41]

Kin selection theory has also been applied to the behavior of human beings, who are said to inherit from their evolutionary ancestors a general emotional predisposition of kin preference. We all know that human beings are capable of kindness, sympathy, and care, that they can assist those in distress, and that they can endure hardship and inconvenience for the sake of others (they are, of course, capable of selfish and cruel behavior as well). Sociobiologists argue, however, that human beings, like other animals, are much more likely to deny their own individual good for their offspring or mate than for anyone else. Parental care may detract from the parent's own individual health, for instance, but it may also contribute to the health of its offspring. It is, in fact, a tendency that has been selected by nature because it contributes to the survival and well-being of its off-spring. Parental caregiving promotes the possibility that some day these children will reproduce their own viable children and thereby contribute to the perdurance of copies of the grandparents' genes.

Reciprocity

Thomas recognized the importance of reciprocity in human social life. Whereas irrational animals are spontaneously directed by natural instinct toward the simple activities needed to secure their own survival and reproduction, human beings must rely on one another to attain these basic goods. As "political animals," human beings flourish through mutual assistance and participation in communal life. Human beings depend for their very existence on intelligence rather than instinct, of course, which makes thoughtful and just social organization necessary. The efficient ordering of economic life can only be pursued through collaboration and cooperative effort, and the division of labor found in social cooperation reflects the intelligent employment of diverse talents and natural capacities.[42] Given this large social backdrop for relations between individuals, Thomas was not one to collapse the sphere of human interaction to the intersubjective, nor was he inclined to understand human connections purely in terms of self-disclosing mutuality or human relations as the exclusive product of interpersonal attraction and voluntary commitment.

The second major evolutionary theory of assistance-giving comes from reciprocity theory, which attempts to account for forms of cooperation among not related or distantly related individuals. According to Robert Trivers, the foremost proponent of reciprocity theory, reciprocity is common in the animal world, from cleaning symbioses in fish and bird "alarm calls" to rescue behavior and "mating coalitions."[43] To account for the extension of helping and caregiving to nonkin (or distantly related kin), Trivers attempts to explain the adaptive advantages accruing to systems of exchange that he terms "reciprocal." Put in simplest terms, he hypothesizes that reciprocity evolved because of the evolutionary advantages it provided to those who practiced it, "advantages" being understood primarily in terms of cost and benefit to the "altruist."[44] The risk of "altruistic" rescue behavior makes sense because the costs of energy and the danger posed by the risk involved are outweighed by the potential benefit of future assistance to the agent.

Two typical avenues to reciprocity are found in the literature. In "direct reciprocity," the altruist's act is typically conditioned on a direct return of benefit, as in, for example, food sharing and baboon "mating coalitions."[45] This type of bilateral reciprocity is dependent on direct exchange. It is crudely expressed by David Barash as, "you scratch my back, and I'll scratch your's,"[46] and in Wilson's definition of reciprocal altruism as "the trading of altruistic acts by individuals at different times."[47]

"Indirect reciprocity" is a more general form of exchange. It depends on some form of potential for return, the benefit of which outweighs the cost entailed in the "altruistic" behavior or at least in the risk undertaken in the behavior, for example, some forms of alarm calling and group defense. Return is not necessarily given by the beneficiary but by others within a particular network of interdependent agents. University of Michigan evolutionary theorist Richard Alexander maintains the morality itself is essentially a system of indirect reciprocity.[48] An agent may benefit another person without expecting any immediate or direct reciprocation, though the actual cost to the agent must not exceed the benefits obtained in the potential return of assistance, for example, the "reputational" benefit given to a person who rescues another from drowning.[49] Indirect reciprocity thus transcends the narrow and overly simple quid pro quo strategy implied in direct reciprocity.

Cooperative and helping behavior are viewed in this context as functioning to provide forms of cumulative investment in a social network within which the agent is a beneficiary, at least over the "long haul." As such, it seems to depend on the establishment and maintenance of a trust that the agent will be reciprocated from others in the future. Wilson maintains that reciprocity, or what he calls "soft core" altruism, is distinctive in that the "altruist" expects a return from society for himself or herself, or at least for his or her closest relatives. As Ruse puts it:

I help you, but do not necessarily expect you personally to help me. Rather, my help is thrown into the general pool, as it were, and then I am free to draw on help as needed.[50]

Parental Love and Filial Love

Thomas examined the biological aspects of familial bonds with detailed specificity, which led him away from any temptation to "angelism" and any tendency to regard love in purely and exclusively spiritual terms. To illustrate a functional equivalence within contemporary evolutionary theory regarding the use of scientific information to shed light on some concrete and specific biological connections, I turn now to the topic of parental and filial love.

Question 26 of the *Secunda secundae*, "The Order of Charity" includes a biologically informed analysis of various types of familial relations. In article 9 of question 26 Thomas asks, "Whether one, out of charity, ought to love one's child more than one's father?"[51] Biological connection is not incidental to human relations in Thomas's perspective; it makes a difference for the relations between people, even though it is not always a predominant feature of human relations. His answer to this question was twofold: one ought to love one's father with greater respect, because of his greater honor, and one's child with greater care, because of his or her greater connection to the self. Love is fundamentally proportioned to the good. Thomas maintained that as the "principle of our being," one's father is a higher good and more like God than one's child is; thus the former deserves greater respect than the latter. On biological grounds alone a child is in a fundamentally different relation to his or her parent than the parent is to his or her own mother and father. Priority of care for one's child is justified by appealing to three biological, or biologically based, factors: (1) natural self-love; (2) knowledge of paternity; and (3) longevity.[52]

Each of these factors presents or relies on some form of biological evidence, usually derived either from direct informal observation or Aristotelian texts, to provide assistance in determining the natural order of familial love and care. Thus, because a father provides the "seed" for the child's being, the latter can be described as a "separated part" of the former.[53] As the reader will recall, Thomas understood this order to be abstract, and knowledge of it to be a necessary but not sufficient condition for comprehending the proper concrete order of love in personal life.

In the concrete, Thomas noted, the personal virtue of the parties involved makes all the difference. This qualification is a critical one to note, for it indicates Thomas's avoidance of simplistic appeals to biological ordering for concrete moral reasoning.

Evolutionary theorists attend to forms of "parenting effort" expended on increasing an offspring's chances of survival and reproduction. Parent-offspring relations are analyzed in terms of "parental investment," which Trivers defines as "any investment by the parent in an individual offspring that increases the offspring's chance of surviving [and hence reproductive success] at the cost of the parent's ability to invest in other offspring."[54] "Parental investment" is typically displayed in direct childcare (e.g., feeding, cleaning, comforting, carrying, and socializing with children), but also in more indirect forms of care such as "proximity maintenance" (e.g., supervision) and "economic provisioning" (providing clothing, food, water, and shelter).[55]

Parental investment theory considers factors parallel to those identified by Thomas—though not, of course, to precisely replicate Thomas's theory. It may therefore be able to inform a contemporary interpretation of the ordering of love. The three factors are understood as follows:

1. Thomas's central argument identified a father's love for his child as similar to self-love. He maintained that because the child is "part" of his or her father and not vice versa, the love of a father for his child is more like self-love than is any other love. By "father" Thomas here meant not only *pater*, or socially acknowledged paternity, but also more precisely *genitor*, or biological paternity.[56] He used several images to depict the parent-child relation. Children are generated by their parents' seed[57] and "split off" from them, and hence parental love is the form of friendship closest to self-love.[58] Until they reach maturity—that is, until they become "wholes" in their own right—children are "parts" of their fathers.[59] Because they are "parts" of the same parents, siblings are said to be "the same thing" though in "separate individuals." Moreover, as Thomas observed in his *Commentary on the Nicomachean Ethics*, other relatives are bound together to the degree that they share common ancestors.[60] Children are described as "products" of their parents, and since the product belongs to the producer, children belong to their parents. Parents do not, however, belong to their children, or if they do, Thomas noted, it is to a much lesser extent; the parents' unique status is that of "principle" or "source." For this reason Thomas observed elsewhere, for example, that a father naturally loves his own child more than his own brother.[61]

Sociobiologists employ biological information in a functionally equivalent way to argue that children are "parts" of their parents, at least in the sense that they are formed from copies of approximately fifty percent of each parent's genes. The effect of genetic proximity is reflected in a variety of ways. In his analysis of differential treatment in parent-offspring relations, for example, anthropologist Michael Flinn discovered a higher proportion of interactions between parents and their biological children, a higher proportion of "agonistic" or conflictual interactions between parents and their stepchildren, and a generally more amicable relationship between the former than the latter.[62] In a related finding, sociobiologists Martin Daly and Margo Wilson have contributed to a growing literature that finds child abuse and neglect disproportionately among stepparents.[63]

Though he was convinced of the unitive effect of love, Thomas maintained that unity with oneself can never be exactly replicated in the union between two separate individuals. From a sociobiological point of view, complete solidarity with another person is impossible because, strictly speaking, identical reproductive interests only coincide with genetic identity. All the same, parental care is a function of "nearness." Sociobiologists offer a genetic rationale for the close connection between self-love and parental love. While it is true by definition that all biological fathers are genetically tied to their offspring it is more to the point that each father's particular constellation of genes—his particular genotype—is more closely replicated in his direct offspring than it is in any other human being, *including the genotypes his own parents.* This position is strikingly analogous to Thomas's premodern assumption about parent-child biological bonds. In this sense at least Thomas was correct to claim not only that "a man's love for his children is like his love for himself" but also parental love is more akin to self-love than is filial love. More important, on this basis we can conclude that sociobiology can offer empirical details in a way functionally equivalent to the role Aristotelian biology played in Thomas's *ordo amoris.*

2. Thomas also maintained that the priority of parental love is grounded in knowledge of paternity. Just as knowledge is a cause of love,[64] so identification precedes and reinforces familial forms of love. Parents thus love their children more strongly because parents are more likely to identify their biological children as such than vice versa. Thomas also held that mothers love their children more than fathers do because their maternal certainty is greater than paternal certainty.[65] It might also be mentioned that in the *Summa contra Gentiles* Thomas maintained that

monogamy promotes greater paternal responsibility by allowing fathers to more readily identify their children as such.[66]

Evolutionary theory again provides biological information functionally equivalent to Thomas's observations regarding the importance of knowledge of paternity. Females with internal gestation are of course confident of their offspring, but males can never be certain. According to sociobiology, reliability of parentage, that is, the probability that a given individual is in fact one's biological offspring, is a highly significant factor in "parental investment strategies."[67] Similarly, a strong positive correlation exists between certainty of paternity and paternal infant care in nonhuman primates, which is no surprise given the disadvantage that would accompany behavior that leads a parent to care equally for its own and others' offspring under conditions of limited resources.[68] Male care of infants is displayed in species of primates characterized by pair-bonding or "monogamous" mating systems, where paternal confidence is much higher than in promiscuous species (though "mating effort" in some cases leads to male paternal assistance for unrelated infants[69]).

If extent of care is proportionate to genetic relatedness, we can see the adaptive significance of "kin recognition," an ability to identify biological kin and to distinguish them from nonkin.[70] As Flinn points out, "Regardless of the precise mechanisms, paternity, and nonpaternity, appear to be universally recognized in human societies."[71] Women, unlike men, are absolutely certain that they share genes with their children and men in many cultures have gone to extremes to achieve reasonable confidence of parentage. Sociobiologists hypothesize that certainty of paternity has been promoted through sexual jealousy in males, the inculcation of modesty in females, and the sexual double standard (harsh sanctions against promiscuous females with tolerance of promiscuous males), and through practices such as footbinding, veiling, and the enforced seclusion of women.[72]

"Kin recognition" is achieved by various means in different species, for example, by physical proximity, early associative experience, phenotypic resemblance, and intuitive recognition. Human beings, of course, lack innate recognition mechanisms (such as the "imprinting" studied by Konrad Lorenz[73]) and instead rely on more complex and flexible, if less reliable, methods. Knowledge of paternity is pursued primarily through controlling and monitoring sexual behavior, comparison of physical resemblances (called "phenotype matching"[74]), and attention to other social factors, including residential location. Monogamous marriage clearly functions to enhance paternity confidence. Over the course of our evolutionary history familiarity may have been a cue so strongly and consistently correlated with kinship that it could have led to the extension of kin-like bonds to other members of a small community. Interestingly, these "proximate mechanisms" for paternity identification can support preferences for nonkin, for example, adopted children, in-laws, and foster children who happen to display one of these appropriate features, particularly prolonged shared residential location.

3. The third factor to which Thomas appealed in his analysis of parental love is "longevity," the comparatively longer period of time that parents love their children than vice versa. According to Thomas, fathers begin to love their children from the moment of birth, whereas children love their parents only after a period of some time over the course of which the child undergoes sufficient physiological and cognitive growth, to develop, for example, the capacity to distinguish parents from other caregivers.

Thomas's observations pertain to our culture, or at least to significant sectors of it, but is it true of all cultures? In some cultures male care of newborns is highly valued;[75] in others this is not the case. For example, in some preindustrial cultures men and their sons forge a bond after the latter have reached an age at which they are capable of learning hunting skills. Fathers are here biologically capable of emotional attachment to newborns, but cultural factors work for a significantly delayed bonding.

According to sociobiology, direct care of offspring plays a different role in male and female reproductive strategies, with males typically concentrating more effort on mating and females on parenting.[76] It is a descriptive not a normative statement to claim that females have been assigned the bulk of child-rearing responsibilities in the majority of societies,[77] even in the most egalitarian of hunter-gatherer cultures, for example, the Aka Pygmies of the Central African Republic,[78] the Cagayan Agta of the Philippines,[79] and the Batek of the rain forest of Malaysia.[80] Thomas's observations would thus have had more cross-cultural validity had they been directed at maternal rather than paternal love. However, both parents are, of course, biologically capable of this longevity in a way that the newborn is not. Thus, Thomas's generalization is still valid biologically.

Thomas's observation that parents love their children longer and therefore more strongly than the reverse finds a functionally equivalent treatment in the biological language of "K-selection" parenting strategy employed by evolutionary theorists. Human beings have evolved to invest heavily in individual offspring. Rather than produce a large number of offspring and render little assistance (the "r-selection" strategy of most invertebrates and many fish, reptiles, and amphibians), humans along with many other mammals have evolved to bear a relatively small number of offspring and to provide extensive caregiving (the "K-selection" strategy characteristic of mammals and birds). These terms actually describe a spectrum rather than two pure types of parental investment. The actual form that "K-selection strategy" takes in the concrete, moreover, varies greatly from culture to culture, and among individuals; and there are always exceptions to the general pattern, for example, the small-sized American nuclear family takes a different path from that of extreme polygamists of other times and places.

Simple observation confirms the claim that fathers in many settings do begin to love their children from birth, and that when they do so their love is characterized by greater longevity than is the filial love that ideally emerges through the developmental process. In social settings in which biological fathers are discouraged from developing strong affective attachments to their children, the comparative question driving Thomas's reflections—should we love our parents more than our children?—is rendered moot. The same is also obviously true to the extent that a given culture discourages or diminishes filial love. But in cultures where both loves are found, Thomas's observations can be said to be supported by sociobiological theory: biological conditions do facilitate greater "longevity" of parental love, which in turn contributes to affective asymmetry noted by Thomas.

Conclusion

In this chapter I have argued that the use of biological information by neo-Darwinians to account for aspects of the ordering of attachment and assistance-giving provides functionally equivalent accounts of some important features of Thomas's *ordo amoris*. I have not argued that kin selection and other evolutionary theories should be naively taken to provide a blueprint of the real ordering of natural relations in ordinary life—structured according to the precise mathematical percentage of "coefficients of relation"—which in turn ought to function as a clear guide for ordering human affections and moral responsibilities. Behavioral biology cannot function in this simple and directly normative manner, as one suspects Aristotle's biology does in Thomas's *ordo amoris*, for a number of reasons, one of which is that inclusive fitness is naturally pursued in different ways in different cultures. Matrifocal cultures and patrifocal cultures, to use one example, constitute alternative ways in which kin preference is promoted in different cultures. Both patterns of residence reflect complex patterns of interaction. While one may in a concrete instance be less successful than the other in promoting inclusive fitness, neither can be said to be more or less "natural" than the other according to evolutionary uses of "nature."

Kin selection and reciprocity theories can be said to offer functional equivalences to Thomas's *ordo amoris* in other significant ways, however, including as an empirical and scientifically based source of information into specific kinds of ordering, fundamental human emotional predispositions, and degrees of natural connection. Evolutionary theory also offers contemporary scientific grounds for understanding the biological context within which emerge various kinds of appropriate virtues—specifically, intimacy, honor, and care—within relations characterized by deep personal love and commitment. These virtues, of course, are not exclusive to these particular kind of relationships; moreover, they are complemented by the full range of virtues appropriate to any human life lived well, for example, prudence, courage, honesty, fidelity, and temperance.

Evolutionary theory offers biologically based reasons functionally equivalent to those adduced by Thomas to support the ordering of nature, human sociality, the natural roots of self-love, the natural gradation of love, the importance of reciprocity for social life, and the biological supports for familial bonding. Sociobiologists argue that we have evolved to be intensely social beings. We live in societies, form alliances and partnerships, and provide care for others, particularly close kin. According to Michael Ruse:

> As part of our biology, we have feelings of sympathy and caring for others. We do desire the well-being—the happiness—of others, as well as of ourselves, and judge that this desire is a good thing. That is one of the key conclusions of modern evolutionary biology.[81]

Most important among our evolved tendencies is kin preference, the evolved general tendency to favor kin over nonkin, and close kin over distant kin, in the allocation of caregiving. Ruse points out that "biologically, our major concern has to be towards our own kin, then to those in at least some sort of relationship to us (not necessarily a blood relationship), and only finally to complete strangers."[82] Within kin relations, attachment to one's own children is like self-love. Parental investment and sexual selection theory seem to offer contemporary scientific explanations of the natural roots of behavior that can help correct the abstraction of contemporary Catholic interpretations of love, whether personalist or liberationist in form.

These functional equivalences have indeed been introduced to suggest that they might be used to overcome the deficiencies in contemporary Catholic ethics. The next chapter offers an expanded examination and assessment of evolutionary theories of altruism in order to prepare the ground for its appropriation in the fifth and culminating chapter of this book.

NOTES

1.   For this distinction, see Konrad Z. Lorenz, "Analogy as a Source of Knowledge," *Science* 185 (1974): 229–34.

2.   See Irenaus Eibl-Eibesfeldt, *Ethology: The Biology of Behavior* (New York: Holt, Rinehart, and Winston, 1975), 87–88.

3.   See Wilson, *Sociobiology*, 177–78.

4.   On the significance of time and space frameworks, see Gustafson, "Ethical Issues in the Human Future," 497–98.

5.   Midgley, *Beast and Man*, 94–95.

6.   Ibid., *xiii*.

7.   Ibid., 58.

8.   ST I.II27.3.

9.   ST I.II.94.2.

10.   Major works on attachment include John Bowlby, *Attachment and Loss*, 3 vols. (N.Y.: Basic Books, 1969, 1973, and 1980) and Colin Murray Park c.s. and Joan Stevenson-Hinde, eds., *The Place of Attachment in Human Behavior* (N.Y.: Basic Books, 1982). On sociobiology and attachment, see M. E. Lamb, R. A. Thompson, N. P. Gardner, E. L. Charnov, and D. Estes, "Security in Infantile Attachment as Assessed in the 'Strange Situation': Its Study and Biological Interpretation," *Behavioral and Brain Sciences* 7 (1984): 127–71.

11.   See Eibl-Eibesfeldt, *Love and Hate*, 119–28 and 212–24.

12.   Sigmund Freud, *The Interpretation of Dreams*, trans. James Strachey (New York: Avon, 1965), 283. Freud's view is replicated by contemporaries as well, for example, in Alberta Siegal's statement that, "A horde of untutored savages arrives in our midst annually; these are our infants, who come among us knowing nothing of our language, our culture, our values. . . . The child starts life totally ignorant of . . . decency, gentleness, compassion, sympathy, kindness. . . . Twenty years are all we have to civilize these barbarians." (Cited by Dennis Krebs, "Commentary and Critique: Psychological and Philosophical Approaches to Prosocial Development," in *The Nature of Prosocial Development*, ed. Diane Bridgeman [New York: Academic Press, 1983], 203.)

13.   Abraham Sagi and Martin L. Hoffman, "Empathic Distress in the Newborn," *Developmental Psychology* 12(1976): 175–76.

14.   Jane Allyn Piliavin and Hong-Wen Chang, "Altruism: A Review of Recent Theory and Research," *Annual Review of Sociology* 16 (1990): 27-65.

15.   Mellen, *Evolution of Love*, 276.

16.   According to Alexander, "When we speak favorably to our children about Good Samaritanism, we are telling them about a behavior that has a strong likelihood of being reproductively profitable" (*Darwinism and Human Affairs* [Seattle: University of Washington, 1979], 102).

17.   See Hoffman, "Is Altruism Part of Human Nature?" It should also be noted that sociobiologists often espouse psychological egoism. For further discussion see Stephen J. Pope, "Agape and Human Nature: Contributions from Neo-Darwinism," *Social Science Information* 31 (1992):509-29, Don S. Browning, "Altruism and Christian Love," *Zygon* 27 (1992):421-36, and Paul Rigby and Paul O'Grady, "Agape and Altruism: Debates in Theology and Social Psychology," *Journal of the American Academy of Religion* LVII (1989):719-37.

18.   Ruse, "Morality of the Gene," 180.

19.   Singer, *Expanding Circle*, 47.

20.   Midgley, "Toward a New Understanding of Human Nature," 525–26.

21.   Michael Ruse, "Evolutionary Ethics: A Phoenix Arisen," *Zygon* 21 (March 1986): 106.

22.   ST I.II.28.1.

23.   ST I.60.3. The ultimate object of the will, though, is not the good of the self but rather the *bonum in communi*, as will be seen below.   See I.II.10.1; and I.60.2.

24.   The term "self" should be taken here to refer not to self-consciousness or personality but more broadly to any living, integrated entity.

25.   See George C. Williams, *Adaptation and Natural Selection: A Critique of Some Current Evolutionary Theory* (Princeton, New Jersey: Princeton University Press, 1966).

26.   van den Berghe, *Human Family Systems*, 182–83.

27.   According to Wilson, "When a person (or animal) increases the fitness of another at the expense of his own fitness, he can be said to have performed an act of altruism" (*Sociobiology*, 117). Mark Ridley and Richard Dawkins offer a virtually identical definition: "An altruistic act is one that has the *effect* of increasing the chance of survival (some would prefer to say 'reproductive success') of another organism at the expense of the altruist's" (in "The Natural Selection of Altruism" in *Altruism and Helping Behavior: Social, Personality, and Developmental Perspectives*, ed. J. Philippe Rushton and Richard M. Sorrentino [Hillsdale, New Jersey: Lawrence Erlbaum Associates, 1981],19).

28.   See Barash, *Sociobiology and Behavior*, 69–71, 83–88.

29.   See B.C.R. Bertram, "Kin Selection in Lions and in Evolution," in P. P. G. Bateson and R. A. Hinde, eds., *Growing Points in Ethology* (Cambridge: Cambridge University Press, 1976), 281–301.

30.   See Ridley and Dawkins, "Natural Selection of Altruism," 42–43.

31.   See, for example, J. B. Silk, A. Samuels, and P. Rodman, "The Influences of Kinship, Rank, and Sex on Affiliations and Aggression between Adult Female and Immature Bonnet Macaques (*Macaca radiata*)," *Behaviour* 78(1981): 111–77.

32.   Wilson, *Sociobiology*, 3.

33.   The term "kin selection" was coined by J. Maynard Smith in "Group Selection and Kin Selection," *Nature* 201 (1964): 1145–47.

34.   See W. D. Hamilton, "The Genetical Evolution of Social Behavior: I and II," *Journal of Theoretical Biology* 7 (1964): 1–52; and "Selection of Selfish and Altruistic Behavior in Some Extreme Models," in J. F. Eisenberg and W. S. Dillon, eds., *Man and Beast*, 57–91. Hamilton's first article on the subject was "The Evolution of Altruistic Behavior," *American Naturalist* 97 (1963): 354–56. Sociobiological attempts to account for the evolution of human altruism continue a line of investigation begun in Charles Darwin's *The Descent of Man and Selection in Relation to Sex* (New York: The Modern Library, 1936), especially chapters IV and V.

35.   See Hamilton, "Genetical Evolution of Social Behavior."

36.   See, for example, Mary Jane West Eberhard, "The Evolution of Social Behavior by Kin Selection," *Quarterly Review of Biology* 50 (1975): 1–33.

37.   Wilson, *Sociobiology*, 11.

38.   Trivers, *Social Evolution*, 57.

39.   For the meaning of phenotypical and genotypical altruism see fn. 27 of Introduction.

40.   Despite the author's explicit disclaimers, Dawkins's *Selfish Gene* has given many readers the impression that "selfish gene" is meant in a quasi-literal sense. For further assessment, see below ch. IV.

41.   This literature is vast. In addition to the sociobiological sources listed above, see James H. Hunt, ed., *Selected Readings in Sociobiology* (New York: McGraw-Hill, 1980); Richard D. Alexander and Donald W. Tinkle, eds., *Natural Selection and Social Behavior: Recent Research and New Theory* (New York and Concord: Chiron Press, 1981); Scott A. Boorman and Paul R. Levitt, *The Genetics of Altruism* (New York: Academic Press, 1980); and John Alcock, *Animal Behavior: An Evolutionary Approach.* 4th ed. (Sunderland, Mass.:Sinaver Associates, 1989).

42.   See Thomas Aquinas, *De regno* I.6. See also *Quodl.* vii.17; SCG III.132.

43.   Ibid., 45. See also Trivers, "Evolution of Reciprocal Altruism," 51, and Robert Axelrod, *The Evolution of Cooperation* (New York: Basic Books, 1984). Reciprocity theory was also anticipated by Darwin in *Descent of Man*, ch. V, 499: "Each man would soon learn that if he aided his fellow-men, he would commonly receive aid in return. From this low motive he might acquire the habit of aiding his fellows." It should also be noted that one other theory of "altruism"—"parasitism"—has been advanced by some neo-Darwinians. In parasitic altruism," the "recipient induces altruism that would normally be directed elsewhere or not displayed at all" (Trivers, *Social Evolution*, 49). A bird who is deceived by "egg mimicry" into hatching and rearing another bird's egg (and perhaps ejecting its own) is said to be behaving "altruistically" in genetic terms—its behavior benefits another organism's fitness at cost to its own. This is a clear illustration of the distance that stands between our ordinary (moral) use of altruism and that employed by sociobiology. On "altruistic parasitism," see ibid., 49–52.

44.   Ibid., 36. According to Trivers, "There is no direct evidence regarding the degree of reciprocal altruism practiced during human evolution nor its genetic basis today" (ibid., 48). Gould criticizes Trivers for not showing why reciprocal altruism could not be simply the product of cultural rather than biological evolution ("Biological Potential vs. Biological Determinism," 348). Stephen Jay Gould, "Biological Potential

vs. Biological Determinism," in *The Sociobiology Debate: Readings on the Ethical and Scientific Issues concerning Sociobiology,* ed. Arthur L. Caplan (N.Y.:Harper and Row, 1978), pp. 343-51.

45.   On food sharing, see B. C. R. Bertram, "Living in Groups: Predators and Prey," in J. R. Krebs and N. B. Davies, eds., *Behavioral Ecology* (Oxford: Blackwell, 1972), 92. On baboon coalitions, C. Paker, "Reciprocal Altruism in *Papio anubis,*" *Nature* 265 (1977): 441-43.

46.   Barash, *Sociobiology and Behavior,* 116.

47.   Wilson, *Sociobiology,* 593.

48.   Alexander, *Biology of Moral Systems,* ch. 2.

49.   Trivers, "Evolution of Reciprocal Altruism," 35–36, 48.

50.   Ruse, "Evolutionary Ethics," 105.

51.   ST II.II.26.9: "Utrum homo ex caritate magis debeat diligere filiam quam patrem."

52.   Thomas follows Aristotle in mentioning four, but the first and third are identical, that is, the "part-whole" argument applied to child and parent. Thomas's treatment of the natural basis of familial bonds closely follows Aristotle's *Nicomachean Ethics* VIII1161b12–33.

53.   See *In Ethic.* VIII, lect. 12, 1161b27.

54.   Robert L. Trivers, "Parental Investment and Sexual Selection," in B. Campbell, ed., *Sexual Selection and the Descent of Man: 1871-1971* (Chicago: Aldine, 1972), 139. See also Laura Betzig, Monique Horgerhoff Mulder, and Paul Turke, eds., *Human Reproductive Behavior: A Darwinian Perspective* (New York: Cambridge University Press, 1988).

55.   Classification of parental investment is given in Raymond Hames, "Variations on Paternal Care," in *Father-Child Relations: Cultural and Biosocial Contexts,* ed. Barry S. Hewlett (New York: Aldine de Gruyter, 1992), 89–91.

56.   See *In Ethic.* VIII, lect. 12.

57.   See also *De Gen. An.* 734b14f.

58.   See *In Ethic.* VIII, lect. 12.

59.   Ibid. See also *Ethics* V, 1134b10.

60.   Ibid.

61.   ST I.96.4ad2.

62.   Flinn, "Parental Care in a Caribbean Village," in Hewlett, ed., *Father-Child Relations,* 68–71. It might be objected that the significance of this study is limited to its sample; that is, that it demonstrates that in the village of Grande Anse fathers distribute investment preferentially toward genetic offspring. Sociobiologists would no doubt argue in response that Flinn's findings have been confirmed in a variety of other studies drawing on other diverse samples.

63.   See Martin Daly and Margo Wilson, "Discriminative Parental Solicitude: A Biological Perspective, *Journal of Marriage and the Family* 42 (1980): 277–88; and "Abuse and Neglect of Children in Evolutionary Perspective," in R. D. Alexander and D. W. Tinkle, eds., *Natural Selection and Social Behavior* (New York: Chiron Press, 1981).

64.   See I.II.27.2.

65.   II.II.26.10.

66. SCGIII, 123.
67. Trivers, "Parental Investment and Sexual Selection." See also L. Betzig, M. Borgerhoff Mulder, and P. Turke, eds., *Human Reproductive Behavior.*
68. See K. B. Bales, "Cumulative Scaling of Paternalistic Behavior in Primates," *American Naturalist* 116 (1980): 454–61.
69. Barbara B. Smuts and David J. Gubernick argue that paternal care must be understood in terms of both paternal confidence and mating effort. See their "Male-Infant Relationships in Nonhuman Primates: Parental Investment or Mating Effort?" in *Father-Child Relations,* ed. Hewlett, 1–30.
70. See Richard H. Porter, "Kin Recognition: Functions and Mediating Mechanisms," in Charles Crawford, Martin Smith, and Dennis Krebs, eds., *Sociobiology and Psychology: Ideas, Issues, and Applications* (Hillsdale, New Jersey: Lawrence Erlbaum Associates, 1987), 175–223.
71. Mark V. Flinn, "Parental Care in a Caribbean Village," in *Father-Child Relations,* ed. Hewlett, 57–84. See also J. Kurland, "Paternity, Mother's Brother, and Human Sociality," in *Evolutionary Biology and Human Social Behavior,* ed., Chagnon and Irons, 145–80.
72. See M. Dickemann, "Paternal Confidence and Dowry Competition: A Biocultural Analysis of Purdah," in *Natural Selection and Social Behavior,* ed. Alexander and Tinkle; M. Daly, M. Wilson, and S. J. Weghorst, "Male Sexual Jealousy," *Ethology and Sociobiology* 3(1982): 11–27.
73. See Konrad Lorenz, "Der Kumpen in der Umwelt des Vogels," *Journal fur Ornithologie* (83 [1935]): 137–213.
74. P.W. Sherman and W. G. Homes, "Kin Recognition: Issues and Evidence," in *Experimental Behavioral Ecology and Sociobiology,* ed. B. Holldobler and M. Lindauer (Sutherland, Massachusetts: Sinauer, 1985).
75. Betzig and Turke argue that, "Because the father's role *is* so potentially important, women appear to have been selected to choose mates for their ability to provide parental care. . . . Men, on the other hand, may be able to attract more males *to the extent* that they are willing to care more for children" ("Fatherhood by Rank on Ifaluk," in Hewlett, ed, *Father-Child Relations,* 126).
76. See, *inter alia,* L. Betzig, "Mating and Parenting in Darwinian Perspective," in *Human Reproductive Behavior,* ed. L. Betzig, M. Borgerhoff Mulder and P. Turke, 3–20; Betzig and Turke, "Fatherhood by Rank on Ifaluk," in Hewlett, ed, *Father-Child Relations,* 126.
77. It is interesting to note that the founder of "attachment theory" relies upon neo-Darwinism in this regard. See Bowlby, *Attachment,* 1: 37–57.
78. See Barry S. Hewlett, *Intimate Fathers: The Nature and Content of Aka Pygmy Paternal Infant Care* (Ann Arbor, Michigan: University of Michigan Press, 1991).
79. See P. Bion Griffin and Marcus B. Griffin, "Fathers and Childcare among the Cagayan Agta," in Hewlett, ed., *Father-Son Relations,* 297–320.
80. See Karen Endicott, "Fathering in an Egalitarian Society," in Hewlett, ed., *Father-Son Relations,* 281–95.
81. Ruse, "Morality of the Gene," 180.
82. Ruse, "Evolutionary Ethics," 106.

4

Evolution and Altruism:
An Interpretation and Assessment

This chapter provides a further interpretation and critical assessment of evolutionary theories of altruism, reciprocity, and related behaviors. The perception that sociobiology is populated by members of the "lunatic fringe" in evolutionary theory is in part the result of impressions created by the popular writings of the sociobiologists themselves, whose rhetoric (especially in the early popular literature) has been too often marked by confusion, unsubstantiated conjecture, and unjustified metaphysical interpolation. Sociobiologists have been at times their own worst enemies, but, as Midgley sensibly notes,

> we cannot deal with sociobiology on tribal lines. It is neither a heresy to be hunted down, nor a revealed doctrine necessary to academic salvation. It is instead the usual mixture of the nutritious and the uneatable, insights and mistakes, old and new material.[1]

Rather than a blanket dismissal of sociobiology, then, we would be better off to follow the spirit of Thomas in carefully identifying and drawing sustenance from the "nutritious" aspects of sociobiology, and other insights of behavioral biology where appropriate, while avoiding its "unpalatable" and "inedible" elements. In this chapter I will examine several prominent objections to sociobiological theories of prosocial behavior and discuss some important features of its account of altruism, with an eye to their relevance for the constructive argument of this book.

Reductionism

Even the most casual reader of the literature is aware of the standard criticism that sociobiology suffers from deeply reductionistic tendencies. The biological reductionist does not simply claim that human behavior is sustained by a biological substrate, but argues that what seem to be "higher" capacities can in fact be explained on grounds of "lower" biological or genetic principles. The reductionist insists, for example, that what seems to distinguish human love from animal bonding is itself explicable in terms of genetic facts.

A sample citation from Wilson's *Sociobiology* provides an illustration of this tendency:

> . . . self-knowledge is constrained and shaped by the emotional control centers in the hypothalamus and limbic system of the brain. These centers flood our consciousness with all the emotions—hate, love, guilt, fear, and others—that are consulted by ethical philosophers who wish to intuit the standards of good and evil. What, we are compelled to ask, made the hypothalamus and limbic system? They evolved by natural selection. That simple biological statement must be pursued to explain ethics and ethical philosophers, if not epistemology and epistemologists, at all depths.[2]

Here the reader encounters several philosophical problems, including the "genetic fallacy" (the confusion of causal origins with moral justification) and an unjustified mechanistic materialism. Wilson is known for substituting purely speculative suggestions in the place of rigorous scientific argument. The previous citation displays a false reductionistic ambition to "biologicize" the humanities, a tendency also seen in Wilson's claim that "scientists and humanists should consider together the possibility that the time has come for ethics to be removed temporarily from the hands of philosophers and biologicized."[3]

Reductionism is also apparent in sociobiology's most provocative single text, Richard Dawkins's *The Selfish Gene*. Dawkins is aware of the fact that genes cannot really be "selfish" since they are microscopic molecules rather than "selves." He alerts the reader to the fact that this phrase is intended to be understood in a purely metaphorical way, to indicate that genes are organized to replicate themselves rather than contribute to the replication of other genes at a net cost to their own replication.[4]

This metaphor creatively joins two dissimilar and, taken literally, incompatible concepts in a way that provides a single interpretive key for understanding wide ranges of previously unconnected behavior, from aggression to family planning, and challenges conventional assumptions about biology and animal behavior. Yet the proper use of metaphor always retains a sense of its intrinsic tension, a sense of dissimilarity as well as similarity, between the object and what it is said to resemble.

Even though he says explicitly that it is a metaphor, Dawkins consistently uses the "selfish gene" in a literal manner as the interpretive key to understanding all animal behavior and indeed a good deal of human behavior as well (though not all, to be sure, because he recognizes that culture also shapes human behavior). Genes are said to be "survival machines,"[5] to provide "the ultimate rationale for our existence,"[6] to exist as "colonies,"[7] to "manipulate" the world by controlling protein synthesis,[8] and to be the "masters" of the body,[9] indeed, to be "our creators."[10] Dawkins extends the description of "selfishness" from genes to humans without hesitation, a tendency that seems to reflect his belief that, as Midgley puts it, "individual motivation is only an expression of some profounder, metaphysical motivation, which he attributes to genes."[11] His use of the "selfish gene" thus carries no sense of abiding tension, or what Paul Ricoeur calls the "is and is not" quality of metaphor.[12] The widespread reaction against Dawkins's image in the humanities results in part from a reductionistic overextension of this interesting but limited metaphor.

Jeffrie Murphy, a philosopher deeply sympathetic to sociobiology, points to problems with its use of language:

> Wilson is—it must be acknowledged—sometimes outrageous in the extent to which he is willing to use the same concept (e.g., aggression, altruism, etc.) to describe both the behavior of animals in nature and humans in culture without even seeming to notice that there might be some serious problems involved in doing this (e.g., simple anthropomorphic projection).[13]

Wilson claims, for example, that, "murder and cannibalism are commonplace among the vertebrates."[14] "Murder" as an unjust taking of life involves a voluntary and deliberate choice to do something that is known to be immoral; nonhuman animals are obviously incapable of the internal act of bad will and therefore also of "murder." This kind of slippery use of moral language is worrisome to many people not because it distorts animal behavior but because it suggests that human murder is simply in line with our animal past, that it is to be expected as a natural behavioral tendency, and that we should be resigned to it. Sociobiologists often explicitly reject this fatalistic inference, but critics fear that it, rather than the proposed corrective, tends to be the practical moral upshot of sociobiology. The same is true of other anthropormic terms, such as "aggression," "male sexual promiscuity," and "female domesticity."

Sociobiologists strive to provide a theoretical framework within which behavior that appears to result partly from to nonbiological factors can be construed in biological terms. Morality is a case in point. Consider Wilson's claim:

> The brain is a product of evolution. Human behavior—like the deepest capacities for emotional response which drive and guide it— is the circuitous technique by which human genetic material has been and will keep intact. Morality has no other demonstrable ultimate function.[15]

At times, he even suggests that particular moral beliefs have been caused by natural selection.[16] Morality has no other "ultimate demonstrable function" under the criteria established by inclusive fitness; other criteria that might recognize other functions of morality are methodologically excluded from consideration. The belief that one's behavior might reflect love for what is good for its own sake is not only excluded on methodological grounds; sociobiology suggests that this kind of motive is illusory.

To attempt to account for all friendship and hatred, conciliation and fighting, peace and aggression, by reducing them to genetic interests and biological drives is to ignore characteristic features of human nature itself: the rich diversity of our social life, the communication of knowledge and moral wisdom through tradition, and the ability of human intelligence to creatively adapt to new conditions. The basis of such reductionism, in my judgment, is the sociobiological tendency to reduce all goods to one, inclusive fitness. Trivers collapses the full range of human goods into differential reproduction: "Instead of a disorganized list of items that we may care to invest ourselves in, such as children, leisure time, sexual enjoyment, food, friendship, and so on, . . . all of these activities are expected to be organized eventually toward the production of surviving offspring."[17] Indeed, James Gustafson's judgment regarding Wilson's project is true of other sociobiological works as well—they represent at times a secular equivalent of systematic theology in their ambitious coverage of the scope of human life and meaning rather than pure science.[18]

In sociobiological analyses of human behavior, the participants' view of their own action is ignored on methodological grounds. A self-critical person can be aware of the temptation to instrumentalize others and to the near constant working of mixed motives, yet nonetheless insist that love for another person can be a predominant if not exclusive motive of particular actions. Thus, the reductionist analysis of human behavior by definition cannot properly grasp its true nature. Such a priori constraints do not facilitate understanding the complexity of human motivation. Given this defect, sociobiology cannot be expected to provide a sufficient basis for understanding either human love or altruism.

Determinism

For many people, "genetic" means "fixed" and "fixed" implies "inevitable." Perhaps the most serious criticism of sociobiology for ethicists pertains to its "genetic determinism" or "biological determinism" that undermines the human freedom and responsibility that is the *sine qua non* of morality.[19] Unfortunately, in its early stages at least, sociobiology failed to examine ways in which biological tendencies are reshaped within human behavior, and so it often seemed to imply that human beings are genetic automatons and the unthinking slaves of their deep biological masters. When sociobiologists discuss behavior genetics and topics like morality, innate aggression, social stratification, and fixed gender roles, the human mind seems to be no more than a biological means by which irresistible genetic forces determine external acts. According to Wilson, for example, "Human emotional responses and more general ethical practices based on them have been programmed to a substantial degree by natural selection over thousands of generations."[20] Again, the use of language may not be helpful here, since whatever is "programmed," at least in the strict sense of the term, is outside the control of the agent and therefore *ipso facto* neither a properly human act (Thomas's *actus humani*) nor in the realm of morality.

Sociobiologists stand on an opposite extreme from the almost exclusive emphasis on subjectivity found in personalism and existentialism. The factors affecting human behavior are multiple, and the particularities of individual lives immeasurably more complex than is captured by sociobiology. Altruism is a case in point. Individuals vary in the intensity of their affective responses to others who are in need, their willingness to deny themselves in order to provide assistance, and their motivation to help those outside their immediate circle. A person's willingness to perform altruistic acts is deeply affected by temperament, moral norms internalized during childhood, moral development and character, responses to suffering learned through the example of role models, level of self-esteem and sense of security, and willingness to take risks. These obvious facts seem at times to escape sociobiology.

One critical means of avoiding unnecessary reductionism is to properly distinguish "cause" and "function." According to Professor Roger Masters, a causal process or mechanism "explains the material factors which produce phenotypical structures or behaviors. For example, one can say that, under stated conditions, a chromosomal sequence of nucleotide bases causes the production of a protein in particular cells."[21] "Functions," on the other hand, refer to effects of a behavior or structure that might provide reasons for the evolution of this structure or behavior. "Functional adaptations" must not be confused with "causes." This distinction is sometimes compromised in sociobiological analyses of altruism. It may be the case that certain forms of altruism have provided and continue to provide a selective advantage to members of the species (i.e., they may contribute to survival and reproduction), but one may not infer from the fact of adaptation that the cause of particular assistance-giving acts is genetic or biological.

Scientists of course strive for a comprehensive account of both cause and function in natural phenomena but the complexity of human behavior renders this goal highly elusive in our case. As Masters points out, "a causal analysis of human acts would have to specify neurological, developmental, and social factors involved in the behaviors defined. . . . A functional analysis serves to explain the extent to which such behaviors—as well as the causal mechanisms related to them—might be adaptive."[22] Kin selection analysis of assistance-giving examines ways in which genes whose phenotypical effects incline individuals to favor kin will spread throughout the gene pool more successfully than those that do not. This analysis is clearly functional; it focuses on the selective advantages provided by kin favoritism rather than identifying the precise physiological and biochemical mechanisms that "cause" individuals to do so.

Confusion of cause and function has contributed to the common complaint that sociobiologists are genetic determinists.[23] Those guilty of this flaw include both popular sociobiologists who do not clearly differentiate these levels and their opponents who fail to recognize the distinction when it is made by more careful sociobiologists, for example, Masters. Analysis of causes normally does imply a kind of determinism, but sociobiologists at their best offer *functional* explanations that assess statistical probability rather than provide comprehensive or exhaustive accounts of behavior. As Masters points out, sociobiologists and ethologists, "sometimes seem to claim that observed behavior is inevitable and unchange-able, when all they are saying is that—under given conditions—it is probable."[24]

Human behavior is not directly coded by specific genes, but is the result of an extremely complex interaction of events. Even in early works on human sociobiology we find implicit contradictions of this simple-minded genetic determinism, for example, in Wilson's own exhortations that we ought to use our intelligence and freedom to guide future human evolution as much as possible. Here Wilson recognizes that the person is a causal agent not directly controlled by genes,[25] a realization which dis-tances him from positions which suggest that every human act is, at least unconsciously, directed at maximizing genetic fitness. As philosopher Philip Kitcher, one of the strongest critics of sociobiology, correctly observes:

> There is no evidence to lead us away from the natural idea that, given the traits with which evolution has equipped us, we are able to set ourselves personal goals and to perform actions that detract from our inclusive fitness. It is possible to take the evolution of *Homo sapiens* seriously and yet to deny that natural selection has fashioned dispositions to behavior that lead us always (or almost always) to maximize our inclusive fitness.[26]

Human love has a biological basis—in the sense that biological and genetic causes provide the necessary if not sufficient basis for the exercise of human moral and emotional capacities—but this basis implies neither that human reason, will, and choices are only genetically controlled "neu-ronal machinery" nor that human beings are nothing more than "survival machines—robot vehicles blindly programmed to preserve the selfish molecules known as genes."[27] The error of sociobiological fatalism lies not in its simple recognition of biological causality, but in taking it to refer to a quasi-exclusive causal factor and in minimizing the force of a multitude of other causal factors (personal, cultural, and economic). Bio-logical determinism shares with the contradictory position, cultural deter-minism, the same fault of "tunnel vision, the belief that one kind of explanation necessarily excludes another."[28] Against this fatalism, it is more reasonable to recognize that human motivation is pluralistic and best understood through the examination of multiple and interacting causes.

Human Behavior, Genes, and Culture

Most people are at least vaguely aware of the fact that prosocial traits such as generosity, kindness, helpfulness, and tolerance vary enormously across the spectrum of human societies, and that culture influences the way in which our intrinsic human tendencies are shaped, channeled, and given a certain precision and clarity. Culture profoundly shapes the norms of altruism and family loyalty held in a given society. It goes without saying that within particular societies the sense of family loyalty held by different individuals may vary greatly, depending on environmental variables, and the experiences to which they are exposed in childhood. Cultural and social context deeply influence what we think about ourselves, our relations with and connections to others, our moral responsibilities, and the kinds and degrees of care we ought to provide to those in need. An obvious example is the tremendous difference in the significance of extended "blood ties" for social organization in preindustrial agricultural societies and in postindustrial societies like our own.[29]

The view that the human emotional constitution has biological foundations and origins need not be taken to imply that human affections and behavior are genetically fixed. Innate biological orientations to favor kin can be distorted, manipulated, exaggerated, or even, in some extreme cases, nearly extinguished;[30] and no doubt our natural orientations need to be cultivated and supplemented by habituation within an appropriate upbringing, as Aristotle noted. People are shaped by both biology and culture to care for some persons more than others.

The human biogram by itself is only an abstraction, and it does not exist outside concrete cultural and social contexts. Research from a variety of fields points to the amazing plasticity and variety of the human emotional constitution, which in fact needs culture of some kind or another to be actualized. Thus, in Alasdair MacIntyre's observation: "Man without culture is a myth. Our biological nature certainly places constraints on all cultural possibility; but man who has nothing but a biological nature is a creature of whom we know nothing."[31] Erik Erikson expresses this point from the perspective of developmental psychology:

> As an animal, man is nothing. It is meaningless to speak of a human child as if it were an animal in the process of domestication; or of his instincts as set patterns encroached upon or molded by the autocratic environment. Man's 'inborn instincts' are drive fragments to be assembled, given meaning, and organized during a prolonged

childhood by methods of child training and schooling which vary from culture to culture and are determined by tradition. In this lies his chance as an organism, as a member of a society, as an individual. In this also lies his limitation. For while the animal survives where his segment of nature remains predictable enough to fit his inborn patterns of instinctive response or where these responses contain the elements for necessary mutation, man survives only where traditional child training provides him with a conscience which will guide him without crushing him and which is firm and flexible enough to fit the vicissitudes of his historical era. . . . The human child learns to exist in space and time as he learns to be an organism in the space-time of his culture. Every part function thus learned is based on some integration of all the organ modes with one another and with the world image of their culture.[32]

Sociobiological "gene-culture" theory attempts to incorporate a deeper recognition of the fact that history and culture do not replace but shape and inform concrete actualizations of human nature.[33] After his early work, Wilson and his colleague Charles Lumsden began to see the distorting effects that an assumption of monocausal genetic determinism had on attempts to understand human behavior. They recognized that culture is not just an epiphenomenal layer merely reflecting genetic imperatives: "Culture is not just a passive entity. It is a force so powerful in its own right that it drags the genes along. Working as a rapid mutator, it throws new variations into the teeth of natural selection and changes the epigenetic rules across generations."[34]

"Gene-culture" theory recognizes that culture is not just an extension of human biology, but interacts with biology as an independent variable. Sociobiologists have thus attempted to correct their own reductive and deterministic elimination of human freedom from their accounts of human nature, and to recognize that the person is faced with a very wide range of options available within cultural parameters and biological restraints.

Gene-culture theory recognizes that even fundamental genetically based inclinations can be overridden by other factors. Lumsden and Wilson, for example, argue that human beings have a strong genetically based inclination toward outbreeding and away from inbreeding (at least within the nuclear family or household); however, they also recognize that human beings have a choice as to whether they will respect the incest taboo (the near universal cultural enforcer of our genetic inclination to avoid inbreeding) or violate it.[35] Religiously inspired virginity or celibacy overrides an evolved trait which has obviously been essential to the reproduction of human life. Basic human compassion can obviously be overridden, as happened in the famous Kitty Genevose case in which thirty-eight bystanders refused to respond in any way—not even to request police intervention—to the screams of a woman who was repeatedly assaulted for thirty minutes on a street in New York City (social psychologists tend to maintain that the "bystander effect" neutralized human sympathy in this case).[36] On the other hand, our natural "in-group bias" can be overridden and corrected by other components of human nature, such as compassion, particularly if reinforced by culture and exhorted by moral authorities.

Rather than viewing human acts as blindly directed by biological instinct and drives, Wilson and Lumsden recognize that mind and culture make a qualitative difference to the way our species functions. They would agree at least in a general way with Stephen Jay Gould, one of the most vociferous opponents of human sociobiology, when he argues that "flexibility may well be the most important determinant of human consciousness; the direct programming of behavior has probably become inadaptive."[37] Sociobiologists have not adequately developed a philosophical account of human freedom and related it to biological causes and natural selection but they illustrate an increasing sociobiological appreciation of freedom when they claim:

> Moral reasoning is based on the epigenetic rules that channel the development of the mind. Such reasoning appears to be ultimately dependent on the genes as well as on culture and self-conscious decision, but the rules only bias development; they do not determine ethical precepts or the necessary decisions in a fixed manner. They still require that a choice be made, and in this sense they preserve free will.[38]

"Biased development" can be discussed in terms of "prepared learning." The theory of "prepared learning," Mary Maxwell argues:

> is deterministic to the extent that it says the child would have difficulty learning any ethical rule of culture that "goes against the grain." For instance, most cultures have a rule "Love thy Mother and thy Father." If, say, in some social engineering experiment a culture adopted the rule "Hate thy Mother and thy Father," children

would tend not to obey that rule. . . . The idea here is that culture will *invent* only certain rules and not others, because of innate human traits.[39]

Cultures allow a certain range of types of attachment systems, from our own nuclear family to the avuncular system of the south Pacific. Yet all cultures resist the Platonic dream of abolishing particular ties and natural preferences.[40] Our nature "prepares" us to favor some persons over others and it does so because this pattern has played an important role in our survival and flourishing.

Biologist Ernst Mayr's distinction between "closed" and "open behavior programs" helps to clarify the role of genes in human behavior. "Closed behavior programs" are seen in the rigidly stereotyped stimulus-response behavior of lower animals; it reflects strict control of behavior by genetically coded instructions. Higher animals with more complex brains, in contrast, are able to store learned information in their memories and so are said to possess "open behavior programs." "Open behavior programs" bestow on us a degree of flexibility not found in other species.[41] *Homo sapiens* has the most open behavioral program of any species, but our freedom here is still more restricted than some existentialists admit—human behavior still reflects its genetic heritage. Neither are we free, as Gutiérrez puts it, to create a "new humanity."[42]

Egoism

The issues of reductionism and determinism are related to egoism, which is understood here as the claim that all or most actions are predominantly motivated by self-concern. Most sociobiologists espouse some form of egoism, a position that I believe fails to appreciate sufficiently the full complexity of human nature. Before broaching the issue of egoism and altruism, however, I should note that for all their discussion of altruism, parental care, cooperation, and the like, sociobiologists by and large tend to disclaim any interest in human psychology and motivation. Thus Dawkins comments in the *Selfish Gene:*

I am not concerned here with the psychology of motives. I am not going to argue about whether people who behave altruistically are "really" doing it for secret or subconscious selfish motives. Maybe they are and maybe they aren't, and maybe we can never know, but in any case that is not what this book is about. My definition is concerned only with whether the effect of an act is to lower or raise the survival prospects of the presumed altruist and the survival prospects of the presumed beneficiary.[43]

No matter how many disclaimers are offered, the language of "selfishness" expresses a certain feature of human motivation, of the state of mind shared by all agents acting in certain ways. Indeed, despite occasional statements to the contrary, sociobiologists frequently tend to attribute selfish motives to human agents. Maxwell asserts that while people can be "trained to take a genuine interest in leading moral lives . . . much of human morality is motivated by a desire on the part of the individual to get something in return for his goodness."[44] Dawkins himself admonishes, "Much as we might wish to believe otherwise, universal love and the welfare of the species as a whole are concepts which simply do not make evolutionary sense. . . . Let us try to teach generosity and altruism, because we are born selfish."[45]

Dawkins may announce that his attribution of "selfishness" to genes is merely metaphorical, but this is belied by a persistent psychological egoism, the basis for which is an assumed but undemonstrated direct reflection of the "selfishness" of the genes in the human being's own psychological-emotional constitution. Sociobiologists do not argue that people always consciously engage in cost-benefit calculations to determine which of several courses of action will "pay off" the best.[46] Yet they seem required, in order to avoid the obviously erroneous assumption that agents determine their courses of action by a deliberate, case-by-case assessment of self-interest, to assume that this opportunistic practice is promoted by some kind of an unconscious process geared to the same end of maximizing self-interest. Without positing some kind of unconscious process, they would have no way to connect genes and action.

I would like to argue that human sociobiologists do provide grounds for a view of human nature that is not egoistic—one that accounts for genuinely altruistic as well as egoistic motivations.[47] The predominant assumption in sociobiology is egoistic, maintaining that human behavior is always or almost always motivated ultimately (often unconsciously) by self-concern and that apparent altruism is illusory.[48] Michael Ghiselin provides one of the most provocative citations in this regard:

Given a full chance to act in his own interest, nothing but expediency will restrain him from brutalizing, from maiming, from murdering—his brother, his mate, his parent, or his child. Scratch an "altruist," and watch a "hypocrite" bleed. No hint of genuine charity ameliorates our vision of society, once sentimentalism has been laid aside. What passes for cooperation turns out to be a mixture of opportunism and exploitation.[49]

In Alexander's view, altruistic behavior is desirable because it allows one to appear to be a trustworthy and attractive and thereby to advance one's own inclusive fitness, but in reality, he argues, individuals always seek a net gain in their interactions with others (at least over the long haul).

Wilson is somewhat more generous than other sociobiologists. In his homespun terminology, "hard-core" altruism does involve genuine moral altruism in that it is not motivated by desire for personal reward or punishment; yet he also maintains that "soft-core" altruism is fundamentally selfish: "The 'altruist' expects reciprocation from society for himself and his closest relatives. His good behavior is calculating, often in a wholly unconscious way."[50] Given these egoistic presuppositions, one can understand why Wilson asserts (without explanation) that Mother Theresa's heroically self-sacrificial devotion to the poor of Calcutta is somehow "cheerfully subordinate" to her "biological imperatives"(!).[51]

Some of the authors who endorse this position seem to project the egoism of classical liberalism onto nature. Alexander asserts that "ethics, morality, human conduct, and the human psyche are to be understood *only* if societies are seen as collections of individuals seeking their own self-interests."[52] Even acts of apparently "indiscriminate beneficence" are engaged in because, one way or another, they contribute to the interests of benefactors by contributing to their reputation, building up social unity, and tacitly encouraging others to act in a self-sacrificing manner.[53] The subjective experience of genuinely altruistic motives is one of evolution's masterpieces: self-deception regarding our own deepest (i.e., egoistic) motives best advances our own inclusive fitness. It is conceded that we might occasionally run across a genuinely altruistic person but with the qualification that they are exceedingly rare.[54]

This egoism, it seems to me, is confused. When discussing human action we need to distinguish (1) stated reasons for actions, (2) conscious intentions, desires, and motives, (3) unconscious desires and motivations, and (4) biologically based instinctual proclivities, inclinations, and drives. Descriptions of human behavior as "altruistic" in ordinary discourse normally refer to level 2, that is to actions reflecting an agent's conscious desire to help another. Sociobiological analyses of "altruism" refer primarily to consequences of acts that benefit the recipient at some expense to the agent's inclusive fitness. However, the strong commitment to the primacy of evolutionary forces is seldom accompanied by attention to features of human behavior that cannot be explained as unconsciously directed toward the agent's inclusive fitness. Sociobiologists often imply that people seldom, if ever, transcend the evolutionary pressures that earlier shaped their hominid ancestors' characteristic behavior. Evolution has shaped human nature at levels 3 and 4, the level of unconscious desires, and the level of our instinctual drives, so that, as a species, we are not habitually drawn to actions that are self-destructive or systematically reduce our inclusive fitness.

Many sociobiological accounts of altruism fail to provide an adequate account of the links between these four levels of human being and do not sufficiently distinguish unconscious desires from conscious intentions. The effort to debunk altruism relies on the belief that other-regarding reasons for action (level 1) and conscious motives (level 2) reflect the deeper working of unconscious egoistic desires (level 3). However, even if unconscious motivations are primarily self-regarding (level 3)—a claim that one may reasonably debate—this fact by no means entails that the conscious experience of other-regard is illusory or self-deceptive. Those who make the latter claim seem to be conflating levels that should be distinguished. In doing so sociobiologists tend to make what I think is a highly dubious assumption, namely, that it is nearly impossible for humans to act consistently from genuinely moral motives and with deliberate benevolence toward strangers. But according to sociobiologist Ian Vine, "We surely know nothing like enough about the specificity of the human genome to assert from sociobiological theory alone that we lack the power willingly and knowingly to transcend fitness-maximizing dispositions in motivationally authentic ways."[55]

Distinguishing these levels allows one to claim that an act may be both morally altruistic and "genetically egoistic," that is, motivated by genuine concern for another person (level 2) yet yielding consequences (the object of level 4) that contribute to the agent's inclusive fitness (e.g., the altruism of a parent who spends the night caring for a sick child). Acts of kin favoritism or reciprocity can be either egoistic or altruistic, depending on the quality of the agent's conscious motivation (the mixed motives of real life complicate the matter but do not invalidate the point).

A second way of reading evolutionary approaches to human nature maintains that, alongside self-regard, genuinely altruistic motivations do exist. Some sociobiologists maintain that this flexible structure of motivation evolved to include the capacity for both altruism and egoism because it provides the optimal avenue for securing reproductive advantage.[56] Ruse writes, for example, that "in the case of humans, biology achieves its ends by making us altruistic in the literal sense."[57]

> As part of our biology, we have feelings of sympathy and caring for others. We do desire the well-being—the happiness—of others, as well as of ourselves, and judge that this desire is a good thing. That is one of the key conclusions of modern evolutionary biology.[58]

Maxwell argues similarly that kin selection theory does not claim that

> each parent calculates his or her advantage. . . . And it doesn't mean that love and genuine care in fact are not involved. It means that emotions such as love and genuine care in fact evolved because of underlying causes: principally, the biological need to maximize the probability that *Homo sapiens* will survive.[59]

Even Alexander, who often speaks as an unabashed egoist, is close to these authors when he argues that "generosity and altruism are older than Dawkins implies, and far more complex. I hypothesize that they are as integral a part of human nature as being 'born selfish'."[60] In this view, complexity, mixed motives, and deep seated ambivalence—rather than pure egoism—characterize human nature: some tendencies incline us to service, empathy, and communion, others to aggression, indifference, and isolation.

I maintain that the second approach to altruism is the most plausible on three grounds. First, sociobiological egoism is at odds with the mounting evidence from social scientific sources that supports a capacity of genuine altruism.[61] Attempts to provide credible explanations of every kind of well-known altruism have not been successful. On the contrary, studies such as Richard Titmuss's famous analysis of the altruism of blood donors indicates the performance of authentic moral altruism directed toward nonkin and nonreciprocators.[62] Alexander's assertion that each and every one of Titmuss's blood donors were motivated (consciously or unconsciously) by the desire for social reputation is not convincing.[63]

Second, some version of "genetic selfishness" examined by sociobiologists may be compatible with moral altruism as long as the distinction between "self" and "genes" is carefully maintained. A loving parent caring for a child is acting from altruistic motives and contributing to his or her inclusive fitness. When this distinction collapses, as it often seems to do in popular sociobiology, the self is identified with its genes or with copies of its genes, and every act that affects the self, relatives, or friends in even a remotely positive manner is described as "selfish." As philosopher John Chandler points out, however, when we scrupulously retain the distinction between self and genes, "it becomes clear that the attribution of 'selfishness' to genes in the sociobiological sense of the term is perfectly compatible with genuine altruism on the part of the individual."[64] This is simply to say that conscious motives and desires (level 2) cannot be simplistically identified with unconscious desires (level 3), let alone biological inclinations (level 4).

Third, sociobiological egoism does not account for the genuine altruism that is experienced by most normal emotionally developed people at least some of the time. In many theological and philosophical circles, sociobiology has been dismissed because, among other reasons, it is perceived as attempting to force human motives into a Procrustean bed of egoism that betrays the testimony of ordinary moral experience. A great deal of human experience seems to make sense only if human nature has evolved in such a way as to include not only egoistic inclinations but also capacities for genuine altruism and related affective capacities like empathy, sympathy, and compassion. We are not simply indifferent to the suffering of others who are nonkin and nonreciprocators. Not unlike the work of the great "masters of suspicion," Nietzsche, Marx, and Freud, the "unmasking" potential of sociobiology which discovers the self-serving nature of some of our ostensibly other-regarding actions, provides lines for interpreting some human behavior but not all.

Kin Preference

The two major theories of assistance-giving, kin preference and reciprocity, do not logically depend on rigidly egoistic presuppositions. The term "kin" in sociobiology refers only to genetic relationships, whereas the notion of kin in human societies often includes those who are not genetically related. An adopted child, for example, or another member of a communal household, may well be considered "kin" and granted every privilege of being a family member, equal in status to genetically connected family members. Indeed, in antiquity the term *familia* included not only two parents and their biological children but all members of their household and possibly others. More broadly, some social arrangements not characterized by legal or biological ties have over time come to be construed in familial terms, for example, as a "strategy for survival."[65]

The status of "coefficients of relationship," that is, the significance of degrees of genetic relatedness to human behavior, must therefore be properly understood. Sociobiologists argue not only that we are biologically disposed to assist our own offspring more than strangers—a noncontroversial claim if every there was one—but also that we have a genetic interest in favoring close kin over distant kin, for example, to assist first cousins, with whom we share copies of approximately one-eighth of our genes, more than second cousins, with whom we share a sixteenth of our genes. Inclusive fitness theory maintains that these cousins also possess a certain pull on our attention ultimately because of our genetic relation to them. Sociobiology here is apparently subject to a refutation by *reductio ad absurdum:* that we should, say, care more for a third cousin three times removed than for a nonrelated individual, since we at least share some of the same genes with the former compared to none with the latter. Kin favoritism is after all only one of the variables in human assistance-giving. It seems more reasonable to distinguish between abstract genetic interests and actual emotional predispositions, since life experience and interpersonal history so profoundly qualifies degrees of caregiving.

This qualification having been noted, it still seems to be the case that kin preference may be one of the most intuitively plausible claims of sociobiology. Natural parents are normally expected to feel the most powerful obligations to meet the needs of their own children; when others are called on to act for a considerable time as substitute parents, biological parents are regarded as significantly deficient. Familial obligations tend to be more "diffuse" than other kinds of obligations, in the sense that people are rarely able to discharge completely their obligations to family members. And as psychologist Lillian Rubin maintains, regardless of degrees of liking, kin can normally be relied on to provide services and material assistance, a "bottom line" not found so consistently with friends.[66]

It is crucial to recognize that kin favoritism refers to behavioral predispositions rather than to a rigid mechanism controlling human assistance-giving behavior. It does not imply that each discrete act of human helping directly results from the deliberate calculation of inclusive fitness. The attempt to understand altruism in terms of biology should not be taken to imply that there is a biological "drive" for altruism analogous to sexual desire or hunger. We are not driven to assist others by a primal instinct, a specific form of stored energy released for a single purpose.[67] We clearly do not apportion care on the basis of a simplistic and rigid arithmetical calculation of "coefficient of relationship," and no sociobiologist argues that we do. We are emotionally *predisposed* to form affective bonds with and to devote the greatest care to close family; as Maxwell puts it, "emotions such as love and genuine care in fact evolved because of underlying causes: principally, the biological need to maximize the probability that *Homo sapiens* will survive."[68] Wilson grants that

> the form and intensity of altruistic acts are to a large extent cultur-
> ally determined. Human social evolution is obviously more cultural
> than genetic. The point is that the *underlying emotion*, powerfully
> manifested in virtually all human societies, is what is considered to
> evolve through the genes.[69]

Psychologist Martin Hoffman maintains that the prime mediator of human altruistic behavior is "empathy," which he defines as "a vicarious affective response to others; that is, an affective response appropriate to someone else's situation rather than one's own."[70] Hoffman's extensive research on empathic distress has lead him to the conclusion that children move through four distinct stages: "global empathy," "egocentric empa-thy," "empathy for another's feelings," and finally "empathy for another's general plight."[71] Hoffman, explicitly drawing on sociobiology, argues that empathy evolved as a proximate means for the promotion of altruism.

Parents obviously have a powerful emotional proclivity to love their children, not their children's genes. When a parent jumps into a river to save a drowning child, he or she intends to save the child, not the assem-blage of the child's genes. The distinction between ultimate and proxi-mate levels of causation is critical here. What immediately "causes" the parent to save a drowning child is a complex interaction of physiological and psychological responses that are the parents' immediate response to seeing his or her child in immanent and mortal danger. A very complex emotional constitution, rooted in physiology and also no doubt influ-enced by individual identity (and, to some extent, human freedom), induces the parent to rush to the aid of the child without a second thought. The parent's choice to save the child is in this instance undeni-ably influenced, if not strongly "determined," by very powerful emotions (e.g., protectiveness and fear) and desires (e.g., to protect and rescue) rooted in but not reducible to human physiology—a complex array of "proximate causes" of the rescue behavior.

Behavioral biologists argue that the "ultimate" cause lying behind and informing the human emotional constitution is natural selection:

early hominids that manifested emotions of protectiveness and fear and rescue behavior were, over the long run, more likely to leave more collateral relatives than were those who did not. The parent's desire to save his or her child from drowning is not directly caused by genes nor is it motivated by some kind of an unconscious desire to protect his or her "genetic investment," parental love being a helpful illusion to this end. Rather, the parent's genuine love for the child motivates the rescue behavior. The emotional predispositions underlying this motivational structure, however, are said to reflect the shaping influence of millions of years of evolution. That, in fact, is why so many other social species display similar kinds of behavior when faced with endangered offspring.

These dispositions may lead to acts that enhance one's inclusive reproductive fitness even though detracting from individual fitness—acts that are both genuinely altruistic and also contribute to one's own reproductive fitness. A parent performing an act at some cost to herself for the benefit of her daughters may be simultaneously both detracting from her personal well-being (or individual fitness) and promoting her own reproductive fitness. By being disposed to benefit her daughters, the theory runs, the mother also tends to benefit those who carry copies of approximately fifty percent of her own genes.

Reciprocity

Evolutionary accounts of reciprocity theory speculate that the inclination to engage in cooperative behavior with nonkin is a natural orientation of the human psyche. It is commonly argued that prior to the neolithic revolution, early hominids lived in small groups of hunter-gatherers. Over the course of millions of years, those individuals who cooperated with others tended to produce more than the average number of offspring and hence gained an advantage in "differential reproduction." Living in groups provided advantages of group defense and resource acquisition, and as group living expanded, language and culture emerged as a symbolic means of social coordination. Human nature in this view is oriented to both competitive and cooperative, aggressive and altruistic modes of behavior, depending on which happens to promote inclusive reproductive fitness at any given time. Morality in this perspective is often regarded as a complex symbolic system that ensures cooperation within the group and protection from threats issued by outsiders and their groups.

"Reciprocity" can be distinguished from "cooperation" in that the former involves the acceptance of some immediate cost with the expectation of attaining greater long-term benefit. Trivers maintains that the ubiquity of reciprocity in human behavior results from the widespread but often unacknowledged expectation that by acting on one another's behalf agents can attain greater benefit as individuals than would be otherwise obtainable. Indeed, according to Trivers, each individual aims to attain a greater benefit than his or her reciprocator.

Though "cost-efficiency" plays some role in assistance giving, it need not have the dominance ascribed to it by sociobiologists. "Do unto others" will never be confused with, "what have you done for me lately?" In the Christian ethic, Wilson's "hard-core" as well as "soft-core" altruism must be extended to nonreciprocators.[72] It must include both people who will never be in a position to reciprocate (e.g., strangers in need), as well as those who are, in a more general sense, socially and economically "unproductive" (e.g., the elderly and the mentally and physically handicapped). In this sense, as noted previously, we work against "nature" as sociobiologists depict it.[73]

Reciprocity theories are mistaken in striving to explain each and every act of nonkin assistance giving in terms of either direct or at least potential return of benefit to the agent. Reciprocity need not be taken as the conscious aim of every act, nor does assistance giving have to be requited to be performed. As Alexander confesses, "I am not assuming that all (or even most) apparently selfish acts are in fact reciprocated, but that such acts would not be performed unless, during evolutionary history, the rewards were *on average* greater than the costs."[74] Reciprocity, like kin preference, is best understood as one emotional predisposition among others that evolved through natural selection over the millions of years of our evolutionary past. It is not a theory of how each discrete act of reciprocity is somehow consciously or unconsciously calculated to play to the agent's inclusive fitness advantage.

The major shortcoming of reciprocity theory is its inability to recognize the self-transcendence of love, which is expressed in its excessively narrow understanding of human interaction and behavior. Simple care for another regardless of benefit to self may be "accidental" to evolutionary purposes or a "mistake" according to the evolutionary logic of fitness maximization (i.e., the transmission of genes to the succeeding generation), but it is not accidental or mistaken according to human love.

The internal methodological constraints of behavioral biology in general and sociobiology in particular make it incapable of comprehending the full range of the human emotional repertoire, including the teleo-logical thrust of love in which self-love is transcended in love for the friend. Sociobiology frequently ignores the closer union of affections that characterizes the mutuality of friendship in contrast to the mere reciproc-ity of two self-interested individuals. Reciprocity theory fails to grasp properly both the nature of trust, which is evoked by an awareness that another person cares for the self and the nature of personal commitment engaged in for the sake of another, precisely because the self cares for a friend for his or her own sake. Another way of saying this is that the com-mon sociobiological tendency to pit self against others can obscure the interpersonal union that is an essential effect of true love in its fullness, Thomas's *amor amicitiae*.

Ethicists hold that action performed primarily for the benefit to the self thought to be forthcoming disqualifies reciprocity as a genuine form of moral altruism. Trivers's rather mercenary model of "reciprocal altru-ism" (the term itself as he uses it is oxymoronic) obviously cannot be iden-tified with the personalist analogue of reciprocity.[75] As we have seen, the impracticability implied in Trivers's quid pro quo account of reciprocity is one reason why some sociobiologists prefer to speak of a less immediate but more plausible "indirect reciprocity."[76] Ethicists might object on grounds of its opportunism and narrow individualism. Yet the kind of helpful behavior that flows from a sense of gratitude for past benefits—rather than expectation of future returns, with interest—is absent from all sociobiological models of reciprocity because it does not fit into a rigidly egoistic model of human behavior, one based on the assumption that behavior has been selected to favor inclusive fitness.

Buber's "I-Thou" relations transcend the simple exchange model common to reciprocity theories, and involve a deep interconnection and relationality that transcends the atomistic division between self-interest and other-interest that is presupposed in reciprocity theory. Reciprocity is one form of prosocial behavior, it accounts for some but by no means all assistance giving not directed to kin; it comprises a significant but only partial subset of human social behavior. The egoistic presuppositions held by many sociobiologists makes them uneasy with the simple and straight-forward claim that we have evolved emotional predispositions to help oth-ers, including both nonkin and nonreciprocators. In many ways, the ethic promoted by sociobiology is equivalent to Polemarchus' ethic of reciproc-ity: "justice is helping friends and harming enemies,"[77] or Freud's version of the golden rule, "love thy neighbor as thy neighbor loves thee."[78] This ethic is, of course, a far cry from the profound mutuality of Christian communion (*koinonia*). Needless to say, from a Christian standpoint the ordering of love must never be collapsed into the shallow reciprocity ethic that was the target of Jesus' criticisms (e.g., Matt 5:38, 44, 46; Luke 6:35–36).

Conclusion

The primary flaw found in sociobiology is its tendency to see the human organism and not the human person. In their book, *The Creative Process in Science and Medicine*, H. Krebs and J. Shelly report that Einstein was asked whether he believed that everything could ultimately be expressed in scientific terms. "Einstein replied: 'Yes, that is conceivable, but it would make no sense. It would be as if one were to reproduce Beethoven's Ninth symphony in the form of an air pressure curve.'"[79] Because the sociobiologists view human caregiving strictly in terms of genes, they miss the core of human love even more than would Einstein's reproduction of the Ninth symphony in an air pressure curve. The capacity genuinely to love another person, or to care for a stranger, reflects human transcendence of elemental concern for survival and reproduction.

The human emotional constitution does function as a "proximate cause" of human action that reflects in some way our evolutionary past. But this does not necessarily imply that it is *nothing but* a mechanism for inclusive fitness. Indeed, it seems more accurate to say that the human emotional constitution, as well as human intelligence, now induces forms of human behavior that are, at least often enough, totally unrelated to any genetic interests. We are intellectually capable not only of planning for our material security but also of creating, in nearly complete transcendence of "biological imperatives" (whatever this phrase may mean), music, art, poetry, and metaphysics. Similarly, we are capable of caring not only for family and friends but also for strangers and even enemies. Human nature includes "inclusive fitness" concerns but extends far beyond their conceivable range.

The egoism that is assumed by many sociobiologists conflicts sharply with the kind of interpersonal mutuality that is examined by Rahner, Farley, and others; mutuality in the view of these Catholic authors is based on noninstrumental love of the other for his or her own sake, on what Johann refers to as "direct love." Nevertheless, several important features of evolutionary accounts of altruism can be coordinated with a nonreductionistic approach to human nature. First, simplistic, one-dimensional accounts of altruism are unacceptable; indeed, they distort more than they illumine. Appropriations of behavioral biology must proceed in a nonreductionist way, in full recognition of the fact that natural selection is but one of several factors producing stability and change. Altruism and other forms of social behavior are influenced by a wide variety of factors, including among others the temperament and emotional state of the agent, the concrete environment, the presence of third party witnesses, the particular pattern of the relationship between the agent and the recipient (e.g., history of reciprocity), and social roles.

Second, an understanding of altruism must be complex and hierarchical; it must incorporate an awareness of the different ways in which genetic, somatic, social, and cultural factors influence human behavior. Above all, it must account for the importance of personality and intentions on human actions. Assessing the significance of biology on altruism by no means entails locating a single variable, an isolated "gene for altruism" or an "altruistic drive," then attributing its affects to all human behavior.

Third, sociobiology need not support a relentless and opportunistic egoism but a more complex view of human nature that helps account for its genuine albeit limited capacity for altruism. Against those who detect in sociobiology a revival of the social Darwinism that was deployed to justify predatory capitalism in the nineteenth century, Midgley correctly argues that sociobiology "shows plainly that there is no reason at all why creatures need be unmitigatingly selfish and deliberately competitive in order to succeed in evolution."[80] We are naturally oriented to care for others and to care for ourselves. This notion is in keeping with the claim that spontaneous empathy, rather than a one-sided calculation of reproductive profitability,[81] is one of the emotional predispositions produced by our evolutionary heritage.[82]

Fourth, kin preference and reciprocity can be understood as evolved emotional predispositions that shape human prosocial motivations. Evolution has inclined human beings naturally to love some people with a particularly intense affective attachment and to care for some more than others. Nature, in other words, has built into the human emotional repertoire a basic affective partiality.

Having reviewed various objections to sociobiological accounts of altruism, noted certain of their deficiencies, and briefly interpreted their most plausible elements, I turn now to the constructive argument of the book, the particular significance of sociobiology for a contemporary Catholic ethics of love.

NOTES

1.   Midgley, "Rival Fatalisms," 17.

2.   Ibid., 3.

3.   Wilson, *Sociobiology*, 562. Another problem associated with reductionism is "adaptionism," the assumption that every trait or behavior provides a functional adaptation to the agent

4.   E.g., Dawkins, *Selfish Gene*, 48, 95, 210. Critiques include Mary Midgley, "Gene Juggling," *Philosophy* 54 (1979): 439–58; Stephen Jay Gould, "Caring Groups and Selfish Genes," in *The Panda's Thumb: More Reflections on Natural History* (New York and London: W. W. Norton, 1982), ch. 8.

5.   Dawkins, *Selfish Gene*, 21.

6.   Ibid.

7.   Ibid., 49

8.   Ibid., 58.

9.   Ibid., 63

10.   Ibid., 215.

11.   Midgley, "Gene Juggling," 455.

12.   Paul Ricoeur, *Interpretation Theory: Discourse and the Surplus of Meaning* (Fort Worth, Texas: Texas Christian University Press, 1976), 68.

13.   Murphy, *Evolution, Morality, and the Meaning of Life*, 93.

14.   Wilson, *Sociobiology*, 246.

15.   Wilson, *On Human Nature*, 167.

16.   Wilson, *Sociobiology*, 129: "A science of sociobiology, if coupled with neurophysiology, might transform the insights of ancient religions into a precise account of the evolutionary origin of ethics and hence explain the reasons why we make certain moral choices instead of others at particular times." A critical treatment of this claim is found in Ruth Mattern, "Altruism, Ethics, and Sociobiology," in *The Sociobiology Debate*, ed. Arthur Caplan (New York: Harper and Row, 1978), 466–67.

17.   Trivers, *Social Evolution*, 21.

18.   James M. Gustafson, "Sociobiology: A Secular Theology," *Hastings Center Report*, February 1979, 44–45. For a more extended treatment of this theme, see Howard L. Kaye, *The Social Meaning of Modern Biology: From Social Darwinism to Sociobiology* (New York and London: Yale University Press, 1986), ch. 4: "Sociobiology: The Natural Theology of E. O. Wilson," 95–135.

19.   This is the primary criticism of Gould in "Biological Potential vs. Biological Determinism," in *Sociobiology Debate*, ed. Caplan, 343–51. See also R. C. Lewontin, Steven Rose, and Leon J. Kamin, *Not in Our Genes: Biology, Ideology, and Human Nature* (New York: Random House, 1984).

20.   Wilson, *On Human Nature*, 6.

21.   Roger Masters, "Beyond Reductionism: Five Basic Concepts in Human Ethology," in *Human Ethology: Claims and Limits of a New Discipline*, ed. M. von Cranach, K. Foppa, W. Lepenies and D. Ploog (New York: Cambridge University Press, 1979), 266.

22.   Ibid., 267.

23.   See Roger D. Masters, "Of Marmots and Men: Animal Behavior and

Human Altruism." In Lauren Wispé, ed., *Altruism, Sympathy, and Helping Behavior* (New York: Academic Press, 1978).

    24.   Ibid., 268.

    25.   For example, Wilson, *On Human Nature*, 6.

    26.   Philip Kitcher, *Vaulting Ambition: Sociobiology and the Quest for Human Nature* (Cambridge, Massachusetts: MIT Press, 1985), 402.

    27.   Dawkins, *Selfish Gene*, ix.

    28.   Midgley, "Rival Fatalisms," 34. The "soft determinism" espoused here by no means demands a complete rejection of recent Roman Catholic appropriations of personalist, existentialist, and phenomenological descriptions of subjectivity and freedom; rather it provides a resource for balancing these descriptions with a greater appreciation of our biologically based limits, possibilities, conditions, and grounds.

    29.   van den Berghe, *Human Family Systems*, 171–98 provides a sociobiological account of this difference; see also Sahlins, "The Sociology of Primitive Exchange" and *The Use and Abuse of Biology.*

    30.   For an extreme case of disintegrated family ties, see Colin M. Turnbull, *The Mountain People* (New York: Simon and Schuster, 1972).

    31.   Alasdair MacIntyre, *After Virtue: A Study in Moral Theory* (Notre Dame, Indiana: University of Notre Dame Press, 1981), 150–51.

    32.   Erik Erikson, *Childhood and Society* (New York: Norton, 1963), 95–96.

    33.   See Charles J. Lumsden and Edward O. Wilson, *Genes, Mind, and Culture: The Coevolutionary Process* (Cambridge, Massachusetts: Harvard University Press, 1981); and *Promethean Fire: Reflections on the Origins of Mind* (Cambridge, Massachusetts: Harvard University Press, 1983).

    34.   Lumsden and Wilson, *Promethean Fire*, 154. On kin selection in cross-cultural perspective, see Chagnon, "Mate Competition, Favoring Close Kin, and Village Fissioning Among the Yanomono Indians" in *Evolutionary Biology and Human Social Behavior*, eds., Chagnon and Irons; and "Kin Selection Theory, Kinship, Marriage, and Fitness Among the Yanomono Indians," in *Sociobiology: Beyond Nature/Nurture*, eds. Barlow and Silverberg.

    35.   See Lumsden and Wilson, *Genes, Mind, and Culture*, 87. The relation between culturally-based incest taboos of various kinds and a naturally-based aversion to incest (promoting inbreeding avoidance) is more complex than can be or need be discussed here. For sociobiological treatment see J. Shepher, *Incest: A Biosocial View* (Orlando, Florida: Academic Press, 1983) and Pierre van der Berghe, "Incest Taboos and Avoidance: Some African Applications," in *Sociobiology and Psychology: Ideas, Issues, and Applications*, ed. Charles Crawford, Martin Smith, and Dennis Krebs (Hillsdale, New Jersey: Lawrence Erlbaum Associates, 1987), 353–71.

    36.   See Bibb Latane and John Darley, *The Unresponsive Bystander: Why Doesn't He Help?* (New York: Appleton-Century-Crofts, 1970).

    37.   Gould, "Biological Potential vs. Biological Determinism," 348–49. Lumsden and Wilson would disagree with Gould in their theory of "epigenic rules," which channel human learning patterns and therefore lie between strict programming and pure potential. Gould holds that the brain is "capable of the full range of human behaviors and predisposed toward none," whereas Lumsden and Wilson argue for genetically based predispositions, such as kin preference, that may or may not be actualized. Lums-

den and Wilson's "gene-culture" theory recognizes a degree of freedom that takes the inevitability out of what is "natural" and therefore undercuts Gould's political criticism of sociobiological social conservatism regarding, for example, sexism and classism.

38.   Lumsden and Wilson, *Promethean Fire*, 179. Needless to say, Wilson has not developed an account of the difference that this developing view of human freedom makes for his metaphysical materialism.

39.   Mary Maxwell, *Morality among Nations* (Albany, New York: State University of New York Press, 1990), 89.

40.   See Plato, *The Republic* V. 457–65.

41.   Ernst Mayr, "Evolution and Ethics," ch. 2 in *Darwin, Marx, and Freud: Their Influence on Moral Theory* (New York: Plenum Press, 1984), 43.

42.   Gutiérrez, *Theology of Liberation*, 81.

43.   Dawkins, *Selfish Gene*, 4–5.

44.   Maxwell, *Morality among Nations*, 113.

45.   Ibid., 3–4.

46.   Ibid., 104f.

47.   The distinction between moral altruism (as it is usually understood in ordinary discourse) and "genetic altruism" is important to maintain in spite of its awkwardness. In ordinary language "altruism" is action motivated by concern for another person for his or her own good, whereas "egoism" is the doctrine that human actions are primarily motivated by self-interest. "Genetic altruism," one will recall from the previous chapter, prescinds from motives and concerns only behavior that somehow contributes to the benefit of another at some expense to the agent's inclusive fitness. See Wilson, *Sociobiology*, 3. In my view, "love" is not to be equated with either sense of "altruism." For a helpful analysis of altruism in sociobiology, see Brian C. R. Bertram, "Problems with Altruism," in *Current Problems in Sociobiology*, ed. King's College Sociobiology Group (Cambridge, England: Cambridge University Press, 1982), 252–67. Some sociobiologists, for example, van den Berghe, *Human Family Systems*, also speak of manipulation and coerced altruism in addition to reciprocity and kin favoritism. In my view these theories are less credible than the latter so I do not entertain them in this book.

48.   See, for example, Dawkins, *Selfish Gene*, 3–4; Alexander, *Moral Systems*, 191; Campbell, "On the Conflict Between Biological and Social Evolution and Between Psychology and Moral Tradition," *American Psychologist* 30 (1975): 1102–26; and J. L. Makie, "The Law of the Jungle," *Philosophy* 53 (1978): 553–73. Thus Wilson, *On Human Nature*, 154: "The evolutionary theory of human altruism is greatly complicated by the ultimately self-serving quality of most forms of that altruism. No sustained form of human altruism is explicitly and totally self-annihilating." Wilson does not explain why actions that are not "totally self-annihilating" are ultimately self-serving. He continues: "The 'altruist' expects reciprocation from society for himself and his closest relatives. His good behavior is calculating, often in a wholly conscious way, and his maneuvers are orchestrated by the excruciatingly intricate sanctions and demands of society." Wilson does not reconcile the apparent contradiction implied in the twofold claim that altruistic actions are both "orchestrated" by society and at the same time reflect self-serving calculation of self-interest.

49.   Michael T. Ghiselin, *The Economy of Nature and the Evolution of Sex* (Berkeley: University of California, 1974), 247.

50. Ibid., 155.
51. Ibid., 166.
52. Alexander, *Biology of Moral Systems*, 3. My italics. Alexander argues that the golden rule is an "admirable goal" but "clearly contrary to a tendency to behave in a reproductively selfish manner. 'Thou shalt give the impression that thou lovest thy neighbor as thyself' might be closer to the truth" (in R. D. Alexander, "The Search for a General Theory of Behavior," *Behavioral Science* 20 [1975]: 96–97).
53. Ibid., 101–102. Acts of "indiscriminate beneficence" can be self-regarding, but need they always be such? The affirmative has not been demonstrated.
54. Ibid., 191. For a convincing refutation of this egoistic presupposition of sociobiology, see Kitcher, *Vaulting Ambition*, 396–406.
55. Ian Vine, Review of *Evolution and Individual Behavior: Introduction to Human Sociobiology*, Christopher Badcock (Oxford: Basil Blackwell, 1991) in *Human Ethology Newsletter* 7 (1992): 8.
56. See Roger D. Masters, "Of Marmots and Men: Animal Behavior and Human Altruism," in *Altruism, Sympathy, and Helping Behavior: Psychological and Sociological Principles*, ed. Lauren Wispé (New York: Academic Press, 1978).
57. Ruse, *Taking Darwin Seriously*, 237.
58. Ruse, "The Morality of the Gene," *The Monist* 67 (1985): 180.
59. Maxwell, *Human Evolution*, 154.
60. Alexander, *Biology of Moral Systems*, 139. Alexander is not alone in this ambiguity. A number of the authors cited under the first category actually speak at times as if they were in the second. Wilson is a case in point. He claims that acts of kin favoritism are not conducted with expectation of return but acts of "soft core" altruism expect reciprocation from society for either the agent or his or her closest relatives. Wilson thus seems to be claiming that all acts outside kin favoritism are motivated by self-concern. Sociobiologists are either ambiguous or waver incoherently between these two, sometimes claiming that inclusive fitness accounts for the ultimate human motives underlying all external acts and at other times suggesting a more distant relation between genetic fitness and human motivation.
61. See Daniel Batson, *The Altruism Question: Toward a Social-Psychological Answer* (Hillsdale, New Jersey: Lawrence Erlbaum Associates, 1991), and various works by Dennis L. Krebs and Martin L. Hoffman. In political science, see Jane J. Mansbridge, ed., *Beyond Self-Interest* (Chicago and London: University of London, 1990): Popular presentations of the case for altruism include Morton Hunt, *The Compassionate Beast: What Science is Discovering About the Humane Side of Humankind* (New York: William Morrow and Co., 1990) and Alfie Kohn, *The Brighter Side of Human Nature: Altruism and Empathy in Everyday Life* (New York: Basic Books, 1990).
62. Richard M. Titmuss, *The Gift Relationship: From Human Blood to Social Policy* (New York: Pantheon Books, 1971).
63. Alexander, *Biology of Moral Systems*, 158. Neither is Barash's account of the "selfishness" of kamikaze pilots convincing (*The Whisperings Within* [New York: Penguin Books, 1979], 167–68).
64. John Chandler, "Ethical Philosophy," in *The Sociobiological Imagination*, ed. Mary Maxwell (Albany: State University of New York Press, 1991), 162.
65. N. Gerstel and H. E. Gross, *Families and Work* (Philadelphia: Temple University Press, 1987), E. Liebow, *Talley's Corner* (Boston: Little, Brown, 1967), and C.

Stack, *All Our Kin—Strategies for Survival in A Black Community* (New York: Harper and Row, 1974).

66.   See Lillian B. Rubin, *Just Friends* (New York: Harper and Row, 1985).

67.   This notion of "instinct" is given in W. H. Thorpe, *Learning and Instinct in Animals* (London: Methuen, 1963), 29.

68.   Maxwell, *Human Evolution*, 153.

69.   Wilson, *On Human Nature*, 153. My emphasis.

70.   Martin L. Hoffman, "Is Altruism Part of Human Nature?" *Journal of Personality and Social Psychology* 40 (1981): 128. For another psychological account of empathy as motivator of altruism, see C. Daniel Batson, "Prosocial Motivation: Is It Ever Truly Altruistic?" *Advances in Experimental Social Psychology* 20 (1987): 65–122 and C. Daniel Batson and Jay S. Coke, "Empathic Motivation of Helping Behavior," in J. Philippe Rushton and Richard M. Sorrentino, eds., *Altruism and Helping Behavior: Social, Personality, and Developmental Perspectives* (Hillsdale, New Jersey: Lawrence Erlbaum Associates, 1981). Hoffman and Bateson oppose the view predominant among behavioral scientists that all acts of ostensible altruism are in fact egoistic, that is, intended to benefit the self in some way (e.g., distress relief, mood elevation, moralistic self-satisfaction). The egoistic view is found, *inter alia*, in Anna Freud, "A Form of Altruism," in Anna Freud, ed., *The Ego and the Mechanism of Defense* (New York: International Universities Press, 1946) and, in Robert B. Cialdini and Douglas T. Kenrick, "Altruism as Hedonism: A Social Development Perspective on the Relationship of Negative Mood State and Helping," *Journal of Personality and Social Psychology* 34 (1976): 907–14.

71.   Martin Hoffman, "Empathy and Prosocial Activism," in Nancy Eisenberg, Janusz Reykowski, and Ervin Staub, eds., *Social and Moral Values: Individual and Societal Perspectives* (Hillsdale, New Jersey: Lawrence Erlbaum Associates, 1988), 4–6. The development of empathy as a mediator for altruism is confirmed in a number of sources, including the early childhood studies of Carolyn Zahn-Waxler and Robert A. King, "Child Rearing and Children's Prosocial Initiations Towards Victims of Distress," *Child Development* 50 (1979) 2: 319–30.

72.   According to Wilson, for the good of the human race we must work against "pure, hard-core altruism based upon kin selection" and build social harmony through the extension of "soft-core" reciprocity (*On Human Nature*, 155–59).

73.   Sociobiologists themselves propose that we work against those aspects of our nature that threaten our present social and biological existence. They are not social Darwinians who claim that what has evolved is ipso facto morally good. One of the tasks of culture, in fact, is to correct the antisocial tendencies that evolved over the course of our primate and especially hunter-gatherer past. Wilson, for example, hopes that "New patterns of sociality could be installed in bits and pieces" into human nature, despite the fact that it rests on a "jerrybuilt foundation of partly obsolete Ice-Age adaptations" (*On Human Nature*, 208).

74.   Alexander, *Biology of Moral Systems*, 160; my emphasis.

75.   See Johann, *Meaning of Love*, 45–46.

76.   See Alexander, *Biology of Moral Systems*.

77.   Plato, *The Republic*, trans. Francis MacDonald Cornford (Oxford: Oxford University Press, 1945), I.331E–336A, 7–14.

78.   Freud, *Civilization and Its Discontents*, 64.

79. H. A. Krebs and J. H. Shelley, *The Creative Process in Science and Medicine* (Amsterdam: Excerpta Medica, 195), 24.

80. Midgely, "Toward a New Understanding of Human Nature," 525–26.

81. According to Alexander, "When we speak favorably to our children about Good Samaritanism, we are telling them about a behavior that has a strong likelihood of being reproductively profitable" (*Darwinism and Human Affairs*, 102).

82. For this reason some philosophers have attempted to draw a connection between sociobiological accounts of altruism and Hume's notion of "sympathy." David Hume, *An Enquiry concerning the Principles of Morals*, in *British Moralists 1650-1800*, ed. D.D. Raphael, 2 vols. (Oxford: The Clarendon Press, 1969), 2:74. Sociobiologists are thus divided over allegiance to Hume or to Hobbes, his antagonist in this matter.

5

Human Nature, the Ordering of Love, and Evolutionary Theory

Contemporary evolutionary theory can provide an empirical basis on which to develop a contemporary restatement of the order of love. Behavioral biology gives a natural explanation of the deeply partial character of human love, the fact that human beings naturally love some people more than others and that their affectional bonds are particular and cannot be extended to encompass all human beings. It provides evolutionary bases for the claim that self-love is in some sense naturally prior to love for others, that the intimacy and shared life between spouses constitutes the greatest friendship of which human beings are capable in this life, and that one has a debt of gratitude for one's parents. It offers an understanding of the biological underpinning of the particularly intense love that parents tend to feel for their children and their willingness to sacrifice everything for their well-being. These notions are all part of "order of love" as I interpret it.

As we saw in the second chapter, Aristotelian science enabled Thomas Aquinas to avoid the major deficiencies that mark contemporary Catholic interpretations of love. It provided a comprehensive account of the wider natural world within which human nature can be understood. It recognized that human beings are "rational animals" and that some of the emotional proclivities underlying human behavior show affinities with those of other animals. An awareness of biological forms of ordering supported Thomas's perception of the limits to love, and his need to acknowledge an ordering of love and beneficence. It realized that we have deeply natural, prerational, prepersonal predispositions for selective, intense, particular care for kin. These predispositions are modified by cultural influences, of course, but more often than not, they play a central role in the formation of familial bonds across cultures.

In this chapter I argue that evolutionary science can help us avoid the deficiencies that characterize contemporary Catholic ethics. The discussion begins with kin altruism and reciprocity.

Kin Preference

The evolutionary basis of kin preference may be the most intuitively plausible contribution of sociobiological theory. Most people would agree with the claim that natural parents ought to feel the most powerful obligations to the needs of their own children, that "rules of prescriptive altruism"[1] are most stringent within the family circle, and that human beings are naturally predisposed to form affective bonds with and to devote the greatest care to close family. Though one may have doubts about other aspects of sociobiology, it seems reasonable enough to agree with Wilson's claim that, "emotions such as love and genuine care in fact evolved because of underlying causes: principally, the biological need to maximize the probability that *Homo sapiens* will survive."[2]

Knowledge of the emotional capacities and social behavioral tendencies of nonhuman animals provides a wide backdrop against which the distinctive features of human love stand out—particularly aspects of love that reflect a substantial sense of identity and personal history, for example, intimacy, trust, fidelity, and love of the other for his or her own sake. In this sense, such knowledge confirms personalist interpretations of love. Fully human love is in fact unparalleled in the animal world, and it is among the most recent and uncommon of evolutionary adaptations.

There are, however, a number of functions that kin selection theory cannot be said to perform within a reasonable account of the ordering of love. First, kin selection theory provides no direct assistance in moral decision making. Kin favoritism cannot be assumed to be always and everywhere ethically right or even permissible, for the obvious reason that in certain circumstances the needs of family members ought to be subordinated to meet the more urgent needs of others. Kin favoritism abstracted from concrete personal, cultural, and social factors cannot be expected to provide help in sorting out concrete moral priorities.

Second, there is no biological blueprint for an ideally correct moral order, some kind of a model based on the exact percent of "coefficient of relationship" between various blood relatives. Sociobiology is helpful in explaining, in evolutionary terms, why is it that humans are a "bond-forming" species, and, for that matter, why they tend to adopt "moderately polygynous" "mating patterns" and devote a great deal of time and energy on their children (the "K-selection" strategy mentioned above). Yet obviously this information will not determine how one treats one's own spouse or enable one to properly weigh various courses of action regarding assistance giving within one's family. There is no abstract, universal order of love that can be used to guide or judge the operative priorities of all persons at all times. The less substantive, more interactionist views of the human person that appear in Rahner, Johann, and Farley correctly militate against the notion that there is one order of good valid and binding for all persons at all times and places. Indications taken from the perceived ordering of human nature should therefore be seen as necessary but not sufficient sources of moral insight. Biological facts and tendencies by themselves cannot be taken as determinative of who ought to be loved and cared for, but as significant factors that support and shape some persisting and morally significant relationships. Clearly, the particularities of individual lives make all the difference regarding the concrete, existential relevance of the order of nature.

Third, kin preference by no means eliminates human freedom. Sociobiologists do not suggest that everyone automatically loves his or her family members and will take pains to ensure their security and well-being. Sadly but perhaps not unexpectedly, recent studies indicate that at times biological families have refused to fulfill their natural obligations to a family member who has contracted AIDS.[3] Although families are often marked by deep interpersonal bonds and sustained by healthy patterns of interaction of the kind said by personalists to characterize mature mutual love, ordinary experience provides abundant testimony of an expansive range of human affections toward kin, from the most devoted and intimate to quite detached or even hateful. A psychologically and physically abused sister will not automatically develop the normal genetically based emotional disposition to love and care for her abusive brother solely because they share copies of approximately fifty percent of their genes. And obviously in many cases—for example, the affective attachment between adoptive parents and their children—the most intense love reflects no genetic relatedness whatsoever. Biological relatedness obviously counts for very little without complementary affective and social ties that mark fully human, interpersonal relations.

Any attempt to incorporate kin preference within an ordering of love must recognize that authentic love is finally grounded in the free decision of the person to love another for his or her own sake and know that people are not purely "inclusive fitness maximizing organisms," but feeling, thinking human beings. The core insight of existentialism that so influences Johann and Rahner must be called to mind here: we must respect "our own proper and incommunicable interiority."[4] The rough patterns of affective and moral priorities that we develop implicitly over the course of our lifetimes give little weight to biological relatedness per se as a conscious motive for care and self-sacrifice. It is the development of affective bonds and social connections with other people that lead us and them to act in caring ways.

The positive significance of kin selection theory for contemporary Catholic interpretations of love can be seen in several areas. First, kin selection theory emphatically underscores human finitude in general and the limits to human love in particular. It highlights the fact that we are incorrigibly finite creatures who are unable to love all human beings with the full mutuality extolled by personalism and feminism or with the radical solidarity of liberation theology. As ethologist Eibl-Eibesfeldt points out:

> Our reason can fully grasp the commandment to love all fellowmen, but, as we are now constructed, we are not capable of fulfilling this commandment. We experience warm feelings of love and friendship only as a bond with individuals, and with the best will in the world, this cannot be altered.[5]

Neither Catholic personalists nor liberation theologians would claim that neighbor love mandates "warm feelings of love and friendship" for all people in the world, but Eibl-Eibesfeldt's comment can be taken to register a valid caution regarding our capacity to extend genuine mutuality and solidarity beyond a certain point in our relations to others.

Second, kin selection theory encourages us to acknowledge the persistence of conflict in human relations. Sociobiologists tend to maintain that conflict and competition have been literally built into the human condition because of the genetic diversity of interests. In the animal world, the ubiquity of cooperative strategies, alliances, and bonds reflects the multitude of strategies through which natural organisms pursue inclusive reproductive success. This heightened awareness of natural conflict and competition has in the past taken extreme ideological form in social Darwinism, but the basic perspective was powerfully expressed in the scientific writings of Darwin himself.[6] The "competitive" aspects of human motivation pose special problems for the development and maintenance of prosocial bonds and to the kinds of trust, acceptance, openness, and fidelity analyzed and promoted by advocates of mutuality and solidarity.

Sociobiologists argue that the evolutionary process has not led to a preestablished harmony of human values. On the contrary, human nature is marked by conflict and ambivalence. According to Wilson, "the individual is forced to make imperfect choices based on irreconcilable loyalties—between the 'rights' and 'duties' of self and those of family, tribe, and other units of selection, each of which evolves its own code of honor."[7] In a similar vein, Trivers's analysis of "parent-offspring conflict" systematically explicates ways in which intergenerational conflict has been built into the genetic basis of love by the evolutionary process. Sociobiologists can be appreciated for alerting us to the myopia and narrow exclusivity of kin preference, which encourages assistance only to close kin; and to the instrumentalism and prudentialism of reciprocity considerations as well as the dangers stemming from pressures to advance within various "dominance hierarchies," particularly when they are amplified in highly competitive urban technological societies.

Third, kin selection theory challenges Catholic ethics to recognize that a universal human need for some kind of ordering of affections and moral responsibility has been built into human nature by millions of years of natural selection. According to the laws of the evolutionary process, "discrimination is a necessary part of a persisting altruism."[8] Human beings cannot engage in unlimited beneficence or practice altruism, "without discrimination of kinship, acquaintanceship, shared values, or propinquity in time or space."[9] The ethics of love must acknowledge and respond constructively to this need for priorities. Because deep bonds cannot be developed with many human beings, some workable priority system must be employed to organize moral obligations in a reasonable way. Moral imperatives should not require what is impossible to human agents; if "ought implies can," the limits to human nature are significant for the ethics of love, especially because they demand that we prioritize our responsibilities.

Fourth, kin selection theory corrects the exclusive focus on the purely conscious and deliberate sources of love that marks personalism's and liberation theology's appeals to the preferential option. It underscores the fact that not all forms of love can be encompassed under the rubric of fully mature adult mutuality, the form highlighted by "I-Thou" friendship. Parental love is the prototypical case of love that is not founded on self-disclosure and the "reciprocity of consciousness." Rather than being exclusively the result of fully self-conscious human self-disposal, parental love is rooted in deeper features of the human emotional repertoire (though of course it cannot develop without affective consent). The existential realization that to love someone involves a risk and entails a commitment based on trust must be balanced with awareness that love is not always exclusively the product of the spiritual interaction of two free-floating, fully self-determining transcendental subjectivities.

Fifth, kin selection theory underscores the extent to which partiality pervades human sociality. Evolutionary theorists acknowledge the natural basis of the ubiquitous channeling of human affections and assistance giving. Kin preference of some kind normally plays a role in what it means for human beings to live satisfying lives. Sociologists Elaine Cumming and David Schneider, for example, observe that "sibling solidarity would seem . . . to have little chance of outlasting early childhood . . the evidence shows that it remains a dominant affective and moral force for most people throughout life."[10] People naturally tend to love some more than others and give special preference to close kin. Admitting the moral centrality of this natural partiality challenges the radical egalitarianism implied in Gutiérrez's preferential option. Acknowledging the moral priority of kinfolk or friends implies that the intensities of love will be unequal in some fundamental ways.

The critical distinction here is between proper and improper inequality. "Nepotism" implies an inappropriate inequality, the favoring of family members in the assignment of public responsibilities and privileges with insufficient regard to requisite skills and standard qualifications. Favoritism within families is the source of lifelong grudges and resentment, and signifies an improper preference of affection or action on behalf of some children over others. The proper ordering of love may at times legitimately involve the unequal distribution of family resources but it ought to proceed in a manner that strives to accommodate the needs of all its members. Partiality for primary relations, however, is unavoidable because deeply rooted in human nature. The accompanying moral challenge includes differentiating proper from improper forms of partiality.

Sixth, kin selection theory indicates evolutionary reasons behind the value of kin preference for human well-being, a contribution that ought to be morally recognized by Catholic ethicists. Child rearing requires a tremendous time commitment and exertion of energy that is promoted through affectional bonding and attachment. Stable and consistent parental affection provides the psychological security necessary for exploratory behavior in small children, a necessary condition for further emotional and cognitive development. Kin preference is valuable for parents and their children, but also, if balanced with other goods and properly ordered to other ends, for their communities, their societies, and the human species as a whole.[11] It is good that people feel strongly about their families and take care of family members, especially children; families must teach their children to love and care for their own when the time is right, and to work for a society in which families thrive and children are loved and respected.

These attitudes and behaviors are morally good for children themselves and for others partly because they provide the context for the development in adult life of both intimacy and moral commitment between spouses and moral concern for those who lie outside the circle of primary relationships. As John Henry Newman observed, "the best preparation for loving the world at large, and loving it duly and wisely, is to cultivate an intimate friendship and affection toward those who are immediately about us."[12] There are good psychological and biological grounds for affirming that relatively stable and secure bonds of love within the family create the emotional basis for a later extension of love to persons outside the family and continue to powerfully inform subsequent adult affectional bonds.[13]

Ties of blood or marriage do not of course guarantee a sense of affective connection, and obviously at times people linked by consanguinity or marriage or both, possess little or no love for one another and do not perceive themselves to be part of the lives of others with whom they have a biological or legal connection. This lack confirms in some detail the common sense intuition that mature interpersonal love depends on affective and social capacities cultivated in some form of family life. Most of us recognize that "father absence" constitutes, among other things, a form of emotional deprivation that may or may not be compensated for by siblings, surrogate fathers, or other people in the social environment.[14] Ordinary human experience discloses the sharp contrast between the effects on children of loving and predictable parental care and parental indifference or rejection. People who are deprived of intimate familial love as children often lack the full capacity for intimacy and social concern as adults—capacities simply taken for granted by both personalism and liberation theology.

Seventh, kin preference is due a fundamental place in any ethic built on the conviction that nature is perfected by grace. Gutiérrez's language of solidarity and of "reversing the usual priority system" corrects the apparently pervasive human tendency to attend to those who are proximate to the self and to ignore those who are more distant, but it gives no clear and proper appreciation to the legitimate and morally obligatory application of kin preference. Christian love must include both concerns. In keeping with their emphasis on mutuality rather than self-sacrifice or equal regard, Rahner and Johann, among others, are in a position to see intrafamilial love as a central locus of the ethics of love rather than as merely peripheral because of its preferential nature. Ties of family are central to every culture, precisely because kin preference is such a fundamental feature of human nature. As such, and despite its present neglect, it would seem to have a major role in Catholic ethics.

Reciprocity

Evolutionary accounts of reciprocity speculate that the inclination to engage in cooperative behavior with nonkin has evolved to become a natural orientation of the human psyche. It was argued in the previous chapter that personalist "I-Thou" relations need to be distinguished from the simple exchange model common to reciprocity theories, and to involve a level of relationality that transcends the atomistic division between the interests of self and others presupposed in reciprocity theory. It was also argued, nevertheless, that reciprocity theory does capture an important dimension of the natural human motivation to engage in prosocial behavior; it can thus be said to account for a significant if limited subset of human social behavior.

Purged of the underlying egoism assumed by some of its exponents, what does reciprocity theory contribute to the ethics of love? It seems to me that reciprocity theory can make a significant contribution to contemporary Catholic interpretations of love in several ways. First, it calls attention to the many ways in which love and caregiving are bound up with various kinds of biological and psychological interdependence that are the bases of "I-Thou" relationships.

As we saw earlier, recent studies show that from the very beginning the infant-caregiver relationship is marked not only by dependence but also by complex and subtle kinds of preconscious interdependence and forms of what biologist Robert Hinde calls "proto-intersubjectivity."[15] Reciprocity theory provides analysis of the extent to which human social life from its earliest moments is built on a basic if not fully developed reciprocal interaction and interdependence. If parent-child love provides the roots of trust, intimacy, and caring in adult life, later peer relations, marked by greater equality and less asymmetry, similarly enhance the development of important emotional aspects of adult mutuality. The ability to sustain and extend reciprocity in a variety of relationships is integrally related to mature affective and social competence—the condition of the kind of mutuality that Rahner and Johann so eloquently describe. These are, to be sure, psychological traits, but they are made possible by biological capacities and, sociobiologists would maintain, unconsciously encouraged by the human psyche.

Second, sociobiology here underscores the fact that cooperation and reciprocity are much more common forms of interpersonal interaction than either unmitigating altruism or pure self-sacrifice, the inflated moralistic rhetoric of some ethicists notwithstanding. They are clearly essential to human flourishing, at least in the sense that they provide the basis for moving beyond moment-by-moment concern for meeting subsistence needs. One need not accept the oversimplified claim that "almost all the higher ethics—such as friendship, gratitude, trust, sympathy, and so on—can be derived from [reciprocal altruism],"[16] to see that reciprocity does indeed play a very important role in the moral life. To the extent that it is ignored by proponents of the preferential option, their interpretation of love is incomplete and therefore inadequate.

Ordinary experience seems to confirm Trivers's claim that the golden rule is found most frequently in relationships between reciprocators. Considerations of cost effectiveness are not totally foreign to ordinary human caregiving—far from it. It seems reasonable that most people are more willing, for example, to give something that entails a small personal cost and helps another a great deal than they are to give something that requires great sacrifice but helps another to a negligible degree. This is not to claim, of course, that exercise of the golden rule ought to be restricted to reciprocators, a position which seems implied in the writings of some sociobiologists.

Third, the pervasiveness of "indirect reciprocity" underscores the fact that as individuals, human beings are able to flourish only in a social and communal context—an awareness that corrects the more narrowly dyadic sphere of human interaction assumed by personalists. The person is constituted not only in relation to other dialoguing subjects but also to various groups and as part of larger social wholes, the fact, as Midgley puts it, that "We are incurably members one of another."[17] Focus on assistance giving as ultimately contributing to a social network as well as being immediately directed to a needy individual leads us to see the person not as an isolated individual, as in "social atomism," but as a participant embedded in a much larger social whole. Sociobiological sensitivity to the dependence of persons on larger communities thus brings a much needed corrective to the excessive emphasis on the interpersonal realm and the occasional suggestion of its self-sufficiency.

The sense of moral responsibility that accords with the personalist dyad is narrowly directed toward immediate objects of love; love itself is understood primarily in terms of friendship, and love of community or wider social groups is given little attention. A single-minded preoccupation with mutuality suggests that the sphere of moral concern extends only to those persons with whom one shares a relationship of deep interpersonal mutuality and "reciprocal consciousness," and hence indicates the temptation to an *égoisme à deux* that is indifferent to others and to the reality of the larger community and the common good. The theory of "indirect reciprocity" helps to correct this excessively narrow moral context.

Moral Inclusiveness

The theories of kin preference and reciprocity provide reasonably plausible evolutionary grounds for understanding the natural centrality of primary relations in ordinary life. Sociobiologists claim as a sheer matter of fact, that human beings tend to be most generous toward close relatives (parents, offspring, siblings) and more restrictive in their caring for others (i.e., to "familialistically" subordinate the good of others to that of one's kin). Contemporary evolutionary theory points to the natural ground for this general pattern of ordering.

"Wilson's own ethic," Ruse explains

> has to be one where we feel a greater obligation toward those near and dear to us, than to others, and (most probably) to countrymen than to foreigners. I have an obligation to help my own two children over my obligations to others and I am not doing wrong when (as I do) I act in this way. I have an obligation to the helpless in my own society, above that obligation to other societies.[18]

Ruse clearly softens the "selfishness" with which sociobiologists generally claim we regard those who are most distant by saying that we feel a *greater* sense of moral obligation toward those who are closest to us and a *less intense* sense of obligation toward the more distant. All cultures tend to apply "the rule of prescriptive altruism" to family members and much less, if at all, to others.[19] Thus, according to Ruse: "In a very real sense, I think I [as a Canadian] have a stronger obligation to the poor of Canada than say, to the poor of Chad. I certainly have a stronger obligation to the poor of Canada, than I have to the poor of Australia."[20] In the Catholic theological perspective, which understands that nature is perfected by grace, it seems reasonable to affirm that this natural prioritization—properly balanced with other goods—will be incorporated in a Christian ethics of love.

This general pattern of ordering is characterized by certain distinct possibilities of good, but also by certain distinct capacities for evil. Reciprocity, for example, as a primary basis for human interaction beyond the kinship circle raises the issue of whether the most powerful in society will always be favored.[21] Sociobiologists tend to maintain that human behavior reflects a "natural morality" of cooperating with cooperators and defecting against defectors—an ethic hardly inspiring moral concern for the stranger. This is especially the case if the stranger is depicted as one whom Gutiérrez calls a "nonperson," a member of a marginal group rather than a person with prestige or other resources whose recognition would be valued by the agent within a system of indirect reciprocity.

The evolutionary process has resulted in a widespread human proclivity to be biased toward kin and reciprocators and in favor of a certain kind of solidarity, namely, "in-group" affiliation, which some sociobiologists argue, emerged as an evolutionary extension of kin selection.[22] Alexander maintains that in-group bias, along with greater cooperation, communication skills, and other social advances, resulted from alliances originally forged as a method by which Pleistocene groups competed against one another.[23]

Kin selection theory maintains that in-group affiliation tends to be accompanied by out-group bias, a tendency to respond with suspicion to those to whom we are not bound by ties of kinship or connections of reciprocal obligations and an evolved capacity, elicited in many circumstances, "to partition other people into friends and aliens."[24] What are now taken to be undesirable traits, such as conformism, suggestibility, nepotism, ethnocentrism, self-deception, racism, excessive competitiveness, and "moralistic aggression," are, according to sociobiologists, based on evolved human tendencies that at an earlier stage in our evolutionary history might have provided adaptive advantages to members of the species, particularly in settings marked by intense and persistent group versus group conflict.[25] This position offers scant basis for openness to those belonging to other groups. The indifference to, or outright suspicion of, people from other groups that is said to accompany in-group loyalty thus presents special challenges for the universalism implied in the preferential option.

How to morally evaluate these tendencies and their relation to human action lies outside the perview of behavioral biology qua science. Sociobiologists qua scientists do not argue that we ought to be concerned about the wider human community, or that we ought to forget our narrow "in-group" loyalties and develop a universal ethic that includes all human beings (or all sentient beings, for that matter).[26] It should be noted for the record that in their moral reflections, sociobiologists generally argue for the need to expand moral horizons beyond conventional boundaries of kin and direct reciprocators.[27] How far beyond one's immediate circle of kin and reciprocators is a matter of debate among sociobiologists, though many argue that out of survival interests alone, human beings need to be more critical of the generally prevailing sharp restriction of beneficence beyond conventional boundaries, whether of the family, clan, neighborhood, or nation-state.

From a Catholic perspective, however, sociobiology can be said to alert us to the fact that the extension of a sense of moral responsibility from the interpersonal to the communal level may at times be subverted by natural unconscious desires and biases and to provide grounds for criticizing overidealized moralities of universal beneficence, illustrated in Gutiérrez's work. It thus insists on interpreting the meaning and requirements of love with a certain realism.

Sociobiologists question any moral perspectives that assert that genuine moral concern, by a pure act of the will encouraged by moral exhortation, can be simply extended beyond the kinship group and beyond the circle of those with whom one has reciprocal relations without going against the grain of human nature. At the same time, they do not imply that human beings are simply fated to distorted moral parochialism. Kin favoritism accompanied by in-group loyalty is not an inexorable outcome of human genes but the result of human choices. Natural proclivities need not automatically be taken as normative; as Alexander points out, "to say that we are evolved to serve the interests of our genes in no way suggests that we are obliged to serve them."[28] It is important to acknowledge the complexity and profound ambivalence of human nature, to recognize not only the innate tendency toward in-group bias but also the weaker but nonetheless real human capacity to care about, and for, strangers.

I suspect that few readers would doubt that human affections are largely centripetal rather than centrifugal; that is, they move predominantly inward toward self, friends, and family rather than out toward strangers and enemies. Awareness of the evolved proclivity to reciprocal affiliation and kin preference can be enlisted to increase our control over the centripetal direction of moral concern and especially its myopic tendencies. Such awareness calls attention to the need to develop countervailing skills and to encourage the expansion of corrective emotional capacities such as empathy, kindness, and sympathy. The natural predis-position to help strangers who are needy may be fainter and more diffuse than kin preference, but it can be amplified and extended under the proper social and cultural conditions, those promoted, for example, within religious communities.[29]

Biology alone does not provide sufficient grounds for recognizing and affirming the dignity of every human being or for supporting disin-terested care for others not connected to us by kinship or reciprocity. Johann is certainly correct to insist on the irreducible interiority of every person. The biblical view of the person as made in the "image of God" inspires a deep regard for human dignity that sharply contrasts with Dawkins's view of human beings as "survival machines—robot vehicles blindly programmed to preserve the selfish molecules known as genes."[30] Morality reduced to a means for internalizing and monitoring reciprocity leaves little or no place, for example, for caring for the severely mentally handicapped or the destitute, whose ability to engage in productive activ-ity or to contribute to the well-being of others is significantly compro-mised. Biology is not all of nature, and there may be other natural grounds, most notably natural human capacities for intelligence and love, upon which to establish what Charles Taylor calls, "the universal attribu-tion of moral personality: in fundamental ethical matters, everyone ought to count, and all ought to count in the same way."[31]

Because human beings are cultural animals with "open programs," we are not fated to moral parochialism and myopia. People are able to extend moral concern (at least in the sense of nonmaleficence) to all human beings, even though the human biological substrate may not strongly incline people to act in this direction. Most behavioral biologists regard the basis for extending altruism beyond kin and friends to be largely cultural rather than biological; that is, commitment to the well-being of those with whom one has no bonds of blood or reciprocity is encouraged by cultural sources rather than evolved human propensities. According to Mary Maxwell, the kinds of "gratuitous altruism" that in most societies provide care for helpless individuals, including those who will never be able to reciprocate, are "definitely not based on any system of altruism that evolved by natural selection."[32] Put in sociological language, the church can be said to function as a "socializing" agent that expands the circle of concern to include all human beings and all communities, regardless of genetic similarities, cultural ties, racial identity, and national allegiance.[33] Though, in general, natural priorities are retained in the Catholic moral tradition, the significance of the needs of others are given more weight than the sociobiologists would regard as warranted on strictly natural, that is, inclusive fitness, grounds.

Two avenues have been viewed as correctives to in-group bias, one predominantly affective and the other predominantly cognitive. Some authors focus on the development and extension of our native affective capacities, arousing emotional responses of sympathy or empathy to another person's plight. Some evolutionary thinkers have argued that biologically based capacity for empathy can provide a natural basis for expanding the range of human concern beyond the immediate circle. Others focus on the cognitive capacities for roleplaying and acknowledging the independent perspective of others as the key to extending moral concern.

Darwin's position incorporated both approaches, but clearly favored the extension of sympathy as the central motivating force behind the development of the moral sense. Thus, he argued in the *Descent of Man* that "the social instincts—the prime principle of man's moral constitution—with the aid of active intellectual powers and the effects of habit, naturally lead to the golden rule: 'As ye would that men should do to you, do ye to them likewise'."[34] He believed that three elements comprise our acceptance of the golden rule: our capacity for empathy and altruism ("the social instincts"), cognitive recognition of common humanity ("active intellectual powers"), and social development and proper upbringing ("the effects of habit"). In the *Descent of Man*, he argued:

> The moral nature of man has reached its present standard, partly through the advancement of his reasoning powers and consequently of a just public opinion, but especially from his sympathies having been rendered more tender and widely diffused through the effects of habit, example, instruction, and reflection.[35]

Some philosophers informed by evolutionary theory have speculated that the course of human evolution has witnessed the broadening and extension (or "overgeneralization"[36]) of altruistic behavior and empathic emotions from kin and reciprocators (i.e., members of one's primary group) to other persons and wider communities, and that social and cultural evolution can have the effect of amplifying this capacity even further. Darwin himself maintained (in contrast to Johann) that our natural sympathy for one another is an extension of animals' "love of their own kind,"[37] a position later developed by Russian anarchist Peter Kropotkin and others who argued that evolution has endowed us with an instinct for mutual aid and cooperation, a "feeling or instinct of human solidarity and sociability."[38]

More recently, evolutionary theorists have speculated that what was at one time an adaptive emotional proclivity to engage in altruism within small groups (that is, in Pleistocene hunter-gatherer tribes) is now able to take on a life of its own and transcend its original limits regarding sympathy and care for strangers. And, as Midgley notes, Wilson emphasizes the "likeness of our emotional constitutions," which, among other things, "makes us able to sympathize to some extent with one another's dilemmas."[39] Just as human intelligence is capable of grasping more than is necessary for (or even remotely related to) survival and reproduction, so human altruistic capacities are able to transcend the confines of the behavioral repertoire of early human ancestors. Acknowledging the common species membership of all human beings may thus contribute to what Scheler calls an "emotional realization of the unity of mankind as a species."[40]

This extension of affections has its limits, of course, and a second tack extending moral concern concentrates on promoting a deeper cognitive awareness of shared humanity. Personalist emphasis on the uniqueness of the "other" provides a counterweight to the potentially dehumanizing affect of viewing the individual as a part of a larger whole. Emphasis on the "otherness of the other," however, must be encouraged within the larger context of basic human commonality. Perhaps a clearer consciousness of human connectedness can contribute to solidarity, just as "pseudospeciation"—the objectification of other people by effectively viewing them as outside the human species—creates a distance that facilitates harming, oppressing, and brutalizing enemies.[41]

Maxwell illustrates some of the themes put forward here: "Rule One of reciprocal altruism is: help those who will help you at least equally on a tit-for-tat basis; Rule Two is: help those in great distress if the cost to you is small."[42] Yet she also maintains that though "in its origins altruism was limited to a few categories of people . . . the principles of morality and the feelings of sympathy are potentially extendable to all human beings."[43] She argues that we do not spontaneously extend concern to all human beings but that we have the natural capacity to do so under the certain conditions, including especially an appropriate kind of upbringing. She gives primacy to reason rather than to "moral sentiments," citing Karl Popper to this effect: "'We cannot feel the same emotions toward everybody', he says—even the best Christian cannot feel equal love for all men. 'We can love mankind only in certain concrete individuals. But by the use of thought and imagination [putting ourselves in the other person's shoes] we may become ready to help all who need our help'."[44]

This statement accords with the interpretation of the ordering of love developed here; it accounts for both the centrality of natural human priorities and for a more universal sense of moral concern based on the dignity of every person. It implies a "readiness" to help when possible without an inappropriate "promiscuous" altruism that ignores proper discrimination among objects or even undercuts primary moral responsibilities. It thus extends moral concern beyond the interpersonal mutuality discussed by Johann and Rahner without at the same time falling into the radical "reversal of priorities" sometimes implied by Gutiérrez.

Two extremes have to be avoided. First, no one is permitted to collapse moral concern into a narrow circle of family and friends without regard for other individuals or communities. Moral obligations to one's family or friendships can be grossly exaggerated or inflated in comparison with other responsibilities or considerations. At times an appeal to one's duty to family or friends (or one's social role) can act as a way of evading responsibility for consequences to people who lie outside primary relations. And at the very least the New Testament radically relativizes the priority given to familial bonds. Commenting on the Johannine "new commandment" in John, biblical scholar Raymond Collins comments that "In relation to Lev 19:18, love has a new object, determined by ties of faith, not blood ('one another' rather than 'your neighbor')."[45] (The implication of the position developed in this book, by the way, is that in Christianity the object of love is determined by ties of blood and by ties of faith, as well as by a multitude of other kinds of connection. Faith is the most important bond, but it by no means eradicates the others.) Though the general pattern of caring for one's own takes precedence over care for others, it is also necessary to guard against the apparently persistent temptation to minimize or ignore the claims by those who are more remote.

Second, neighbor love should not be simply identified with the generalized care for the needy. Proper neighbor love is not a matter of caring for needy strangers rather than those to one is bound with special ties of affection, though one can get this impression from liberation theology (as well as from other strains of Christian ethics). Indeed, as mentioned above, we should not ignore the fact that the extent to which one is capable of the caring for strangers is itself significantly dependent on the extent to which one have been provided with the opportunity for the caring for family, either through one's natural family or a surrogate family, particularly in the early years of life.

One ought not, therefore, to collapse the broad scope of neighbor love into one of its subsets, in this case, love for strangers. One is not justified in acting altruistically in the fashion of Dickens's Mrs. Jellby, whose "telescopic philanthropy" leads her to neglect her own children in the course of helping unknown needy people in foreign lands.[46] The ethics of love ought not require people to act in ways that human nature makes impossible, including being *equally* concerned for all people, strangers as much as one's own kin, let alone showing a generalized *preferential* concern for the former over the latter. It seems more reasonable to claim that preferential concern ought to be granted to those with whom one shares particular connections but to recognize that this generalized priority scheme is significantly modified, even to the point of being temporarily suspended, in the presence of serious need. I suspect that if asked directly, Gutiérrez himself would not dispute Ruse's claim that we do not have "a moral obligation to beggar our families and to send all to Oxfam."[47] There is, of course, a constant danger that preference for "the nearest and dearest" will effectively neutralize the rightful claims of persons and communities who are the most needy but geographically or socially most remote. Moral myopia is certainly a greater moral temptation than "telescopic philanthropy" (this seems to be ensured by evolution), but ironically, excessive moral preoccupation with the latter contributes to the growth of the former. Thus, because appeals to unlimited moral responsibility appear incredible, they provide the seeds for a rejection of the broadly inclusive aspects of neighbor love.

This tension between particular and inclusive moral claims points to the need for a properly understood ordering of love rather than its abandonment. The Christian ordering of love is in fact a corrective to unbalanced, single-minded, and one-sided interpretations of neighbor love, whether as interpersonal mutuality or as solidarity with the poor. The proper gradation of responsibility recognizes that in general the sense of human solidarity is vague and more diffuse than the love that characterizes intense attachments, but it is nonetheless significant. In a proper understanding of the ordering of obligations, objects of preferential love do not always "trump" objects of nonpreferential love. Both dimensions of neighbor love must be included with a properly balanced ordering of love.

The Catholic authors examined here would certainly admit that natural preferences must be complemented by serious moral responsibilities beyond the narrow circle prescribed by inclusive fitness considerations. Personalists would seem likely to draw a sharp boundary between the biologically based emotional predisposition toward kin preference and interpersonal love in the full sense of the term. Advocates of the preferential option for the poor like Gutiérrez, on the other hand, might acknowledge this evolutionary heritage but insist that the gospel requires transcendence of blood ties—after all, do not the pagans do as much? Neither approach puts its proponents in the position of appropriating scientific information and insights into human sociality, particularly regarding the elemental ordering of love embedded in the human emotional constitution. Both positions are thus correct in what they affirm but incomplete. Whereas the liberation theology ignores, or fails to account for, love in the sphere of friendship, the personalists appreciate friendship but ignore regard for others, particularly the neediest and most oppressed members of society. Both ignore the distinctive nature, the complexity, and the moral significance of love within the family.

Moral Discernment

The term "discrimination" has been employed here in a positive sense, but in our culture it is usually understood in a negative sense, as unjustified bias, usually on the basis of race, gender, religion, or ethnicity. "Discrimination" in its primary sense connotes a legitimate and indeed very praiseworthy capacity to draw proper distinctions between different objects, an ability to differentiate like from unlike and to perceive the peculiar and distinguishing features of different entities. "Undiscriminating" implies a lack of perception, sensitivity, or comprehension, or an absence of sound judgment. Proper discrimination depends on the exercise of discernment, accurately perceiving the distinct kinds of claims made on the agent by various others and for acting in a manner appropriate to different kinds of relations.

I have argued that one problem with sociobiology, at least if taken in a strict sense, is that its single-minded focus on genetic relations undercuts the possibility of perceiving other kinds of goods that are equally important for human well-being. Other kinds of "interests" are recognized, of course, but these "interests" are ultimately regarded as functions of the deeper natural orientation to inclusive reproductive fitness. This genetic reductionism provides no opportunity to distinguish different claims and select the most important among a complex ordering of priorities. The claim that there is, according to nature, one and only one kind of good, the genetic, and that it can be accurately and precisely determined is attractive for its simplicity and parsimony, but ultimately it is illusory, at least when it comes to properly human behavior. Oddly revealing in this regard is J. S. Haldane's famous quip that he would gladly lay down his life—at least for two of his full siblings or eight of his cousins.[48] While obviously intended tongue in cheek, this approach is in fact the logical implication of inclusive fitness thinking unmodified by common sense or humane sensibilities. Acknowledgment of goods, and therefore of multiple connections and bonds of friendship, is a prerequisite to soundness of perception and depth of judgment when it comes to ordering human moral priorities.

A wooden and simplistic appropriation of kin selection theory suggests a moral perspective that is distorted because excessively regimented. Moral and affective priorities result from human decisions. As we have seen, human instincts are "open" rather than "closed," that is, strongly tending to certain kinds of activities, such as taking care of one's own children and siblings, rather than fixed behavior patterns whose details are precisely determined genetically.[49] As a result, human beings have a responsibility to order intelligently human behavior. On the most general level, this includes the conscious decision to elaborate and guide prosocial and altruistic natural tendencies, and also to inhibit, control, or at least channel our egoistic and antisocial inclinations. As Midgley puts it, here "reason" can be said to be precisely "a name for organizing oneself" in the midst of conflicting needs, inclinations, and desires, for choosing concrete priorities in light of some conception of the good.[50] Because the good is always concrete, relative to this particular person in these concrete circumstances, no universal ordering of love, valid for all people in all times and places, can be provided. Determining priorities among objects of love, like establishing the ordering of love generally, requires an exercise of moral discernment.

Love is always related to many neighbors, that is, love for one person is always in the affective and moral context of love for others. Human behavior implies a system of priorities that is applied at least tacitly in specific situations. The ordering of love is in fact a universal human practice, though its forms are relative to cultural, social, psychological, and other factors. The specific interpersonal relation between the self and another person, expressed in the self's action, matters more than the alternative specific actions that may realistically substitute for the action taken. Failure to come to terms with the fundamental human need for ordering affections and obligations leads to disorder and consequences detrimental to self and others, as the reader will recall from the complaint lodged by one of the women in sociologist Lillian Breslow Rubin's book, *Worlds of*

Pain, that her mother, "didn't seem to spend nearly as much time worrying about me or caring that I felt lonely or scared."[51]

Personalists are in no danger of ignoring the value of intimate interpersonal relations and liberation theologians are unlikely to minimize moral obligations to the needy and oppressed. Yet neither of these approaches sufficiently addresses and resolves the question of priority that confronts moral agents faced with specific moral decisions. In concrete life, if one does x, he or she will be subordinating one interpersonal relation to another; if one does Y, he or she will accomplish the reverse. What should the agent do?

Obviously no rigid and exceptionless priority system should be expected, but it seems to me that a reasonably comprehensive ethic of love ought to provide a basis for meeting at least three fundamental requirements: (1) to identify and distinguish among different objects of love or interpersonal relations involved; (2) to determine at least in a general way what weight should normally be given to each person or relation in various situations; and (3) to indicate generally the circumstances in which one consideration may override or outweigh another. It may be the case that this reflection can only be done in the context of a very detailed investigation of specific cases; perhaps it is most adequately examined through film or literature. Nevertheless, the ethics of love ought to provide an explicit framework within which these questions can be engaged and carefully considered for the moral life of every person involves an implicit order of love, according to which various objects have relevance, relative weight, and limits.

Farley's theology provides an exception to the general omission of the ordering of love by recent Catholic authors. She is acutely aware of the complexity and the many possibilities for conflict built into human affectivity. Though she does not develop sufficient warrants to establish the general moral priority of primary relations, she recognizes that conflict between obligations owed to different people is a steady feature of the moral life and that some ordering is necessary.

After introducing the central criteria of priority in the tradition—need and proximity—she highlights the ambiguities attending their application in concrete decisions, which depends on determining, "how great a need, how close a relationship, how great a help or harm, how important the commitment to the one who receives it, how many persons will be aided or injured, etc."[52] There is no consistent hierarchical ordering of criteria; proximity does not always trump need, or vice versa. The criteria help one identify and weigh claims in the process of moral discernment; they do not provide a simple, clear, and reliable basis for resolving conflicting responsibilities.

Perhaps equally as important, Farley realizes that the ordering of love is not primarily about resolving moral quandaries, but about shaping the person's affective and social life to reflect in a morally proper way one's relations to others. Personalists often depict human life in terms of encounters, decisive choices, particular acts and experiences, and momentary events. These categories enable them to discourse effectively on some of love's central features but lead, at the same time, to the omission of other important features. Emphasis on discrete acts of affective affirmation fails to appreciate love as a perduring disposition and continuous affection or, to use Thomistic language, to see charity as a virtue informing and perfecting the emotions. An important element of discernment in the ethics of love involves determining how best to sustain the conditions that promote love in particular contexts, as Farley explains.[53] There is a meaningful sense in which love as a particular affection can itself be the object of moral obligation, for example, a parent should feel strong affection for his or her child, and spouses for one another. Yet the ethics of love should not require an ordering of affections that cannot possibly be approximated given their deeply "preferential" nature.

NOTES

1.   See Meyer Fortes, *Kinship and Social Order: The Legacy of Lewis Henry Morgan* (Chicago: University of Chicago Press, 1969), 309.

2.   Maxwell, *Human Evolution*, 153.

3.   C. Levine, "AIDS and Changing Concepts of Family," *Milbank Quarterly* 68 (1990): 33–58; N. C. Lovejoy, "AIDS: Impact on the Gay Man's Homosexual and Heterosexual Families," *Marriage and Family Review* 14 (1990): 285–316.

4.   Johann, *Meaning of Love*, 212.

5.   Eibl-Eibesfeldt, *Love and Hate*, 97.

6.   The topic of competition is related to the question of individual versus group selection, which I cannot discuss here. The majority of biologists consider the individual rather than the group to be the standard unit of evolution (e.g., John Maynard Smith, *Evolutionary Genetics* [New York: Oxford University Press, 1989], 175–79). This position seems at the very least to call for a careful reinterpretation of Thomas's principle that the part naturally prefers the good of the whole to its own individual good (*inter alia*, ST I.60.5).

7.   Wilson, *Sociobiology*, 129.

8.   Ibid., 167.

9.   Hardin, "Discriminating Altruisms," 172.

10.   Cited in Walzer, *Spheres of Justice*, 242, from Elaine Cumming and David Schneider, "Sibling Solidarity: A Property of American Kinship," *American Anthropologist* 63 (1961): 498–507.

11.   This should not be understood in a sense that implies an illegitimate group selectionism. Sociobiologists have tended to emphasize that group-level interactions and loyalties can be explained in terms of individual inclusive fitness maximization. As a general rule, group selection is only accepted by sociobiologists in the rare event that explanations of behavior at the individual level are unavailable. See George C. Williams, *Adaptation and Natural Selection: A Critique of Some Current Evolutionary Thought* (Princeton, New Jersey: Princeton University Press, 1966). See also Robert Trivers, *Social Evolution* (Menlo Park, California: Benjamin/Cummings, 1985), ch.4.

12.   John Henry Newman, Sermon 5, "Love of Relations and Friends," in *Parochial and Plain Sermons* (San Francisco: Ignatius, 1987), 258.

13.   See Kagan, *Nature of the Child*; Konner, "Biological Aspects of the Mother-Infant Bond"; Rutter, "Early Sources of Security and Competence"; Martin L. Hoffman, "Altruistic Behavior and the Parent-Child Relationship," *Journal of Personality and Social Psychology* 31 (1975): 937–43; and M. H. Ricks, "The Social Transmission of Parental Behavior: Attachment Across Generations," in I. Bretherton and E. Waters, eds., *Growing Points in Attachment and Research*.   Monographs of the Society for Research on Child Development 50(1–2):211–27 (Chicago: University of Chicago Press, 1985).

14.   The connection between "father absence" and gender identity is discussed by M. R. Stevenson and K. N. Black, "Paternal Absence and Sex-Role Development: A Meta-Analysis," *Child Development* 59(1988): 793–814. Cognitive impairment is examined by M. Shinn, "Father Absence and Children's Cognitive Development," *Psychological Bulletin* 85(1978): 295–324.

15.   Robert L. Hinde, *Toward Understanding Relationships* (New York: Academic Press, 1979), 31. See also T. Barry Brazelton, Barbara Koslowski, and Mary Main, "The Origins of Reciprocity: The Early Mother-Infant Interaction" in *The Origins of Behavior: The Effect of the Infant on Its Caregiver*, ed. Michael Lewis and Leonard A. Rosenblum (New York: John Wiley and Sons, 1974); and K. Kaye, "Towards the Origin of Dialogue," in *Studies in Mother-Infant Interaction*, ed., H. R. Schaffer (London: Academic, 1977).

16.   Ernst Mayr, "Evolution and Ethics," ch. 2 in *Darwin, Marx, and Freud: Their Influence on Moral Theory*, ed. Arthur L. Caplan and Bruce Jennings (New York: Plenum Press, 1984), 42.

17.   Midgley, *Animals and Why They Matter*, 21.

18.   Ruse, "Morality of the Gene," 180. Ruse makes the same point elsewhere: "Biologically, our major concern has to be towards our own kin, then to those in at least some sort of relationship to us (not necessarily a blood relationship), and only finally to complete strangers" ("Evolutionary Ethics," 103).

19.   See Fortes, *Kinship and Social Order*, 232.

20.   Ruse, "Morality of the Gene," 188.

21.   See William Irons, "How Did Morality Evolve?" *Zygon* 26 (1991): 49–89.

22.   van den Berghe, *Ethnic Phenomenon*, xi.

23.   See Richard J. Alexander and Donald W. Tickle, "A Comparative Review," *Bioscience* 18 (1986): 245–47.

24.   Wilson, *On Human Nature*, 122–23.

25.   Campbell uses the term "clique selfishness" in "On the Conflicts Between Biological and Social Evolution and Between Psychology and Moral Tradition" and in "Comments on the Sociobiology of Ethics and Moralizing," *Behavioral Science* 24 (1979): 37–45. Wilson argues that we need "a more detached view of the long-range course of evolution [which] should allow us to see beyond the blind decision-making process of natural selection and to envision the history and future of our own genes against the background of the entire human species" (*On Human Nature*, 199). According to Wilson, a more adequate understanding of the human as part of the natural whole provides the proper context for redirecting the human practices that threaten the human good. On in-group affiliation and out-group disaffiliation and its effects, see R. A. Levine and D. T. Campbell, eds., *Ethnocentrism: Theories of Conflict, Ethnic Attitudes, and Group Behavior* (New York: Wiley, 1972); Vernon Reynolds, Vincent Falger, and Ian Vine, eds., *The Sociobiology of Ethnocentrism: Evolutionary Dimensions of Xenophobia, Racism and Nationalism* (London: Croom Helm, 1987); and R. Paul Shaw and Yuwa Wong, *Genetic Seeds of Warfare: Evolution, Nationalism, and Patriotism* (Boston: Unwin Hyman, 1989). For a sociological analysis of "in group" affiliation and "out group" bias, see Harvey A. Hornstein, *Cruelty and Kindness: A New Look at Aggression and Altruism* (Englewood Cliffs, New Jersey: Prentice-Hall, 1976), 16–18.

26.   This approach is found in an opponent of sociobiology, Singer's *Expanding Circle*. According to Singer, impartial reason rather than (and against) biological nature insists on "expanding the circle" of human moral responsibility. Rational impartiality must override the innate bias of spontaneous natural preferences. Peter Singer, *The Expanding Circle: Ethics and Sociobiology* (New York: New American Library, 1981).

27.   For example, Wilson, *On Human Nature*, ch. 7.

28.   Alexander, *Biology of Moral Systems*, 121.

29.   On extending altruism beyond genetic tendencies, see Carolyn Zahn-Waxler in Zahn-Waxler, E. Mark Cummings, and Ronald J. Iannotti, eds., *Altruism and Aggression: Social and Biological Origins* (Cambridge: Cambridge University Press, 1986), 320.

30.   Dawkins, *Selfish Gene*, ix.

31.   Charles Taylor, "The Diversity of Goods," in *Utilitarianism and Beyond*, ed. Amartya Sen and Bernard Williams (New York: Cambridge University Press, 1982), 131.

32.   Maxwell, *Morality among Nations*, 88. An extreme division between selfish nature and altruistic culture is advanced by Campbell, "On the Conflicts between Biological and Social Evolution and between Psychology and Moral Tradition." Others following in a similar but less dichotomous vein include Ralph Wendell Burhoe, "War, Peace, and Religion's Biocultural Evolution," *Zygon: Journal of Religion and Science* 14 (1986): 439–72; Philip Hefner, "Myth and Morality: The Love Command," *Zygon* 26 (1991): 115–36.

33.   See for example, John Paul II, *Sollicitudo rei socialis*.

34.   Darwin, *The Descent of Man and Selection in Relation to Sex* (London: John Murray, new edition, 1901), 194.

35.   Charles Darwin, *Descent of Man*, in *Darwin: A Norton Critical Edition*, 2d. ed., ed. Philip Appleman (New York and London: W.W. Norton and Company, 1979), 201. For two very different critical evaluations of the extension motif see Hardin, "Discriminating Altruisms," and Trigg, *Shaping of Man*, 142–48.

36. As suggested by Eibl-Eibesfeldt and Midgley, this case reflects the extension of behaviors originally learned in the family to a stranger. See, for example, Midgley, *Beast and Man*, 331–44 and Eibl-Eibesfeldt, *Love and Hate*, 224 and 241–42. Dennis Krebs, "Commentary and Critique," in *The Nature of Prosocial Development*, 67: "Four. . . interrelated cues [promoting kinship identification] are physical similarity, proximity, familiarity, and in-group status. I believe it plausible that individuals may behave purely altruistically toward nonrelatives who possess the qualities of relatives as a sort of overgeneralization that has not yet been maladaptive enough to have been weeded out by natural selection during the past few thousands of years."

37. Charles Darwin, *Descent of Man and Selection in Relation to Sex* (London: John Murray, new edition: 1901), 157.

38. Peter Kropotkin, *Mutual Aid*, in *Darwin: A Norton Critical Edition*, 2d. ed., ed. Philip Appleman (New York and London: W. W. Norton, 1970), 407. This citation illustrates a Darwinian approach to wider social concern than that indicated by kin and reciprocal altruism. It should not be taken to endorse Kropotkin's "law of mutual aid." Wilson himself is ambivalent about devotion to community. At times, he seems reluctant to recognize attachment to community, as we see in this citation from *On Human Nature*: "Our societies are based on the mammalian plan: the individual strives for personal reproductive success foremost and that of his immediate kin secondarily; further grudging cooperation represents a compromise struck in order to enjoy the benefits of group membership" (198). Yet he also states elsewhere in the same book that "hard-core" altruism—those unaffected by reward or punishment—has evolved "through kin selection or natural selection operating on entire, competing family or tribal units" (155).

39. Midgley, *Beast and Man*, 173.

40. Scheler, *The Nature of Sympathy,* 98.

41. For example, describing Jews as "vermin" or the Vietcong as "gooks." The former is discussed by Robert Jay Lifton in *The Future of Immortality* (New York: Basic Books, 1987), 79. One American veteran's comment aptly captures the latter example of dehumanization. "A GI was real. But if a gook got killed, it was like me going out here and stepping on a roach." Cited in S. Keen, *Faces of the Enemy: Reflections of the Hostile Imagination* (San Francisco: Harper and Row, 1986), 19.

42. Midgley, *Beast and Man*, 173.

43. Maxwell, *Morality among Nations*, 135.

44. Ibid., 136; from Karl Popper, *The Open Society and Its Enemies*, 2 vols., (London: Routledge and Kegan Paul, 1945), 2:235, 240.

45. Raymond Collins, *Christian Morality: Biblical Foundations* (Notre Dame, Indiana: University of Notre Dame Press, 1986), 114.

46. Dickens, *Bleak House*, ch. 8.

47. Ruse, "Evolutionary Ethics," 106.

48. Cited in Michael J. Reiss, "Human Sociobiology," *Zygon: Journal of Religion and Science* 19(1984): 119.

49. Midgley, *Beast and Man* 51–82 and 331–44.

50. Ibid., 258.

51. Rubin, *Worlds of Pain*, 26.

52. Farley, *Personal Commitments*, 78.

53. Ibid., chs. 4 and 5.

Conclusion:
Human Nature and the Ordering of Love

The "reality" within which the person is conceptually located by theologians guides attention and encourages responsiveness to some features of human experience and not others.[1] The descriptive context of personal and social life lends a particular saliency to some relations and limits the significance of others. The more one's dominant description of human life and its context is restricted, the more focused but narrow and constricted tends to be the framework within which human responsibility is interpreted. As Hans Jonas has observed, the scope of acknowledged responsibility tends to cohere with the range of perceived interactions and available power.[2]

If nothing else, sociobiological perspectives lead us to enlarge our sense of the scope of interhuman and human-natural interdependence. This perspective provides a descriptive basis for a wider and more complex sense of the scope of interpersonal, social, and natural responsibility. Whereas recent personalist and existentialist accounts of human existence give maximum exposure to issues of interpersonal responsibility, for example, responsiveness, fidelity, and acceptance; sociobiology provides a conceptual framework conducive to recognition of wider but usually neglected spheres of moral responsibility. This wider scope would include interpersonal and social topics but also, for example, ecological responsibility.

Love and Human Nature

Earlier in this book, I argued that instead of narrowly concentrating on the isolated relationship between two dialoguing, fully developed adults, we need to attend to the multitude of interacting relations within which we are immersed. I also claimed that human love is typically not only simple and dyadic, but also complex and multiple; it involves our existential encounters and our relationships extended over time. I argued that because the broad spectrum of affective and social life runs from the most superficial and momentary interactions to the most intense, perduring, and significant relationships, we must attend to the plurality of social relations to appreciate those that evoke great love and compassion despite being prior to free choice, full knowledge, and complete self-disclosure. I argued, in short, that Catholic ethicists need to reflect further on the ordering of love.

I also maintained that Catholic ethicists need to recognize more profoundly that we are "human animals" rather than "spirits in the world." Religious idealism sometimes obscures the animality that lies within our humanity. Christians, no matter how spiritual, are creatures of flesh and blood, moved by passions and affections, who act purposefully in pursuit of goods suited to the kind of beings we are. Thus rather than the move from "human nature" to "subjectivity," that many recent Catholic theologians have advocated,[3] I argue that we need properly to appreciate the relative ethical significance of both "human nature" and the "person." Incorporating and understanding both human nature and personhood within a broader natural context can provide a more adequate basis for appreciating the natural channeling of human sociality.

The general theme of this book has been that evolutionary theory provides a helpful corrective to the current temptation to view human beings as transcendental spirits, human love as the exclusive prerogative of two fully self-conscious adults dialoguing in the closed circle of an "I-Thou" relation, and the preferential option for the poor as the focal meaning of Christian love. Recognition of the natural basis of the affections associated with kin preference need not detract from its underlying altruistic motivational component, nor deny proper regard for "the other."

Indeed, one of the major contributions of behavioral biology to ethics is its recognition of the adaptive advantage provided by evolution of the capacity for a mature emotional attachment to and concern for others for their own sakes. There is no need to infer that behavior that serves one's inclusive fitness is motivated by the unconscious desire to do so. Human beings as members of the species share an evolved emotional constitution that under reasonably healthy conditions can motivate us, consciously and unconsciously, to love others for their own sakes. When directed toward kin, this emotional proclivity serves the agent's inclusive fitness. Yet altruistic behavior can also be directed toward nonkin and nonreciprocators so that evolution can be said to have bequeathed human nature the capacity to transcend, at least at times, its own most basic framework.

My general focus has been on neo-Darwinism as a way of thinking about human relations that acknowledges their roots in deeply ingrained motivations and emotional predispositions shaped by natural selection. To claim that human affections are rooted in natural emotional predispositions is by no means to suggest that human affections are simply biological. The personalists would be correct to point out that human behavior cannot be understood without considering motives, intentions, and freedom, and that a purely biological analysis of altruism, like the sort advanced by sociobiologists, by definition ignores its specifically human features.

Odd as it may sound at this point in the book, one implication of this fact, contrary to what some sociobiologists claim, is that evolutionary theory cannot be considered the discipline best suited to provide an account of human altruism. On methodological grounds alone, behavioral biology has less than full competence over this matter. Evolutionary theory can legitimately speculate on the evolutionary function of various deeply rooted human emotions, including kin preference, but it does not supplant the need for a psychological account of human motivations and affections.

One important contribution of behavioral biology is its attentiveness to the complexity and ambiguity of human nature, particularly vis-à-vis morality. It points to a multitude of ways in which human nature has been shaped by its evolutionary past. Earlier chapters criticized Gould's claim that our nature is "capable of the full range of human behaviors and *predisposed toward none*,"[4] and suggested instead that evolution has selected human nature to include certain emotional predispositions. "Predispositions" are by definition not overpowering, and they are always in need of cultural instantiation. The native prosocial affective capacities examined by behavioral biologists can and must be shaped and guided by training and habituation.

Authentic and mature interpersonal love can thus be said to result in part from the development of innate affective and social capacities; love is, as Midgley notes, "part of our animal nature, not a colonial imposition."[5] In other words, love and care may go with rather than against the grain of essential aspects of our nature as human; rather than being simply transcended, suspended, or eliminated, natural human affective capacities can be developed, unfolded, and amplified in an ethic of love. Evolutionary theorists underscore the fact that these prosocial tendencies are directed

most strongly and consistently at family and friends, close kin and reciprocators. From a Christian perspective, the life of charity includes the cul-
tivation of virtue that results among other things, in the proper
development of central aspects of human nature. Thus, Christian virtue
cannot be simply identified with social restraint on individual pleasure or
self-interest.

At the same time, it is the case that universal concern directly con-
tradicts the tendency toward narrow in-group morality. In some ways,
then, the ethic of love works against nature, at least as the sociobiologists
depict it. This seems particularly significant in a Catholic context, which
tends to move in the direction of cooperating with and even conforming
to "the natural." According to Trivers and others, "moral emotions" that
affectively engage us in evaluation of "right" and "wrong" acts evolved as a
means of guarding against the abuse of systems of reciprocity by "cheats"
or "free-riders." Those who could get away with receiving the assistance of
others without any return of benefits to their helpers would be at a great
adaptive advantage. To guard against such exploitation, Trivers argues,
"natural selection will rapidly favor a complex psychological system in
which individuals regulate both their own altruistic and cheating tendencies and their responses to these tendencies in others."[6] Christian moral
exhortation to "give without counting the cost" violates the very nature of
morality as a social institution that monitors reciprocity. If the sociobiologists are correct in this, Christian love, which exhorts us to give to strangers without expectation of return, works against the grain of human
nature and cannot persist in society.

Most readers will agree that we cannot legitimately embrace "normative biologism"—"the view that what is biologically natural is normatively good"[7]—because doing so ignores, for example, the person, human
freedom, intelligence, and creativity. (The same is true of the "physicalism" that has been used in traditional Catholic moral analyses of discrete
human acts, particularly in medical and sexual issues.[8]) The moral status
of what is biologically natural to human beings cannot be determined in
the abstract.[9] Basic human desires indicate that various objects are "good"
in the premoral sense; that is, they constitute means of satisfying certain
human desires. But acting on a natural desire in some contexts is obviously immoral, for example, extramarital sex, even though it is oriented to
a (premoral) good, the satisfaction of sexual desire. What is biologically
natural is not always normatively good, notwithstanding that it constitutes one important basis for human flourishing and indicates certain
goods that will be included in lives lived well.

Rather than reducing the significance of the personal, cultural, or social to the biological, as do many if not all sociobiologists, a more adequate approach to the natural law interprets the ultimate significance of the biological order in terms of its contribution to higher levels of existence—particularly the personal and the intersubjective. The evolutionary process has produced more and more complex levels of existence: from physical to chemical interactions, from chemical to biological activities, from biological to psychological, intellectual, personal, and religious activities. This emergence of more complex forms involves neither a stationary, complete, and unbroken *scala naturae* nor a Spencerian cosmic "escalator" moving all things toward an inevitable progress.[10]

A properly personalist reading of evolution implies that lower activities are given a deeper meaning when comprehended within a higher level, for example, when reproductive biology is understood in terms of the beginning and development of personal life, or when eating a meal contributes to metabolizing energy and to social bonding and familial love. When one moves up the phylogenetic scale to human beings, biology can no longer function as the single comprehensive explanatory principle of all activity.

One premise of this book is that a proper balance is needed between the personal and biological dimensions of human nature, not a one-sided disregard of either component. Mistakes are made by personalists and liberation theologians who ignore "mere biology" and "blood ties" are mistaken as are sociobiologists who dismiss individuality and rational self-consciousness as mere epiphenomena. A balance can be attained in part only by attending to what philosopher Midgley calls the fulfillment of "basic wants"—"the deepest structural constituents of our characters."[11] "We all believe," she writes, "that understanding what we are naturally fit for, capable of, and adapted to will help us to know what is good for us and, therefore, to know what to do."[12] If this is true, we need to strive for a greater openness to the information and insights into the human good available in human behavioral biology—always recognizing, of course, that indications taken from the perceived biological ordering of human nature are necessary for ethics but by no means sufficient.

The ordering of love, then, is based in but not determined by nature. It is "based" in nature in the sense that nature requires that order be brought to human love and that this order will always, without exception, give special affective and moral priority to some people and not others. Often, it seems safe to assert, nature inclines agents to give priority to close family members, though the exact shape of this ordering will reflect cultural variation. At the same time, it is important to acknowledge the moral ambiguity of kin preference—the fact that it can contribute to the disregard of others if not properly balanced with a recognition of the dignity of all people and an appreciation for the value of other goods. An emotional predisposition is obviously not morally legitimate for the sole reason that it has emerged from within the biologically natural order.

In the perspective developed here, then, the "ought" of the ethically proper ordering of love must be grounded in the "is" of natural human behavioral predispositions that have evolved as adaptations to group living. Human emotions and affections require guidance, tutoring, and pruning. Friendship and familial love need to be shaped in a manner appropriate to our relations with a wide range of others, including those to whom Gutiérrez refers as "nonpersons." The ordering of love provides conditions necessary for friendship to develop and be sustained, to take root and grow. It encourages attunement to others and weighs their needs appropriately, avoiding excessive concern for others but attending with sufficient gravity to their needs and desires—and to our own needs. Because of heightened interdependence, mutual relations imply a degree of reciprocal accountability not found in other relations.

The Ordering of Love: A Future Agenda for Theological Ethics

The ordering of love is in some ways the fundamental moral problem of Christian ethics. Theologians concentrating in applied ethics, from sexual and biomedical ethics to social and business ethics, rely, implicitly or explicitly, on some working distinction between proper and improper ways of ordering moral priorities and organizing beneficence. In families, parents of small children determine which among a variety of needs has precedence at particular times and places. In politics, voters and government officials determine policies on the basis of an implicit ranking of priorities among various worthy objectives, for example, education, the environment, and public safety. All ordinary moral problems concern the proper relations among people and between the self and others. The relation of the self to itself, as it is presented in extensive classical discussions of temperance and fortitude, continues to be a sphere of valid moral concern. Yet even here the ordering of love is a prominent issue. All human action regarding the self is from a Christian point of view, also always in relation to God, the primary "object" of the ordering of love. The relationship remains even in cases in which the agent's behavior has negligible impact on other people.

The claims of this book address, at best, only a small portion of even a moderately adequate theory of the ordering of love. A fully explicated theory would have to include a more elaborate account of natural science and attend seriously to relevant social scientific material regarding the human affections, for example, empathy and altruism. It would have to develop a philosophical account not only of love but also of justice, and these accounts would have to be coordinated with the traditional distinction between commands and counsels, duty and supererogation, so that the obligations of love may be differentiated from the selfless generosity of Christian charity. Other philosophical issues would also have to be addressed, perhaps most notably the famous (and sometimes overextended) objection to "naturalistic ethics" known since the time of G. E. Moore as the "naturalistic fallacy."[13] The widespread and entrenched objection to connecting the "is" of human nature with the "ought" of ethics constitutes the major philosophical obstacle that must be negotiated in order to develop a theory of the ordering of love that incorporates natural human affections.

A systematic theory of the ordering of love would also have to address the critical source of the Christian tradition, the bible, and particularly the New Testament texts dealing with *agape* and *philia*. It requires not only an adequate interpretation of the various meanings and implications of these notions within the texts themselves, but also a plausible account of how these various texts ought to be coordinated into a coherent whole and related to doctrinal and theological examinations of related notions, such as nature and grace, Incarnation, Trinity, and church. It requires, in short, nothing less than a thorough grounding in systematic theology and Biblical studies.

The development of a comprehensive theory of the ordering of love from a Catholic perspective would probably have to include some interpretation of the standard, though by no means the only, philosophical tradition employed in Catholic moral theology, the philosophy of Aristotle and Thomas Aquinas. This tradition is enjoying a renaissance at the present time, as witnessed in the recent publication of a number of excellent texts on Thomas's ethics.[14] No major theological work has yet appeared, however, that historically and systematically examines his interpretation of charity, let alone a sophisticated explication of its significance for contemporary ethics. The same lacuna is true, a fortiori, of Thomas's account of the *ordo caritatis*. Thomas's ethics have always been used selectively, of course, and a contemporary development of his notion of the *ordo caritatis* can only proceed after a careful and systematic reflection on the principles and method according to which such selective retrieval and development validly proceeds.

Thus, a great deal of work remains to be done to develop a contemporary analogue to Thomas's *ordo caritatis*. Relating the relevant sources coherently in the context of a theologically grounded and philosophically credible ethics is the only way that a contemporary interpretation of the ordering of love can attain plausibility. To do so in a way that contributes to ethical theory and theological speculation, illumines concrete experience, and provides reasonable guidelines for moral decisionmaking is a project of ambitious proportions. Yet because of the centrality of the ordering of love in the Christian moral life, it seems to me that all moral theologians must contribute to this effort when and where they are able.

Each ethicist in fact implicitly applies an ordering of love in his or her moral reflection, at least in more cases than is typically noted. In the concrete moral life, of course, people ordinarily function reasonably well by applying an implicit ordering of affection and operating on the basis of working assumptions about moral priorities. They do so, however, in an unexamined way, without explicit theoretical justification. They function, often in a fairly effective and responsible manner with the help of a complex and varied mixture of common sense, prudence, traditional wisdom, Christian inspiration, and intuition. If one must choose, clearly the effective practice of a truly Christian ordering of love is preferable to its theoretical elaboration and justification. Fortunately, this choice is not one that we must face; on the contrary, adequate reflection on the ordering of love may yet contribute to the growth in the love of God and neighbor. The task of the theological ethicist is, then, is to bring greater clarity, thoughtfulness, and, I trust, wisdom, to the moral practice that is an essential part of every person's moral life. If this book constitutes a first modest contribution to this effort, it will have achieved its purpose.

NOTES

1.   On the significance of conceptual interpretation for responsiveness, see H. Richard Niebuhr, *The Responsible Self: An Essay in Christian Moral Philosophy* (New York: Harper and Row, 1963).

2.   Hans Jonas, *The Imperative of Responsibility: In Search of an Ethics for the Technological Age* (Chicago: University of Chicago Press, 1984). Many of the themes and insights of Jonas's text are pertinent to this conclusion, but cannot be explicated here for

practical reasons. On the significance of causal efficacy for moral accountability, see H. L. A. Hart, *Punishment and Responsibility* (New York: Oxford University Press, 1968).

3.   See, for example, the representative article by Michael J. Himes, "The Human Person in Contemporary Theology: From Human Nature to Authentic Subjectivity," in *Introduction to Christian Ethics: A Reader*, ed. Ronald P. Hamel and Kenneth R. Himes, O.F.M. (Mahwah, New Jersey: Paulist Press, 1989), 59.

4.   "Biological Potential vs. Biological Determinism," in Caplan, ed., *Sociobiology Debate*, 349. My emphasis.

5.   Midgley, *Beast and Man*, 260.

6.   Trivers, *Social Evolution*, 388.

7.   Donald Campbell, "Social Morality Norms as Evidence of Conflict Between Biological Human Nature and Social Systems Requirements," in Gunther S. Stent, ed., *Morality as a Biological Phenomenon: The Presuppositions of Sociobiological Research* (Berkeley: University of California Press, 1978), 70.

8.   On "physicalism," see Joseph T. C. Arnst, O.P., "The Natural Law and Its History," in *Moral Problems and Christian Personalism*, Concilium 5 (New York: Paulist Press, 1965); Charles Curran, ed., *Absolutes in Moral Theology* (Washington, D.C.: Corpus Books, 1968), and Richard A. McCormick, S.J., "Human Significance and Christian Significance," in G. Outka and P. Ramsey, eds., *Norm and Context in Christian Ethics* (New York: Charles Scribner's Sons, 1968), 233–61. Johann's contribution to the critical literature can be found in "Responsible Parenthood: A Philosophical View," *Proceedings of the Catholic Theological Society of America* 20 (1965): 115–28.

9.   See Bernard Häring, "Dynamism and Continuity in a Personalistic Approach to Natural Law," in *Norm and Context in Christian Ethics*, 199–218. As significant as the "is-ought" and "fact-value" issues have been to contemporary moral philosophy, a philosophical defense of the kind of naturalism presumed here is beyond the scope of this book. This naturalist position however, in which the "ought" is dependent on the "is" though not without remainder, has significant affinities with the philosophical positions provided by Midgley, *Beast and Man*, 177–200; and Gerard J. Hughes, S.J., *Authority in Morals: An Essay in Christian Ethics* (Washington, D.C.: Georgetown University Press, 1978).

10.   The latter is illustrated in the major work of Spencer's disciple, Henry Drummond, *The Ascent of Man*, 3d. ed. (New York: James Pott and Co., 1894).

11.   Midgley, *Beast and Man*, 183. See also Hughes, *Authority in Morals*, 50–60.

12.   Ibid., 177.

13.   See G. E. Moore, *Principia Ethica*. See also *The Is-Ought Question*, ed. W. D. Hudson (New York: St. Martin's Press, 1969).

14.   See Jean Porter, *The Recovery of Virtue: The Relevance of Aquinas for Christian Ethics* (Louisville: Westminster/John Knox, 1990) and James F. Keenan, S.J., *Goodness and Rightness in Thomas Aquinas's Summa Theologiae* (Washington, D.C.: Georgetown University Press, 1992).